MARIA ROMANOV
THIRD DAUGHTER OF THE LAST TSAR

Related Titles

The Diary of Olga Romanov:
Royal Witness to the Russian Revolution by Helen Azar

Tatiana Romanov:
Daughter of the Last Tsar, Diaries and Letters, 1913–1918
by Helen Azar and Nicholas B. A. Nicholson

Maria Romanov

THIRD DAUGHTER
OF THE LAST TSAR
DIARIES AND LETTERS
1908-1918

HELEN AZAR

GEORGE HAWKINS

WESTHOLME
Yardley

Westholme Publishing, LLC
904 Edgewood Road
Yardley, Pennsylvania 19067
Visit our Web site at www.westholmepublishing.com

ISBN: 978-1-59416-322-7
Also available as an eBook.

Printed in the United States of America.

CONTENTS

(A gallery of images appears following page 71)

ACKNOWLEDGMENTS

The authors would like to thank Molly Thatcher for contributing to the Maria biographical chapter, Amanda Madru for transcribing the English language letters, Marlene A. Eilers Koenig and Ferah Arslan for proofreading the manuscript, Vasily Astankov of State Archives of the Russian Federation for his kind assistance with photographs, and the staff at Beinecke Library at Yale University. Many thanks also to Adam Eyre and Victor Hoehnebart for allowing us to translate and include letters and postcards from their private collections. Thanks also to Thomas Aufleger for information about Romanov friends in Hesse, and to Olga Hawkins for helping with Maria's diaries.

INTRODUCTION

GRAND DUCHESS MARIA NIKOLAEVNA

As a middle child and third daughter of the last tsar of Russia, Nicholas II and his wife, Empress Alexandra Feodorovna, Grand Duchess Maria Nikolaevna is often overlooked by Romanov biographers. She is generally described merely as a pretty, kind girl who loved children. While Maria certainly had those qualities, under the surface they belied her incredible bravery and courage, which clearly emerged in the darkest times during the last couple of years of her life. Her deep warmth and interest in everyone's daily lives, from servants to statesmen, arguably made her the most accessible, empathetic, and down-to-earth member of the imperial family.

She was probably least affected by her status as the daughter of the emperor, and her naturally self-deprecating shyness and clumsiness made her endearing to all. She was often overshadowed by the more public roles played by her elder sisters, and in death it was her younger sister Anastasia who gained notoriety; but ultimately Maria proved to have a unique, strong, and solid character. It was no accident that she was the one chosen to accompany her parents on the last journey of their lives: to the unknown destination that turned out to be Ekaterinburg in the "Red Urals."

Unfortunately, in 1918 Maria destroyed the majority of her diaries, and as such only three survive: those from 1912, 1913, and

1916. However, these fragments of her life, along with surviving letters, come together to form a striking portrait of Nicholas II's third daughter. Her writings offer a fascinating insight into the private life of a loving family and detail how the grand duchess changed from an innocent young girl to a pillar of strength and hope for her family, who was able to maintain her kindness and optimism in the face of violence and degradation.

Maria Nikolaevna Romanov was born on June 14, 1899, in Peterhof, in a summer palace near the Gulf of Finland, just outside of St. Petersburg. It had been a difficult pregnancy for Empress Alexandra, and she had spent many of the final months confined to a wheel-chair, as Maria's awkward positioning triggered her back pain. The birth of a third Imperial daughter was signaled by a gun salute from St. Peter and Paul Fortress in St. Petersburg. As the shots rang out across the city, ceasing at 101, they were generally met with disappointment; the general public and extended family members had been anxiously hoping for a male heir after five years of the imperial couple's marriage. Due to the Pauline laws of succession, implemented by Emperor Paul, females were unable to inherit the throne unless there were no more male heirs, hence Maria's birth had little political significance.

Though Nicholas II never verbally expressed disappointment at his wife's delivery of a third daughter, Maria's was the only birth after which he reportedly excused himself for a solitary walk, before seeing Alexandra and the new baby girl. Maria was named after her paternal grandmother, the Dowager Empress Maria Feodorovna, which was fitting since Maria would grow up to closely resemble her—sharing the same large, soulful eyes, as well as her merry, vivacious nature.

Despite any initial disappointment within the imperial family, Maria quickly captured everybody's hearts. The girls' nanny, Margaretta Eagar, wrote that she believed Maria "was born good, I often think, with the very smallest trace of original sin possible." Her placidity came as some surprise, after her more mischievous and active elder sisters—Olga and Tatiana. One often-quoted anecdote from Eagar tells of Maria as a toddler stealing biscuits from her mother's tea table, and instead of punishing her, her father expressed relief, "I was always afraid of the wings growing. I am glad to see she is only a human child."[1]

Maria absolutely adored her father, perhaps even more so than any of his other children. In her memoir, Eagar remembered about the toddler: "When [her father] fell ill in the Crimea, [Maria's] grief at not seeing him was excessive. I had to keep the door of the day nursery locked or she would have escaped into the corridor and disturbed him with her efforts to get to him. Every evening after tea, she sat on the floor just inside the nursery door, listening intently for any sounds from his room. If she heard his voice by any chance, she would stretch her little arms, and call 'Papa, Papa', and her rapture when she [was] allowed to see him was great. When the Empress came to see the children on the first evening after his illness had been pronounced typhoid fever, she happened to be wearing a miniature of the Emperor set as a brooch. In the midst of her sobs and tears, little Marie caught sight of this; she climbed up on the Empress's knee, and covered the pictured face with kisses, and on no evening through his illness would she go to bed without kissing the miniature."

Perhaps because of her goodness, her elder sisters would often exclude or push her in childish play, feeling their baby sister was imposing on what had previously been a tight pair. But, from a young age, Maria's goodness came not from a place of naivety but rather a place of genuine emotional understanding and stoicism. Once, when the older sisters were playing house, they relegated Maria to the role of their footman. Maria quietly refused and instead left, returning with toys, and proclaimed, "I won't be a footman. I'll be the kind aunt who brings presents." Her elder sisters were then ashamed and henceforth included Maria as an equal in their games. Maria had several nicknames among her siblings and other close family members: one was the typically Russian, folksy "Mashka," another the affectionate "fat little bow-wow." She was also occasionally referred to as "Marie."

---

1. All of Margaretta Eagar's recollections are from her memoir, *Six Years at the Russian Court,* except where indicated otherwise.

The affectionate tease "fat little bow-wow" stemmed from Maria's strong build. Maria was considered to have taken after her paternal grandfather Tsar Alexander III in build, who was often likened to a Russian bear, as opposed to her more willowy elder sisters. As she grew, she became remarkably strong and, as Sydney Gibbes recalled, would amuse herself by picking up her tutors. She was also often enlisted to carry Alexei when his official minders were absent.

A friendly, generous child, Maria loved the idea of families and always wanted to know about other people's children. Margaretta Eagar recalled the day when one of the old footmen carried Maria upstairs, and she told him about her doll, which had a laughing face and a crying one and said "Papa" and "Mama." "She asked him if his little girl had such a doll. Now, he was a bachelor, and so he told her that he had no little girl. She was very sorry for him, and he told her, to comfort her, that he had a niece, quite omitting to mention that she was a [grown] woman. Marie wanted to know if his niece had a doll like hers. He said not. So, when she got down to the nursery door she ran in and took her darling doll, and gave it to him for his niece."[2]

With the birth of Anastasia on June 5, 1901, the sisters seemed to split more comfortably into the "Big Pair" and the "Little Pair," the two youngest, Maria and Anastasia, being the latter. However, Maria would sometimes still feel isolated as a middle child. She was "sandwiched" between Olga and Tatiana and Anastasia and the baby and only son Alexei, and can be thought to have developed a true "middle child syndrome" when she was younger. Overpowered by the assertive personality of her younger sister, by the importance of her baby brother as heir to the throne, and by being too young to join Olga and Tatiana on grown-up outings and responsibilities, she felt excluded and imagined her parents had favorites. She was particularly concerned that Alexandra preferred Anastasia, leading to Alexandra having to write in a note, "I have no secrets with Anastasia, I do not like secrets." Her feelings were evidently so strong that Alexandra later wrote her a note reassuring her: "Sweet child,

---

2. Margaretta Eagar, "More About the Little Grand Duchesses of Russia," *The Girl's Own Paper and Woman's Magazine*, 1909.

you must promise me never again to think that nobody loves you. How did such an extraordinary idea get into your little head? Get it quickly out again."

As part of the "Little Pair" Maria and Anastasia shared a bedroom—a simple, light room on the second floor of the Alexander Palace, with a painted motif of pink roses and bronze butterflies circling the walls. The girls were bought up with Spartan simplicity, receiving cold baths in the morning and sleeping on hard camp cots, and they were expected to tidy their own rooms. They were dressed similarly and spent much of their time together.

Growing up, Maria and Anastasia would play games, stage plays, and later even play music and dance to a gramophone in their bedroom. Maria's diaries, as well as letters written by both sisters, are filled with references to their activities together. In a 1915 letter to her father, Maria wrote: "Anastasia and I rode our bicycles for a bit around the house." Anastasia added "[we] just played ping pong with Maria and [were] bustling around and yelling so incredibly much that now my hands are shaking like someone with a head injury."

At times Maria would embrace Anastasia's mischievousness. For example, one common trick was to turn up their gramophone as loud as possible and stomp around their room when they knew their mother had guests downstairs. However, overall their relationship seemed to be a bit more volatile than Olga and Tatiana's. Tatiana recalled to her friend Valentina Chebotareva[3] that even as late as the war years "Nastasya[4] gets mad and pulls [Maria's] hair and tears out clumps of it."

Maria grew up to be considered a beauty; a courtier once noted that she "had the face of one of Botticelli's angels." While Tatiana was considered the classic beauty of the family, with her regal elegance and fine features, many were equally drawn to the more down-to-earth and robust beauty of Maria. She was the most characteristically Russian looking of the four daughters, with a mass of

3. Valentina Ivanovna Chebotareva was a nurse who worked at the Imperial Infirmary with the Empress and the two eldest grand duchesses.
4. Affectionate name for Anastasia.

soft brown hair, romantic lips, and large blue eyes known in the family as "Marie's saucers."

As she grew into a young adult, Maria's beauty became enlivened by her love for life and glowing health. Sofia Ofrosimova, a nurse at one of the imperial infirmaries during the war, described her as "a Russian beauty. Tall, plump with sable brows, a bright blush on her open Russian face, she is especially appealing to a Russian heart. One looks and involuntarily imagines her dressed in a Russian Boyar[5] *sarafan*[6]; around her arms one imagines muslin sleeves, on the high breast—precious stones, and above the high white brow—a *kokoshnik*[7] with exquisite pearls. . . her eyes illuminate her entire face with a unique, radiant luster; they sometimes seem black, as long eyelashes throw shadows over the bright blush of her soft cheeks. She is merry and alive, but she has not yet awakened completely to life; probably concealed in her are the immense forces of a real Russian woman."[8]

When she started regular school lessons, Maria was easily bored in the classroom; having stronger emotional and visual intelligence she preferred conversation or painting to long periods of study and disliked the monotonous recording of events in her diaries. Nevertheless, her report cards show her to have been a good student who usually got the grades of 4s and 5s (Russian equivalents of Bs and As). Maria's writing comes alive through her numerous intimate letters to friends and family, which highlight her skill as a storyteller, as well as her warm nature and lively sense of humor.

In lessons she studied traditional humanities subjects such as Russian history and literature, languages, art, and music. However, Maria and her siblings also attended science lessons and learnt about developing theories and inventions. Perhaps surprisingly to modern readers, Maria's diaries often record her trips to the Realnoe School where she was taught physics. This was perhaps fueled by her father's

5. Russian nobility.

6. Russian traditional dress.

7. Russian traditional women's headwear.

8. All recollections by Ofrosimova were translated from her Russian language memoir, available here: http://xn——7sbavwpxid7bxe5af.xn—p1ai/%D0%BC%D0%B0%D1%80%D0%B8%D1%8F-bio-%D0%B4%D0%B5%D1%82%D1%81%D1%82%D0%B2%D0%BE/.

enthusiasm for physics and aviation, as demonstrated through his interest and patronage of the Russian inventor and aviator Igor Ivanovich Sikorsky.

Maria was arguably the most artistically gifted of her sisters, another talent she inherited from her namesake paternal grandmother, and she sketched using her left hand. Drawings and paintings that survive show she focused on flowers, dogs, and traditional Russian landscapes and architecture. Maria continued making art even in exile, creating sketches of places when cameras were not available. For example, en route to Ekaterinburg, having stopped to change horses at the infamous Grigori Rasputin's native village of Pokrovskoe, Maria made a quick sketch of his house, thus preserving it for posterity.[9] In her letters from Ekaterinburg, Maria would ask her sisters to bring her art supplies when they finally traveled from Tobolsk to join herself and their parents.

In 1913, as tradition dictated, Maria became colonel in chief of her own regiment, the 9th Kazan Dragoons,[10] and she took great delight in the responsibility of patrolling and interacting with "her" soldiers. With her natural friendliness and deep yearning for connection, Maria was drawn to some innocent flirtations with young officers and often expressed the wish to become a soldier's wife and mother to many children. Her maternal nurturing nature also meant that whenever the Romanovs met with their extended cousins, Maria was always drawn to mothering the youngest members. On the imperial family's trip to Romania in 1914, to pursue a possible match between Olga and Prince Carol of Romania, film footage shows Maria swooping in to take a baby from Olga's lap once the official photo had been taken. Similarly, on official trips she would often break rank to interact with children; she recalled in a letter, "The other day we went to the nanny school and squeezed the little children who were already going to bed."

9. This rare sketch was published in *In the Steps of the Romanovs: The Final two Years of the Russian Imperial Family* by Helen Azar.
10. Maria would often proudly sign her letters with "Kazanetz" or "Kazansha," referring to her regiment.

Sadly, it seems that even if Maria had been able to realize her dream of having a family, it would have been plagued with tragedy. Through her great-grandmother Queen Victoria of England, her mother's maternal grandmother, there was the possibility that any one of the four sisters would have been the carrier of the hemophilia gene—the disease that incapacitated their youngest and only brother Alexei. In fact, statistically speaking, one in four females in the affected family would be the carrier of this gene. Many years after the revolution, her paternal aunt, Grand Duchess Olga Alexandrovna, remembered that Maria reportedly hemorrhaged in December 1914 while having her tonsils removed. Her bleeding unnerved the doctor to the point that he refused to complete the operation and had to be ordered to continue by Alexandra. Many years later, tests done on the remains believed to be Maria's showed that she was a carrier of the hemophilia gene and would have probably passed on the disease to at least one of her male children.

The life of imperial family members dramatically changed with the outbreak of the First World War. Everyone was expected to take part and make a contribution to the war effort, including all the grand duchesses. Maria was too young to become a Red Cross nurse like Olga and Tatiana, so instead, during the second part of 1914, she and Anastasia became patrons of the Feodorovsky Infirmary in Tsarskoe Selo. The Little Pair made daily visits to the wounded soldiers at their infirmary, which was located a short distance from the Alexander Palace. They did their best to keep up their patients' spirits by reading to them, helping them write letters, playing games, and of course posing for lots of photographs with them. The infirmary ultimately came to dominate Maria's diaries and letters, as she spent hours talking to the soldiers and asking questions about their families at home. As one soldier remembered, she also had the rather daunting role of trying to control Anastasia's behavior, apologizing and giving warning glances when the latter cheated at board games or teased the soldiers too much.

During the period of the war, Maria developed her first long-term love interest in an officer in the imperial entourage, "Fatso"

Nikolai Demenkov. She made frequent and unabashed references to her affection for him in her diaries and letters, quite the opposite of her more secretive eldest sister, Olga, who devised various codes for her crushes in her diaries. Demenkov remembered an incident from 1914, before the war, that illustrates Maria's natural selflessness and concern: when a button came off his collar "Her Imperial Highness Grand Duchess Maria Nikolaevna, noticing my involuntary embarrassment, with her characteristic kindness and simplicity deigned to come over to me and offer me the use of her handkerchief, which I clearly remember was white with a blue border which matched the white and blue dresses their Highnesses were wearing that day. The handkerchief served as a scarf around my neck and her Highness deigned to draw the Emperor's attention to it." The pair's innocent flirtation only broke off in 1916 when Demenkov transferred to a naval position at sea. Maria saved the letter he wrote to her that year, and it is currently held in the Russian archive. Unfortunately, Maria never saw her "Fatso" again, though Demenkov survived the revolution and died in November 1950 in Paris. Unusually, he never married.

One of Maria's first cousins, Louis "Dickie" Battenberg/Mountbatten, claimed to have had a lifelong crush on his beautiful Russian cousin, from the time he was ten years old and she was eleven. "I was crackers about Marie, and was determined to marry her. She was absolutely lovely. I keep her photograph in my bedroom—always have," Mountbatten would say many years later.[11]

Perhaps the final moments of imperial ceremony and the life Maria once knew occurred on January 9, 1917, when she was officially presented at court at a banquet held to honor the visit of Crown Prince Carol of Romania. In a typically endearing fashion Sophia "Isa" Buxhoeveden recalled how "poor Maria slipped in her new high heels and fell when entering the dining hall on the arm of a tall Grand Duke, and Tatiana recalled Maria laughed "to the point of embarrassment."[12] Maria's endearing clumsiness, friendliness, and beauty caught the attention of Prince Carol, who made

11. Richard Hough, *Mountbatten: Hero of Our Time*, 22-23.
12. Anna Vyrubova, *Memories of the Russian Court*.

an official proposal to the seventeen-year-old Maria before he left St. Petersburg. Nicholas evidently did not take the proposal seriously, laughingly rejecting it, as Maria was far too young to get married and "nothing more than a school girl."[13]

Sadly, Maria's girlish innocence was soon lost forever; just a month later the February revolution broke out and Maria was forced to grow up quickly. At the time Maria was the only imperial sibling not ill with measles. Empress Alexandra was reluctant to upset the ill children with news of the revolution, and as her father's government collapsed around the Romanovs and Nicholas II abdicated, Maria was left alone not only to deal with the news but also to comfort her frantic mother. It was at this time that her great strength, her "immense forces of a real Russian woman," which nurse Ofrosimova had suspected, were revealed.

Viktor Erastovich Zborovsky noted the change in Maria when he came to visit Alexandra, stating, "Nothing remained of the former young girl [. . .] she was now] a serious sensible young woman, who was responding in a deep and thoughtful way to what was going on."

On February 28, 1917, wrapped in a warm simple Russian shawl, Maria accompanied her mother outside the confines of the Alexander Palace to thank the guards who were protecting them. Lili Dehn recalls seeing them through a window "utterly fearless of [their own] safety," smiling and thanking the soldiers as they "passed like dark shadows from line to line."

When news of Nicholas's abdication reached them, Maria told Anna Vyrubova, "I cried [. . .] but no more than I could help it, for poor Mama's sake." While Maria was able to gather her strength in public, in private she remained a terrified teenaged girl. Lili Dehn recalled finding her crouched in the corner of a room crying, scared that the revolutionaries would storm the palace and take her mother away; "She was so young, so helpless, so hurt."

As the other children recovered, Maria fell ill and had a slow recovery under house arrest at the Alexander Palace. Eventually she was able to join her siblings and father outside, in the space sectioned off in Alexander Park for their house arrest. To keep busy,

---

13. Elizaveta Naryshkina, quoted by Anna Vyrubova in *Memories of the Russian Court.*

they broke ice on the canals, took walks, and, when the weather got warmer, planted a kitchen garden.

At this time, still living in their beloved Alexander Palace, it was easy to remain in sort of a denial and pretend that nothing much had changed, that all this was just a temporary situation. For the most part, the family and suite members who elected to stay with them tried to remain optimistic, even Alexandra, who suffered from severe anxiety, retained her sense of humor and optimism.

Having completely recovered from measles, the girls and Alexei had all their hair shaved off in early June, when it started falling out in clumps. As a practical joke they wanted to play on Pierre Gilliard, the children's French tutor who stayed with the family, the four sisters plotted to simultaneously pull off their wigs while posing for a photo and get an "inappropriate" photograph of themselves with bald heads. Subsequently they posed wigless numerous times that summer.

Maria loved taking photographs as much as she loved painting and drawing. Many family photographs, including during captivity, do not include her, because she was most often the photographer. She loved capturing sweet intimate moments of their daily lives in captivity and would later write dates and captions on the backs of printed photos and send them to friends. On the photo of Tatiana and Alexandra sitting on the grass in Alexander Park, which she later sent to Lili Dehn, Maria wrote: "30 June, 1917. I took this photo in the park three days ago. Mama is holding a little bunny which Alexei's dog almost killed."

On the first day of August 1917, the family was led out of Alexander Palace, their home of many years, and put on a train that took them away from their beloved Tsarskoe Selo forever. Their hopes of joining the extended family members in Crimea or receiving asylum in England fell through: they were removed to the faraway Siberian town of Tobolsk to await their future fate.

Maria and her family were settled in a relatively large, comfortable mansion that once belonged to the former governor of the region. There, they initially enjoyed such freedoms as walking to a local church for services. Maria later expressed in a letter that she loved their life in Tobolsk and felt that she could happily stay there forever. But it was not to be: back in Petrograd (as St. Petersburg became known during the war), in November 1917, surprising even themselves, the Bolsheviks took power from the Provisional Government in a virtually bloodless coup.

For a few months, the imperial family were all but forgotten among all the chaos in the capital city and continued to live quietly without much change. The younger children continued to study, and the family put on plays, hand made gifts for each other and the staff, read aloud, wrote letters, took walks, played outside in the snow, and quietly celebrated Orthodox holidays.

However, in the spring of 1918, things changed drastically. Commissar Vasily Yakovlev showed up at the governor's mansion to announce that he must take Nicholas away for important business. It was at this point that Maria burned most of her diaries and Anastasia destroyed all of hers. It is unclear why three of Maria's diaries survived; it is possible that they had been packed away at the time the decision was made.

Alexandra was reluctant to allow her husband to go alone, but at this time Alexei was suffering from another bout of hemophilia and was unable to travel. After the family members discussed which of the sisters should accompany their mother, Maria was put forward. Hence, Alexei and his three sisters would stay behind until the family could be reunited when the boy got better, though they did not yet know where Nicholas, Alexandra, and Maria would ultimately end up. It must have been a terrifying prospect for the eighteen-year-old to leave all her siblings, uncertain if she would ever see them again, and travel with her parents to an undisclosed location, possibly to Moscow and a show-trial ending in execution of her father.

In fact, the three ended up in Ekaterinburg, capital city of the Urals, notoriously hostile to the former emperor and his family. When the train arrived at the main station, an angry mob had formed, swarming around the coaches and demanding, "Show us the Romanovs!" Yakovlev feared that the mob might overpower the coaches and lynch the tsar and the imperial entourage, so the train was moved back to an outer freight station where the prisoners could be handed over safely to the local authorities.

In Ekaterinburg things got significantly worse for the prisoners: the living conditions were much poorer; the house where they were held, which once belonged to engineer Ipatiev, (hence now known as the "Ipatiev house" or "The House of Special Purpose") was damp and cold, and even the windows were later whitewashed to prevent the family signaling or looking out. The guards were not allowed to interact with the prisoners and were instructed to treat them harshly.

Nevertheless, Maria remained optimistic even then. In a letter to her sisters in Tobolsk she described the miserable conditions of their current life but was quick to add that things were still not so bad, because the sun was still shining and she could still hear the birds chirping outside. The hardest thing for all family members was that, for the first time ever, they were separated for Easter—the most important holiday on the Orthodox calendar. Letters flew back and forth almost daily from Ekaterinburg to Tobolsk: Maria wrote long and loving messages to her sisters, in particular her "Little Pair" second half, Anastasia. A few weeks later the family was finally reunited and they were able to once again draw comfort from each other.

As the Romanovs' fate closed in on them, and several members of the family drew inward (notably Alexandra and Olga), the guards at the House of Special Purpose saw Maria as the most well adjusted to her position. One guard, recalling Maria, was reminded of the line by the poet Tyutchev, seeing her as "the incarnation of modesty elevated by suffering."

Maria was murdered along with all members of her family on the night of July 17, 1918, just a few weeks after her nineteenth birthday. Her death was bloody and drawn out; by many accounts she was still alive even as the bodies were being transported into the truck, and she had to be struck again and again.

The telling of the story of the imperial family was not encouraged under the Soviet rule, and Russia's last imperial family was almost airbrushed from official Russian history. It was not until eighty years later, in the 1990s, shortly after the fall of the Soviet Union, that the bodies of five members of the Romanov family were unearthed, and shortly after positively identified via DNA. However, the remains of two family members were still missing: those of Alexei and one of the two youngest sisters, whom the scientists believe to be Maria.

In 1996, the remains of Nicholas, Alexandra, Olga, Tatiana, and Anastasia were buried with official ceremony at the Cathedral of St. Peter and Paul in St. Petersburg, where most of the Romanov family members are interred. Maria and her family were canonized as Orthodox passion bearers in 2000.

It was not until 2007 that the charred remains of two children, later positively identified as Maria and Alexei, were found in a burial site not far from the original shallow grave where the rest of the family was discovered. Due to various political controversies within the Russian Orthodox Church, at the time of this writing, the remains of the two children have not been interred, and it is currently unknown if Maria and Alexei will ever be laid to rest with their family.

We have no way of knowing what kind of life Maria Romanov would have led if she had survived the revolution. She was a humble girl with simple dreams and wishes but had the strength of spirit that would have set her well as a matriarch to any family in exile. Although she is still often presented as a girl uncertain of her place within the most tight-knit of families, who only knew how to give love, her courage and bravery manifested itself when it was most needed by those around her.

In the drama and larger-than-life characters of the Russian Revolution and the fall of the three-hundred-year-old Romanov dynasty, it is easy to lose Maria as an individual, but in this book, through her diaries and letters, her voice can and will be heard, firmly establishing her as much more than an ethereal figure wearing a white dress, or a footnote of history.

FRAGMENTS, 1900–1907

1900

Grand Duchess Elizaveta Feodorovna to Grand Duke Serge Alexandrovich[1]—

Peterhof
23rd July 1900
Darling Serge
The weather is quite splendid. Yesterday we had church and lunch afterwards then I went with Alix to see Olga and Aunt Sanny. Costia was also there, Olga is looking well but very grey and so thankful that her daughter Minny is so happy. All are pleasantly impressioned by the young couple who look so contented and in bright humour. I remember Sophie's conversations and my impressions go deeper— she is so remarkably sweet and loving with me and so often thinks for the past and the present. God bless the dear child. . . . Out of the window I see the sweet children each holding a little parasol and a donkey being led behind them to ride on—too amusing. They ask often after you. Little Marie is marvelously lovely, I have never seen such eyes. The evening we spent the same as yesterday very pleasantly, this stay here is most cozy but without you so empty and then I cannot feel at home, one misses Sacha at every step and I feel so sad that although it is such a joy being with Alix Nicky and children and seeing Minny one cannot forget the past and that one dear

---

1. Grand Duchess Elizabeth (1864-1918) was Empress Alexandra's older sister. She married Nicholas II's uncle, Grand Duke Serge Alexandrovich.

brother that was a rock of love and comfort to lean upon for affection and as guide.

Hearty kisses from your loving Ella.[2]

1901

Nicholas II and Alexandra Feodorovna to Maria—

March 2-th 1901. Papa & Mama kiss Baby sweet many times. March 4-th 1901. If you are a good little girl, we shall come and see you in yr. bath to-night. Papa & Mama kiss you.

1905

Princess Irina Alexandrovna[3] to Maria—

Carnation [written above an embossed picture of carnations]
My dear Miri [sic],
This morning, we went for a walk and picked lilies-of-the-valley. We had a little ball with us and we played with it a bit. One time the ball rolled off into the grass and it was all we could do to find it. Do you like the flowers that are drawn on this? It rained this morning at breakfast time. Tell Anastasia I don't have time to write to her, because I have to prepare for my lesson.
Irina
21 May 1905

1906

Maria to her grandmother, Dowager-Empress Maria Feodorovna—
Dear Babushka[4]
Congratulations on your birthday. How is your health? I miss you. I am studying every day. I have Russian lessons, the Law of God, arithmetic, German, English and music. I really love music lessons. I had such a good time on the Standart.

---

2. Source: Картон 18. Д. 1. Л. 91-92 об.

3. Daughter of Grand Duchess Ksenia (also spelled "Xenia") Alexandrovna and Grand Duke Alexander Mikhailovich, Maria's first cousin and future wife of Prince Felix Yusupov, known for his involvement in murder of Grigori Rasputin.

4. Russian for "grandmother."

Kissing you firmly,
Maria
Tsarskoe Selo
10 November 1906

1907

Pyotr Vasilievich Petrov[5] to Maria—

25 December 1907
I wish for the New Year that You will be such a good student as you
have been this year. Heartfelt greetings. May God protect You!
P.V. P.

Alexandra Feodorovna to Maria [in English[6]]—

[In Maria's hand,[7] Dec. 1907] . . . you—Papa and Olga are reading—I finished drinking cocoa and started to knit a blanket.—
"Lulu and Leander"[8] are lying on the sofa and staring at me
sadly—"where are the merry little children who are enjoying looking at us?"—In a basket, rags and scarf are resting, there is no one
here to play with them. The little cubes are chatting to each other,
trying to figure out why they were forgotten; but the pillows are
happy about the break and that they will not be smashed or torn
for the holidays. Good night, sleep peacefully and get well soon,
Your loving old Mama.

[In Maria's hand]: 29th Dec. 1907. T.S. My sweet Maria, I kiss you
fondly. I hope that your head no longer aches. It's so terribly sad
that you all four are ill and that I cannot be there with you—it's so
quiet around here without . . .

[In Maria's hand in English]: Dec. 30th, 1907. T.S. My darling little
Marie, I hope you will be able to read this letter all alone, tho "it"
is in English. Many thanks for yr nice letter. I am delighted that

5. Imperial children's tutor of Russian.
6. All correspondence in this volume is translated from Russian unless indicated.
7. Maria used to copy letters from her mother, probably as a writing exercise.
8. Dogs.

you are all so much better—God grant I shall soon see you all again.—I am going to have quite a party in my bedroom to luncheon. Papa, Olga & Anastasia; is it not grand? My headache has quite passed; but the head still feels rather tired.—Now I must read the Bible & prayers as I do not go to Church.—I hope you & Tatiana do so too.—Very fondest kisses my little girly dear fr yr boring old Mama. God bless you.

1909

Alexandra Feodorovna to Maria—

10.1.1909 [January 1, in Russian] Darling Maria, I kiss you affectionately and wish you to sleep well—glad that you liked the raspberry tea, hope that you will sweat well—and tomorrow will feel better.—We prayed for you at Church. May the Lord God keep you. Your old Mama.

Maria to Alexandra Feodorovna—

1909. 3rd January. To Mama from Maria. Dear Mama! How is your head? I really want to go to Anya's cathedral and to the nanny school. You after . . .

1909. Dear Mama! I would love to ride out to the cathedral with you one of these days, please or maybe together with Mari and Vikalunyan[1] with all our sisters please [illeg.] I am begging I know that you get a lot of letters and I hope your head doesn't ache today.

Maria to Tatiana—

11th January, 1909. Dear Tatiana! What are you doing? Tell Anastasia that I will not write her a letter because will have no time. My person is sitting in M.I.V.'s[2] room. May little God keep you.

1. Suite members?
2. Maria Ivanovna Vishnyakova.

Pyotr Vasilievich Petrov to Maria—
St Petersburg 29 October 1909
I received your dear letter, Maria Nikolaevna, and I was very happy
to see how successful you are doing in your writing, and, most importantly, your reading. There is just one thing only that I did not
see, that you are so good at using your left hand. I would like to,
but do not know how so I am sending you stamped flowers (=em-
bossed by a machine.) Last time I sent you a photograph of a gen-
tleman who of course you knew and I believe wanted to see, and
today I send you a photograph of the same gentleman, though in a
miniature view. As well as this, I send you a book in which you may
read about your Mama, and about your aunt Gr. Du[chess] Elizaveta Feodorovna, about the sisters of mercy and about your ances-
tors. Ekaterina Adolfovna[3] will find you everything. When you
arrive, we can see if we can read something about our soldiers, how
they fought, what they went through and what kind of warriors
they were.
How often I see all of you in my dreams, and such good it does my
soul after because I always see you good, gentle and sweet. Very soon
now, God grant it, we will see each other. we will start our work
with new strength. Bow to Sofia Ivanovna[4] and Ekaterina Adolfovna
and write to me again. May God protect you!
Your very loving,
PVP

S Petersburg. 9 November 1909.
For the drawing and for the letter, I send you Madame student No.
3, my dearly beloved Maria Nikolaevna, a big thank you, much bigger than the waves of the Black Sea!
"Gazavat" is a very interesting story. No joking, Shamil fought with
us for 30 years and only in his old age got captured. I knew his son
personally. He served in His Majesty's Convoy. And his son, that is,
the grandson studied and lives in Constantinople. We have a picture
at Tsarskoe Selo that shows how 50 years ago prisoner Shamil talked

3. Catherine Schneider, imperial tutor.
4. Sofia Ivanovna Tyutcheva.

with our commander Prince Baryatinsky. You didn't write to tell me if you are correcting the story "Children of the Sun" or who is the author. Who corrects you the most and why? Which institute? Of my books, read "Frostman," "Yegorich," "The Kutkin Couple" and "Ryabinkin's Visit to Osmana-Pasha," "The Lord Had Mercy," "Young Heroes of Sevastopol." I very much want to see you. Now it is not much longer to wait. You will get back to dear Tsarskoe and settle down to your studies. It's time, it's time! And the snow has piled up passionately here. What fun it will be to go sliding on the mountain!
May God keep you! Wishing you all the best,
With heartfelt love,
PVP

S Petersburg. 11 November 1909.
Yesterday the *Feld-Jager*[5] brought me three letters and one of them was from you, dear Maria Nikolaevna. Thank you! I am sending you the same little album I sent Anastasia Nikolaevna. I suppose you have already used up all the paper? About Gazavat, there is yet one more good book of Nemirovich Danchenko's called "Mountain Eagles." Let's read it some time. And the book "Children of the Sun," write to me about all that and how the girls live at the institute. Have you learned how to play lawn-bowls or do you just pick up the balls? Is the sun shining where you are? It seems there is more rain. Well, it is so good here, lots and lots of snow, dear frost, kind— not angry like in January. Don't forget to read "Frostman" from my books, and afterwards write to me whether you liked it or not. Greet Ekaterina Adolfovna. God protect you.
Your loving
PVP

5. Field huntsman.

1910

Maria to Alexandra Feodorovna—

1910. Dear Mama! How are you feeling after the ride, and how is your heart and head? Mama darling do you not understand that I want to get a letter from you? What did Grigori come here for? I kiss you affectionately,
Maria

Alexandra Feodorovna to Maria, copied in Marie's hand [in English]—

Feb. 4, 1910. T.S. Sweet little Marie, your tiny letter touched me very much. Certainly you can hang the ring up at the Immage [icon]—I should keep it for you & then we can think over when & how to do it.—Sleep well & God bless you, try always to love Him above all & to be a good patient little girl, and try never to be disobedient. I kiss you very tenderly. Your own Mama

Maria to Alexandra Feodorovna—

19th February, 1910. Tsarskoe Selo.
My dear Mama! Please give this letter to Anya. Soon Anastasia will write you a letter. Today we got up at 7 o'clock. Anastasia is also writing to Anya. Mama darling how did you sleep last night, how are you feeling how is your heart? Mama darling, I think you already went to Znamenie.[1] And have you been to Anya's?

1. Our Lady of Znamenie (the Sign), a church near Catherine Palace frequented by the imperial family.

Kiss you.
Maria
I wait for a response in a letter.

Alexandra Feodorovna to Maria [in English]—
March 7, 1910. Darling Marie, Loving thanks for several dear letters. Our Friend has come for very short. Try always to be a good
& obedient & gentle girly, then all will love you. I have no secrets
with Anastasia, I do not like secrets. God bless you, many kisses fr
yr old Mama +

Thursday March 11th, 1910 My darling little Marie,
Your letter made me quite sad. Sweet child you must promise me
never again to think that nobody loves you. How did such an extraordinary idea get into your little head? Get it quickly out again.
We all love you very tenderly only when too wild & noughty and
won't listen, then must be scolded; but to scold does not mean that
needs does not love, on the contrary one does it so as that you may
cure your faults & improve.—You generally keep away from the
others, think that you are in the way, & remain alone with Trina
instead of being with them. They imagun [imagine] then that you
do not want to be with then [them]; now you are getting a big girl
it is good that you should be more with them. —Now do not think
any more about it, and remember that you are just as presions [pre-
cious] & dear as the other 4 & that we love you with all our heart.
God bless you Darling Child. I kiss you ever so tenderly. Yr loving
old Mama +

14,3,1910 [March 14, 1910] Darling little Marie Very many thanks
for yr pretty card,—I hope you will be allowed to come down today. I won't come up now, so as to go to Church—yesterday could
not go.—Shall come later. Fondes[t] kisses, blessings Fr yr old
Mama + March 15th 1910. Darling Marie, I hope you will have a
quiet night without any pains—it makes me so sad to know you
suffer so much. I well know the horror of ear ache—shall try to
come up in the morning.—Blessing a & kisses fr yr old Mama +
Do you want to have any of our puzzles?

March 22, 1910 Beloved Child, I cannot come now, got up late as my head ached, have Mme. Brissac[2] & then Church at 11 1/2 at 12 1/2 a general, & then shall come up to kiss you. What do the drs saying wonder will they lett You soon come down again, I do wish they would. God bless you. Many kisses fr yr old Mama +

Ap.22.1910 Marie Darling, A big kiss & thanks for yr dear letter & little presents wh. You like yourself so much, so kind deary, good-night. God bless you. 1000 kisses fr yr old Mama +

Maria to Alexandra Feodorovna—

11th May, 1910

My dear Mama! Are you well? I want to tell you that Olga would really like to have a room of her own in Peterhof, because she and Tatiana have way too many things and way too little space. Mama how old were you when you got your own room? Please tell me if this can be arranged. Mama, how old were you when you started wearing long dresses? You should not think that Olga also wants to wear long dresses. Mama when you transfer both of us or just Olga, I am thinking it would be convenient to same place where Anastasia had diphtheria. [Crossed out] Mama since you wanted Tatiana [the end crossed out]

I kiss you,

Maria

P.S. I made this up to write to you

Princess Louise of Battenberg[3] to Maria [in English]—

Dec 28 1910

Dear Marie,

Thank you so very, very much for the awfully pretty table cover. How most awfully nice of you to do it for me. I am quite delighted to have it. How well you have done it and how busy you must have been to have done such a lot. And thank you also very much for

2. St. Petersburg couturier, one of the empress's dressmakers.

3. Later Lady Louise Alexandra Marie Irene Mountbatten (13 July 1889–7 March 1965), previously Princess Louise of Battenberg, was Queen of Sweden from the accession of her husband, Gustaf VI Adolf, in 1950 until her death.

the nice Xmas card you and Anastasia sent. We spent a very nice Xmas and I got heaps of lovely presents. The whole family is here. C. Louie lives quite close to us in London. We played the game in the dark like at Friedberg two nights ago. On New Year's Eve we are all going to dress up and after dinner we are going to Aunt Helen Albany[4] who is living quite near Windsor at Frogmore. We are going to play games and see the new year in there. Her daughter Alice and husband[5] will also be there. We go back to London on our 2nd. Georgie has to go back to his ship then Dick's holidays last some time longer. I must stop now as I have many other letters to write. Thank you again so much dear Marie for the nice table cover. Lots of love from your very loving cousin Louise.

4. Helena, Duchess of Albany, wife of Queen Victoria's youngest son, Prince Leopold.

5. Princess Alice, Countess of Athlone—Queen Victoria's last surviving grandchild who died in 1981, and her husband Prince Alexander of Teck, brother-in-law of King George V.

1911

Alexandra Feodorovna to Maria [in English]—

9 Jan. 1911 Darling Childie, Thanks for yr note. I have luckily my back aches much, as I am very tired. I have got yr ring still. Yes, we shall all think of him tomorrow. Bless you. 1000 kisses fr yr old Mama+

Feb.15. 1911 Loving thanks, Marie darling for your sweet letter. Yes, I too am very sad our beloved Friend is now leaving—but whilst he is gone we must try & live as He would have wished, then we will feel He is near us in prayers and thoughts. Sleep well. 1000 kisses from yr old Mama Next week I shall take you to Znam[enie]: Church.—Faults in your letter: ofoull—awfull. Ofoon—often, too diner—to dinner, awey—away, sech—such, taom—time, I wood— I would, no—know, wat—what, Communion, angell—angel, we—week, suit—sweet, rite—write.

Feb.25.1911 Marie dear, Don't forget to read before [under] confession & communion the book Batushka[1] gave you, Anya[2] & I have been doing the same. A blessing fr yr old Mama + 21.A.1911 My sweet Maria [in Russian] Olga has written to A.[unt] Xenia[3] & sent 74 r. collected by you. You had 51, Madeleine gave 3 (you must

---

1 ."Little father," Russian reference for a priest.
2. Anna Vyrubova.
3. Ksenia Alexandrovna.

give her a flower tomorrow) & I added 20.—Aunties children collected 22 r. Sleep well. God bless you. A good kiss fr yr old Mama
+

Maria to Alexandra Feodorovna—
Dear Mama!
How do you feel?
I now lie with my whole head bandaged, Trina[4] reads to me. My ear does not hurt. I was told that if I lie there, I can go on Sunday. Firmly kissing You and Papa.
Maria.

Maria to her grandmother, Dowager-Empress Maria Feodorovna—
[19 July 1911—on the Standart]
My dear Babushka!
I congratulate you very much with your holiday. How is your health? I am having such a good time here. I hope to see you soon. I have gone for a swim once—the water was warm. Papa has already been swimming for several days; we weren't able to swim earlier; the water and weather were cold. Every day, morning and afternoon, we go ashore, and go on big walks with Papa or stay on the shore and wait for him. We had two picnics not so long ago with fifteen people. We had an awfully jolly time. I kiss you and Aunt Alix firmly. Lovingly yours, your granddaughter,
Maria

9 November 1911
Livadia
My dear Babushka,
From my soul I congratulate you and kiss you firmly. It is such a pity you are not here with us. It was so wonderful and good at the ball. It went on till one at night. Mama and Papa watched the dances. We had no rain all October, and then yesterday was a thunderstorm with hail; but today it is warm and sunny again. Tonight,

---

4. Catherine Schneider's nickname.

there will be a dance evening at Aunt Minnie's at Kharax. Olga and Tatiana have been invited to it. We go to Kharax and Ai-Todor a lot after morning lessons and lunch. We are always back at six o'clock for reading lessons. Olga and Tatiana often play tennis with Papa. Anastasia and I are learning how to play. How is your health? I kiss you firmly.

Lovingly yours, your granddaughter
Maria

1912

Maria's diary—

January 1 Sunday Circumcision of the Lord. St Basil the Great Bo-isman.

In the morning, we were at Liturgy. Had breakfast 5 with Mama and Trina. In the afternoon we went for a walk and sledded on the little hill. Had dinner with Anastasia and Alexei.

January 2 Monday. St Sylvester
Sandro
In the morning walked and slid on the mountain. Breakfasted 5 with Papa, Mama and Sandro. Were at Pavlovsk in the day and had tea there. Dinner with Anastasia and Alexei. Played with Trina and Sonia.[1]

January 3 Tuesday St Prophet Malachi
U[ncle] Kirill[2]
Walked and sledding on the little hill. Had breakfast 5 with Papa, Mama and U[ncle] Kirill. Vera came over during the day. After that we played at Trina's. Dinner with Anastasia and Alexei.

January 4 Wednesday Synaxis of the Seventy Apostles Polivanov
We went for a walk and went sledding on the small hill. Breakfast

1. Princess Sonia Orbeliani, Georgian princess at the Russian Court.
2. Grand Duke Kirill Vladimirovich, the Tsar's cousin.

5 with Mama, Papa and A[unt] Ella.[3] Went for a walk with Mama and A[unt] Ella in the day. At 4 o'clock was a *yolka*[4] for the officers. Dinner with Anastasia and Alexei.

January 5 Thursday Martyr Theopempt
Forefeast of Theophany
/No entry on this day/

January 12 Thursday Martyr Tatiana Gr V Dashkov
Stayed home in the morning. At 12 1/2 was a *moleben*.[5] After that, breakfast 5 with Mama, Papa, A[unt] Ella, U[ncle] Andrei[6] and Sashka.[7] Vera[8] came over during the day and had tea with us. Dinner with Anastasia and Alexei.

January 13 Friday Martyr Ermil
Lesson in the morning. Before breakfast, we saw the English. Had breakfast 5 with Papa, A[unt] Ella, U[ncle] Pavel[9] and Dmitri.[10] Went for a walk in the afternoon. After that I had a music lesson. Had tea with Mama, Papa and A[unt] Ella. Dinner with Anastasia and Alexei.

January 14 Saturday Svechin
Had lesson in the morning. Breakfast with Anastasia and Alexei.

January 15 Sunday St Paul of the Thebaid Dmitri
In the morning we were at Church. After that had breakfast 5 with Papa, Mama, A[unt] Ella and Dmitri. In the day we went over to Vera's and had tea. Had dinner with Anastasia, Alexei and the little Ai-Todories.[11]

3. Grand Duchess Elisabeth Feodorovna.

4. Literally "fir tree," refers to a Christmas party.

5. A Russian Orthodox liturgical service of supplication or thanksgiving.

6. Grand Duke Andrei Vladimirovich.

7. Alexander Vorontsov, officer of the suite.

8. Princess Vera Konstaninovna, youngest daughter of Grand Duke Konstantin Konstantinovich.

9. Grand Duke Pavel Alexandrovich, Nicholas II's youngest uncle.

10. Grand Duke Dmitri Pavlovich, Grand Duke Pavel's son, the tsar's first cousin.

11. Family of Grand Duchess Ksenia and Grand Duke Alexander, who had a mansion in Ai-Todor, Crimea.

January 16 Monday Apostle Peter Sergei[12]
In the morning lessons as always. After that breakfast 5 with Mama. In the day I went for a walk with Tatiana, Anastasia and Trina. After that was a music lesson. Had tea 4 with Mama and Papa except Anastasia.
Dinner with Anastasia and Alexei.

January 21 Saturday Venerable Maxim Ioannchik[13]
I had a lesson in the morning. Breakfast 5 with Mama, Papa, B[aron] Fredericks[14] and Ioannchik. In the day 4 went to Anya's with Mama. Kiki[15] was there. Was at the *vsenoshnaya*[16] with the Regiment. Dinner 5 with Mama, Papa and Ioannchik.

February 2 Thursday The Meeting of the Lord Pr. Eristov
Were at Church in the morning. Went to the theater by train. Sat at breakfast with Papa and Pr[ince] Eristov. Saw the ballet "Sleeping Beauty." Later were at the Montenegrin King's.[17]

March 10 Saturday Martyr Kodrat Pr. Engalychev
Had lessons. Breakfast 4 with Mama, Pr[ince] Yusupov and Belevsky. Went for a ride and a walk in the day. Was at the All-Night Vigil. Had tea with Anastasia and Alexei. Dinner 4 with Papa, Mama, Aunt Ksenia, A[unt] Olga and Grandma.

March 11 Sunday St Sophrony Patriarch of Jerusalem Shipov
Went for a walk. Were at Church Liturgy. Breakfast with Lili[18] and M Kututsova. Went for a ride with Irina and Tatiana. There was a cinematograph and lots of guests. Dinner with Anastasia and Alexei.

---

12. Most likely Grand Duke Sergei Mikhailovich.

13. Prince Ioann Konstantinovich, son of Grand Duke Konstantin Konstantinovich.

14. Baron Vladimir Borisovich Fredericks, the imperial household minister, later styled Count Fredericks (9 Feb 1913).

15. Nickname for Nikolai Pavlovich Sablin.

16. All-night vigil, a combination of Vespers, Matins, and First Hour, held the evening before a liturgy in the Russian Orthodox Church.

17. King Nicholas I of Montenegro.

18. Lili Dehn, the empress's lady in waiting.

March 12 Monday Venerable Theophanes Pr. Dolgor.[ukov]
Had lessons. Breakfast 5 with Mama and Papa. Anastasia and I with
S[ofia]. I[vanovna].[19] were at the Nanny School.[20] Had a music lesson. Tea at 3 with Mama and Papa.
Sasha

April 17 Tuesday Holy-martyr. Simeon, Bishop.
Had lessons. At breakfast, I sat with [blank]. During the day I went
for a walk and picked flowers with Mama in the equipage [small
carriage]. Had dinner with Alexei and Anastasia. We went to the
yacht and slept the night there.
Sasha

April 18. Wednesday. Ven. John, Martyr Victor.
Was at the raising of the flag. We went to the "Novaya Zemlya." At
breakfast, I sat with U[ncle] Ernie[21] and Ridheisel. In the afternoon,
we watched "Novaya Zemlya" and [illeg.].

Alexandra P. Schneider to A. A. Dostoevsky[22]—

22 April, 1912. Pansion von Shleier. Recently, two girls came over
to me, whom I suspected to be the youngest grand duchesses, based
on their age, and by how they approached me directly, said hello
and stretched out their hand. But while talking to them, I discarded
this initial thought, and decided these are the children of mere mortals,—as they spoke Russian absolutely perfectly, without any sign
of English burr [accent], as was inherent to aristocratic children;
another sign that led me to a false conclusion was that they were
dressed not just simply, but poorly,—albeit cleanly, in extremely
worn blue skirts, which had apparently been exposed to sand, as
well as sea water, and in knitted blue blouses and similar little hats,
and worn booties—I noticed it all, trying to determine if they were
the grand duchesses or not—and decided, no, I was mistaken.

19. Tyutcheva.

20. An orphanage in Tsarskoe Selo, patronized by the empress.

21. Grand Duke Ernest of Hesse, brother of Empress Alexandra.

22. Source: Письма—больше, чем воспоминания. . .": Из переписки семьи Семёновых-Тян-Шанских и сестёр А. П. и В. П. Шнейдер. М., 2012. Alexandra Schneider (no relation to Catherine) later became the grand duchesses' art tutor.

Maria to Alexandra Feodorovna—

25th June, 1912. The Standart. My dear Mama!
How did you sleep and how do you feel? I didn't sleep since half past five and told Anastasia that I will stay in bed because I slept badly. Mama, where shall I have breakfast, with you or with everyone? I kiss you affectionately. Your Maria.
During the night I went to "the place" [toilet] several times.

Pyotr Petrov to Maria—

Kissingen
July 19, 1912.
Dear name day girl Maria Nikolaevna. I wish you on the day of your Angel all the beautiful things that there are in the world!
I wish you not to know the ailments and sorrows, although you cannot do without them. I wish, therefore, for you to be patient, meek and courageous. May the Lord keep you in all the ways of your life!
This year the weather does not spoil us. The hot days gave way to rainy weather. You have to walk around in a waterproof raincoat. The waters and baths are doing me good, but at the same time they tire one.
I think to do *Nachkur* [aftercare—German] at *Starnberger See* [Lake Starnberger—German] in the environs of Munich. Yesterday I was in the cinema [in German *Kammer—Lichtspiel*] and saw the screening of the Olympic Games in Stockholm. Very interesting.
There are no other entertainments for me here. I walk a lot, get up early and go to bed early.
What are you reading now? It is a pity that you do not write more. Write to me, please.
Bow to everyone and Ekaterina Adolfovna.
Be healthy, cheerful and do not forget your sincerely loving P.V. P.

Telegram to Maria—

19 July 1912
Your Imperial Highness's Kazan Dragoons offer to the Almighty their fervent prayers for the good health of their August Chief, send-

ing congratulations on Your name day and drink to your Imperial Highness with unceasing enthusiasm.
Regimental Commander Colonel
Kuzmin Korovaev

Olga to Maria—

Congratulations to my dear, fat Kazansha.
Olga
Christmas 1912

1913

Maria's diary—

January 1. Tuesday. In the morning went to *obednya*.[1] Had breakfast with Papa and Sergei. In the afternoon took a walk with Papa then went to Countess Hendrikova,[2] Aunt Mops[3] and to Anya's, where Nikolai Pavlovich was. Had tea with Papa and Mama. Had dinner with Anya.

January 2. Wednesday. In the morning went to *obednya*. Had breakfast with Papa, Aunt Olga,[4] Aunt Ksenia and Irina. In the afternoon took a walk with Papa, Aunt Olga and Irina. Had tea with Papa, Mama and Irina. Had dinner with Papa and Irina.

January 3. Thursday. Took a ride in the morning, had breakfast with Papa. In the afternoon slid down the hill near the regimental church and then near the white tower. Had tea with Papa and Mama. Had dinner with Anastasia upstairs.

January 6. Sunday. In the morning went to *obednya*. The four of us had breakfast. Anastasia and I took a ride with Trina and then went to the nanny school. Had tea with Mama and Anya. Had dinner upstairs with Anastasia.

1. The Russian Orthodox service with communion.
2. Countess Hendrikova was Princess Sophia Petrovna Gagarine, mother to "Nastenka" Hendrikova, and an unofficial governess to the four young grand duchesses.
3. Evgenia Maximilianovna, Duchess of Leuchtenberg. Mother-in-law of Grand Duchess Olga Alexandrovna.
4. Grand Duchess Olga Alexandrovna, the tsar's youngest sister.

January 27. Sunday. In the morning to *obednya* at the regiment church. At breakfast sat with Dedulin[5] and [blank space]. In the afternoon took a walk with Papa. Had tea with Irina, Feodor, Rostislav, Georgiy[6] and R[illeg.]. Then we went to [see] a cinematograph. Had dinner with Anastasia and Alexei.

February 7. Thursday. Rode around with Anastasia and Madame Conrad.[7] Then had lessons. Had breakfast four with Mama and Anya. In the afternoon sledded near white tower. Alexei was there too. Had tea with Trina. Had a music [crossed out] dance lesson, then music. Then did homework. Had dinner with Anastasia.

February 10. Sunday. In the morning went to *obednya* with Papa at the regiment church. At breakfast sat with Gavril[8] and Drenteln.[9] Went to Petersburg to Grandmama's from there to Aunt Olga's. Played, had tea and dinner. There were: Irina, Andrusha, Feodor, Sasha, Nadya and their mama, Zoya, Khvoshinsky, Klyucharev, Rodionov, Count Ungengiterberg, Skvortzov, Shvedov, Kulikovsky and Isan[illeg.]. At dinner sat with Skvotzov and Shangin. Then [we] went to the circus with the Cossacks, Nadya, Klyucharev, Kulikovsky, Prince Gagarin and Lili.

February 16. Saturday. Had lessons in the morning. Had breakfast four with Papa, Aunt Olga, Aunt Ella and Mama on the sofa. In the afternoon took a walk with Papa and Aunt Olga and then sledded near the white tower. Had tea with Mama, Papa, Aunt Olga and Aunt Ella. Went to the regiment church for *vsenoshnaya* with Papa, Aunt Olga and Aunt Ella. Then there was a cinematograph. They showed historical films.

February 21. Thursday. In the morning took a walk in the park. Then drove to Kazansky Cathedral for molebna. Had breakfast four

---

5. Presumably V.A. Dedulin, one of the tsar's retinue.

6. Rostislav and Feodor were the sons of Grand Duchess Ksenia, and Maria's first cousins; Georgiy is Prince Georgiy Konstantinovich, youngest son of Grand Duke Konstantin Konstantinovich.

7. Wife of the imperial children's music teacher.

8. Prince Gavril Konstantinovich, second son of Grand Duke Konstantin Konstantinovich.

9. Alexander Alexandrovich Drenteln, the tsar's major-general.

with Papa, Grandmama and Aunt Olga. In the afternoon we were all in Russian dresses and there was a "*baise main.*"[10] Had tea at the children's monastery with Anastasia.

February 23 Saturday. In the morning took a walk with Papa. Then there was a "*baise main*" for the ladies. Had breakfast with Papa and Grandmama.[11] In the afternoon took a walk with Papa. Had tea with all the Ai Todories. Went to Trina's. Had dinner with Olga and Papa. Anastasia and I took a bath in the big bathtub at Papa's. Tatiana has typhus.[12]

February 24 Sunday. In the morning went to *obednya* with Papa. Had breakfast with Papa. In the afternoon went to Aunt Olga's there we had tea, played. At her [place] were: Irina, Andrusha,[13] Sasha, Nadya, Kolya and their mama, Count Ungermeterberg, Shvedov,[14] Yuzik, Skvortsov, Sablin,[15] Klyucharev, Kulikovsky,[16] Zarnekoy, Zoya, [illeg.]. Had dinner with Anastasia.

February 25 Monday. In the morning went to church. Had breakfast with Papa, Uncle Boris,[17] Tatiana and Bagration. Took a walk with Papa on the roof and in the garden. Had tea with Mama and Anya. Went to church. Had dinner with Papa and Bagration. Took a bath in Papa's bathtub. Mama, Papa and Aunt Olga watched.

March 4 Monday. Had lessons in the morning. Had breakfast with Papa and Mama on the sofa. Went to the review of the Albavsky sailors. Had tea alone. Had a music lesson. Went to Realnoe school[18] with Olga and Trina for a physics [lesson]. Did homework. Had dinner with Anastasia and Alexei.

10. Kissing of the hands ceremony.

11. Dowager-Empress Maria Feodorovna.

12. Tatiana later had her hair cut short while convalescing from this.

13. Prince Andrei Alexandrovich, Maria's cousin.

14. Alexander Shvedov, officer.

15. Nicholas Pavlovich Sablin, officer on imperial yacht *The Standart.*

16. Nikolai Kulikovsky, one of the imperial officers, later second husband of Grand Duchess Olga Alexandrovna.

17. Grand Duke Boris Vladimirovich, the tsar's cousin.

18. The Realnoe School was founded by Nicholas II in 1900. The school focused on natural sciences, and the imperial children went there to use laboratory equipment for physics lessons.

March 5 Tuesday. In the morning sledded with Madame Conrad. Had lessons. Had breakfast with Mama on the sofa. In the afternoon stayed home due to a cold. We got haircuts and Tatiana's [hair] got all cut off. Had tea in the playroom. Had dance lessons then did homework. Had dinner with Mama on the sofa.

March 6 Wednesday. Had lessons in the morning. Had breakfast four with Papa, Fabritzky and Mama on the sofa. In the afternoon stayed home. Had a music lesson. Had tea in the playroom. Did homework. Had dinner with Anastasia. The King of Greece has died.[19]

March 10 Sunday. In the morning went to the regiment church with Papa. Had breakfast with Papa and Mama on the sofa and Prince [illeg.]. Went to Petersburg, at first were at Grandmama's and then went to Aunt Olga's. There we had tea and looked at her exhibit. Had dinner upstairs with Anastasia's.

March 15 Friday. Had lessons in the morning. Had breakfast with Papa and Mama on the sofa. In the afternoon broke ice with Papa, Alexei was also there. Had tea alone. Had a music lesson. Anastasia and I had French reading. Did homework. Had dinner with Anastasia and Alexei.

March 17 Sunday. In the morning went to *obednya* with Papa at the regiment church. Had breakfast with Papa, Ioann, Gavril and Mama on the sofa. Went to Petersburg, at first to Grandmama's and then to Aunt Olga's, there were: Irina, Andrei, Feodor, Sasha and her mother, Count Ungershternberg, Shvedov, Skvortzov, Yuzik, and Kulikovsky. We played, had tea and dinner and returned home.

March 24 Sunday. In the morning went to *obednya* at the regiment church with Papa. At breakfast sat with Ioann and Komakov. In the afternoon broke ice with Papa and Irina. Had tea with the little Ai Todories, Georgiy and Vera, and played. Went to *vsenoshnaya* with Papa at the regiment church. Had dinner with Papa, Bagration and Mama on the sofa.

19. King George I of Greece, brother of Maria's paternal grandmother, Dowager Empress Maria Feodorovna, was assassinated on March 18, 1913.

March 25 Monday. In the morning went to Petersburg with Papa. Went to *obednya* at Anichkov[20] with Grandmama. Had breakfast with Grandmama, Aunt Olga and Irina with [her] brothers. Had tea, played and had dinner at Aunt Olga's. There were: Count Ungershternberg, Shvedov, Yuzik, Skvortzov, Zborovsky,[21] Zarbuchalo, Shangin, Kulikovsky, Felix, Irina with [her] brothers, Sasha with mother, Kolya, Nadya and Uncle Petya. And returned home.

March 28 Thursday. In the morning sledded with Madame Conrad. Had one lesson. Went to the *manege*[22] to a parade of the Svodny regiment with Papa and Aunt Olga. At breakfast sat with Sherikhovsky and Kutepov. In the afternoon took a walk and broke ice with Papa and Aunt Olga. Had tea alone. Anastasia and I had a dance lesson. Had a music lesson. Did homework. Had dinner upstairs with Olga and Anastasia.
[This page had a dried flower in it, marked "A rose from the Svodny regiment from the parade."]

March 31 Sunday. In the morning went to *obednya* with Papa at the regiment church. At breakfast sat with Count Rostovtzev and Prince Gotgoselsky. Went to Petersburg, at first to Grandmama's, and then to Aunt Olga's. At her [place] we had tea and played. There were: Uncle Petya, Kulikovsky, Count Ungershternberg, Shvedov, Yuzik, Zborovsky, Kolya and mother, Klyucharev and Shangin.

April 7 Sunday. In the morning five with Papa went to *obednya* at the regiment church. At breakfast sat with Komarov and Count Sheremetiev. In the afternoon rode around with Trina. Had tea and went to a cinematograph with Ritka,[23] Irina and [her] brothers. Had dinner 4 with Papa, Irina, Feodor, Nikita and Mama on the sofa. Looked at the pictures of Prokudin-Gorsky.[24]

---

20. Anichkov Palace in St. Petersburg was one of the main residences of Dowager Empress Maria Feodorovna.
21. Viktor Erastovich Zborovsky, one of the favorite officers of the tsar's daughters.
22. Enclosed area in which horses and riders are trained.
23. Margarita Khitrovo, a friend of Grand Duchess Olga Nikolaevna.
24. Sergei Prokudin-Gorsky was a chemist and photographer, considered to be the pioneer of color photography.

April 9 Tuesday. In the morning rode around 4 with Madame. Went 5 with Papa to the pre-consecrated *obednya* at the lower church. Had breakfast 5 with Papa and Mama on the sofa. Broke ice with Papa. Had tea 4 with Mama, Papa, Aunt Ksenia and Uncle San-dro.[25] Went to church with Papa and Mama. Had dinner 4 with Papa and Mama on the sofa.

April 13 Saturday. In the morning at 5 o'clock went to *pogrebenie*[26] at the regiment church. Had breakfast with Papa and Mama on the sofa. Went to Anya's 4 with Papa and Mama and colored eggs and had tea. There were: Kiki, Isa, Lili, Rodionov, Kozhevnikov and Pi. Had dinner 4 with Papa and Mama. Went 5 with Papa and Mama to *zautrenya*[27] and then to *obednya*, and then prepared for commun-ion. [Dried flower marker "Lilac from *zautrenya* from the regiment church."]

April 14 Easter Sunday. In the morning 5 went to *khristovanie*,[28] Papa and Mama gave out eggs. Had breakfast 5 with Papa and Mama on the sofa. Went to Vera's[29] with Anastasia, had tea played in the garden. Went 4 with Papa to the regiment church. Had din-ner 4 with Papa and Mama on the sofa.

April 15 Monday. In the morning 4 went to *obednya* with Papa at the regiment church. Had breakfast 5 with Papa and Mama on the sofa. In the afternoon we 5 with Papa rode little boats. Had tea with Papa and Mama. Went to Trina's and played with her Sonia. Had dinner with Anastasia and Mama on the sofa.

April 16 Tuesday. Went 5 to a grenadier parade. Had breakfast 5 with Aunt Olga and Mama on the sofa. In the afternoon took a walk and rode little boats with Papa and Aunt Olga. Had tea with Mama, Papa and Aunt Olga. Had dinner 4 with Papa and Mama on the sofa. Kiki sent a letter.

25. Grand Duke Alexander Mikhailovich, husband of Grand Duchess Ksenia Alexandrovna.

26. The Burial Service of Christ, part of the Easter services.

27. Morning prayer service.

28. Easter ceremony of triple kisses.

29. Princess Vera Konstantinovna, daughter of Grand Duke Konstantin Konstantinovich, one of the Romanov cousins.

April 17 Wednesday. Went 5 to the parade of the 1st and 2nd sharp-shooter regiment. Had breakfast 5. Went to the Invalid House and 4 gave out eggs. Went 4 with Lili to Petersburg. Went to Grand-mama's. Then went to Aunt Olga's. We played and had tea and dinner. There were: Sasha and her mother, Irina, Feodor, Count Ungershternberg, Shvedov, Yuzik, Skvortzov, Zborovsky, Klyucharev, Kiki, Kolya, Kulikovsky[30] and Uncle Petya.

April 18 Thursday. In the morning rode around with Trina and then stopped by the nanny school, there we gave out eggs and played with the children. Had breakfast 5 with Papa and Kostya.[31] In the afternoon took a walk 4 with Papa and rode in little boats. Had tea 4 with Mama and Papa. Had dinner 4 with Papa, Kostya and Mama on the sofa.

April 24 Wednesday. Had lessons in the morning. Had breakfast 5 with Papa, Daragan and Mama on the sofa. In the afternoon rode bicycles with Papa and then in canoes. Had tea upstairs with Alexei. Had a music lesson. Read with Trina. Had dinner with Isa[32] and Mama on the sofa.

April 25 Thursday. In the morning rode with Madame. Then had lessons. Had breakfast with Papa, Sergei and Mama on the sofa. In the afternoon rode bicycles with Papa and then in little boats. Had tea alone. Had music [lesson]. Did homework and read with Trina. Had dinner with Alexei.

May 5 Sunday. At breakfast sat with Delsal and Dedulin. In the afternoon 4 took a walk with Papa and Aunt Olga, then sledded with Kiki and Papa with Aunt Olga. Had tea 4 with Papa, Mama and Aunt Olga. We 4 sat with Aunt Olga. Had dinner 4 with Papa, Grandmama, Aunt Olga, Uncle Petya, Aunt Ksenia and Uncle Sandro. Then went to hear the Andreev choir and Kiki was there.

May 6 Monday. 4 with Papa, Grandmama and other relatives went

30. Nikolai Kulikovsky married Maria's paternal aunt Olga in November 1916.
31. Prince Konstantin Konstantinovich, third son of Grand Duke Konstantin Konstantinovich.
32. Sophie Buxhoeveden, one of the empress's ladies in waiting.

to church and had breakfast there too. I sat with Uncle Sandro and Gavril. In the afternoon rode bicycles and canoes 4 with Papa. Had tea 4 with Papa and Mama. Went to Trina's with Anastasia. Had dinner with Anastasia and Alexei.

May 7 Tuesday. Rode around with Anastasia and Madame. Had lessons. Went to the regiment church for molebna 5 with Papa. Had breakfast 5 with Papa and Mama on the sofa. In the afternoon took a walk with Papa, then went in boats. Had tea 4. We 4 had dance lessons. Had music. Had dinner with Anastasia and Alexei. At 11 in the evening Papa left to Berlin for the wedding of the daughter of the German emperor.[33]

May 11 Saturday. Rode around with Anastasia and Madame. Had lessons. Had breakfast with Anastasia, Alexei and Mama on the sofa. In the afternoon I, Anastasia and Alexei [went] to the nanny school and played with the children in the garden and inside. Had tea 5 with Mama and Irina. 4 went to church of the Svodny regiment. Had dinner 4 with Anya and Mama on the sofa.

May 13 Monday. We 5 went to the train station to meet Papa. Had a lesson. Took a walk with Papa. Had lessons. Had breakfast 5 with Papa and Mama on the sofa. In the afternoon 4 with Papa rode our bicycles and in boats. Had music. Had tea with Papa. Went to Trina's. Had dinner 4 with Papa, Grandmama, Aunt Ksenia, Uncle Sandro, Aunt Olga and Uncle Petya.

May 14 Tuesday. I had food poisoning and didn't go to church. Had breakfast 5 with Papa. In the afternoon sat on the balcony with Mama and Anya. Had tea 4 with Papa. Anastasia and I sat at Trina's. Had dinner with Anastasia and Alexei.

May 16 Thursday.[34] At breakfast sat with Count Apraksin and Masolov. Went 5 with Papa to Vladimir to the Uspensky Cathedral.

33. Princess Victoria Louise of Prussia, who married Ernest Augustus, Duke of Brunswick on 24 May 1913.
34. The imperial family went to Moscow for the Tercentennial celebrations of the Romanov Dynasty.

From there 4 with Papa on the motors rode to Suzdal. There went to the Suzdal Cathedral then to Spas-Yefimovsky monastery, went to the grave of Prince Pozharsky,[35] from there to Rizolotsky monastery, to Pokrovsky monastery. Had tea in the Igumania's cell. From there went to Bogolubov were in the Cathedral [there]. Papa received the township heads. Had dinner with Anastasia, Alexei, Nilov and Sablin.

May 17 Friday. In the morning arrived in Nizhny Novgorod, went 5 with Papa and Mama to the cathedral. There was a *litia*[36] at the grave of Minin,[37] then went on a Procession of the Cross, to the laying of the foundation of the memorial to Minin and Pozharsky. Had breakfast 5 with Papa and Mama at the palace. In the afternoon we 5 with Papa and Mama had tea at the Nobility meeting. Had dinner with Anastasia, Alexei, Pogulyaev and Sablin.

May 19 Sunday. In the morning there was *obednya* and *moleben* at the Ipatiev monastery.[38] 5 with Mama and Papa. At breakfast sat with Botkin[39] and Dedulin. In the afternoon we 5 with Papa and Mama saw the Tsar Mikhail Feodorovich's[40] museum. There was tea with the Nobility. Had dinner with Anastasia, Alexei, Nilov and Sablin.

May 20 Monday. In the morning 5 with Mama and Papa to the cathedral. From there went to the laying of the foundation 300 memorial. We 5 with Mama and Aunt Olga went to Bogoyavleisky monastery. At breakfast sat with Dedulin and Botkin. In the afternoon we 4 with Papa went to Resurrection Church in Debryanks. Then looked at the Red Cross hospital, from there went to see the

35. Dmitri Mikhailovich Pozharsky, a Rurikid prince, led Russian forces against Polish-Lithuanian invaders in 1611-1612.

36. A service at the end of Vespers where five loaves of bread are offered.

37. Kuzma Minin was a merchant from Nizhny Novgorod, who together with Prince Pozharsky became a national hero for his role in defending the country against the Polish invasion.

38. Ipatiev Monastery in Kostroma, was where the first Romanov Tsar Michael took refuge as a teenager.

39. Dr. Evgeny Botkin.

40. Tsar Mikhail Feodorovich was the first Romanov tsar, a.k.a. Tsar Michael.

crafts exhibition, where [we] had tea. Had dinner with Anastasia, Alexei, Nilov and Sablin.

May 21 Tuesday. Arrived in Yaroslavl. We 5 with Papa and Mama went to the Uspensky Cathedral from there 4 with Papa to Spassky Monastery.

May 22 Wednesday. Arrived in Rostov. We 5 with Papa went to the Uspensky Cathedral, then walked along Kremlin wall, from there to the White Chamber and Princely Tower. On the way looked at churches. At breakfast sat with Count Benkendorf[41] and Mosolov. In the afternoon we went to the Pokrovsky monastery and church of St Ioann. Had tea 5 with Papa and the suite. Went to *vsenoshnaya* at the Christ's Resurrection church. At dinner sat with Benkendorf and Mosolov.

May 23 Thursday. Arrived in Petrovsk with Papa. Went to *obednya* at the city cathedral. At breakfast sat with Alexei and Trotsky. Drove to Pereslav in motors. Went to Nikitsky monastery where we were blessed by [illeg.]. Then went to Danilovsky monastery and also in Feodorovsky [illeg.] monastery.

May 24 Friday. We 4 with Papa went to *obednya* at the Sergeyev Lavra and had tea with Metropolit. At breakfast sat with Benkendorf and Bulygin. Went to Moscow, from the [train] station we went to the Kremlin to the cathedral [?]. Had tea 4 with Papa, Mama, Aunt Olga and Aunt Ksenia. Had dinner 4 with Papa and Aunt Ella.

May 25 Saturday. There was a [Ceremonial] Exit from the Red Porch and I was walking arm in arm with Uncle Sandro. There was an *obednya* at the Uspensky Cathedral, many people picked up gold coins. At breakfast sat with Uncle Sandro and Uncle Alek[42] [?]. In the afternoon we 4 with Papa looked at antiques, then went to the

41. Count Alexander Benkendorf, Russia's ambassador to the United Kingdom.
42. Alexander Petrovich Oldenburg, father of "Uncle Petya" (Grand Duchess Olga Alexandrovna's husband).

bridge of imprisonment of St Hermogen[43] and looked at the house of the Boyars Romanovs.[44] Had tea 4 with Papa, Dmitri and Marie. Had dinner with Anastasia and Alexei.

May 26 Sunday. In the morning 5 with Papa went to *obednya* at the Novo-Spassky monastery and there was *litia* at the grave. Had breakfast 5 with Papa, Aunt Olga at Aunt Ella's. In the afternoon 4 and Papa with her went to the school of the middle merchant society, had tea there. Had dinner 4 with Papa.

May 27 Monday. In the morning 4 with Papa saw an exhibit at the Stroganoff School. Had breakfast 5 with Mama on the sofa, Aunt Ella and Marie. In the afternoon we 5 with Papa, Mama and Aunt Ella went to the Voznesensky Monastery. From there went to the train. Had tea 4 with Papa and the suite. At dinner sat with Count Benkendorf and Veselkovsky.

May 28 Tuesday. In the morning arrived at T.S. We 5 with Papa went to molebna at the lower regiment church. Had breakfast 5 with Papa, Veselkin and Mama on the sofa. In the afternoon rode around with Trina. Had tea 4 with Papa and Mama. Had dinner 4 with Papa, Veselkin and Mama on the sofa.

May 29 Wednesday. In the morning we had *moleben*. Had breakfast 5 with Papa, Aunt Olga, Aunt Ksenia, Uncle Sandro and the children. In the afternoon I stayed home and read with Trina. Had tea with Mama, Papa and Irina. Had dinner with Anastasia, Alexei and 4 little Ai Todories.

May 30 Thursday. I have fever, in the morning was 38.7 and sore throat and headache. They transferred me to Tatiana's room, I stayed in bed and Shura read to me. Had breakfast in bed. Temp. 38.8. Then Shura again read to me. Had tea. Temp. 38.4. Had dinner. Temp 38.1. [Crossed out] and Papa before dinner.

43. Patriarch of Moscow in the "Time of Troubles," imprisoned during an invasion of Moscow and starved to death in 1612. Proclaimed a saint of 25 May 1913.
44. The sixteenth-century house of the Romanov family. The first Romanov tsar, Michael, was born here in 1596.

May 31 Friday. In the morning temp 36.9. Read with Trina. Had breakfast. Temp. 37. Read with Trina and played cards with Trina [illeg.] and Liza. Sonia was here, Mama was here and Anya. Temp. 36.3. Read with Trina. Had dinner. Fedor was here. Temp 37.7. June 1 Saturday. Dark in the morning, got up from bed and got dressed. Had breakfast with Anastasia, played cards with Alexei. Had tea in bed. [illeg.] at Mama's and Papa's. Had dinner with Alexei. Temp at 6 o'cl. 37. After dinner at 9 o'cl. 36.9

June 2 Sunday. 5 went with Papa to a parade of the Izmailovsky Regiment and Northern Battalion. Had breakfast 5 with Aunt Mavra[45] and Mama on the sofa. In the afternoon 4 went in a motor with Anya to Aunt Olga's in Peterhof. Had tea, took a walk. Played and had dinner. There were: Shvedov, Yuzik, Skvortzov, Zborovsky, Rodionov, Klyucharev, Kulikovsky, Aunt Ksenia with Irina, Andrusha and Feodor and Anya and Semyonov. Returned home.

June 4 Tuesday. In the morning went with Agatha Evgenievna to the nanny school. Had breakfast 5 with Papa, Bagration and Mama on the sofa. In the afternoon drove from T.S. [Tsarskoe Selo] to Peterhof. Had tea 5 with Mama and Papa. Had dinner 4 with Papa, Aunt Olga and Mama on the sofa.

June 6 Thursday. The dentist was here in the morning. Had breakfast 5 Papa, Mama, Aunt Ksenia, Uncle Sandro and their children. Went to Aunt Olga's had tea there and played. [There] were: Shvedov, Yuzik, Skvortzov, Zborovsky, Kulikovsky and Aunt Ksenia with 4 *strannitzy*.[46] Had dinner with Anastasia and Alexei.

Pyotr Petrov to Maria—
Tsarskoe Selo
7, Konyushennaya
June 12, 1913.
Dear Maria Nikolaevna.
For the eleventh time, beginning in 1903, it is my happiness and

---

45. Grand Duchess Elizaveta Mavrikievna, wife of Grand Duke Konstantin Konstantinovich.
46. Strannitzy are wandering holy women.

heartfelt pleasure to congratulate you on your birthday and wish you health, prosperity in everything and constant happiness in the future.

I rejoice with all my heart that the holidays that have come for you are accompanied by clear, sunny days, and you can, as they say "fully," enjoy the charm of sea recreation.

Of course, you read. In this regard, I especially recommend you, in addition to the "Bartholomew's Night," listen with Anastasia Nikolaevna to the very interesting book "The Settlers" by Grigorovich. Without you in Tsarskoe it is very empty and depressing. I spend almost all my time at home and stuffed with iodine. Occasionally I look in at the Palace and I put Alexei Nikolaevich's books in order. The dead silence in the rooms involuntarily takes my thoughts to you, so I remember all of you, you can say—hourly. Give me a happy stream of lines. I ask the same of Anastasia Nikolaevna. Greetings to Alexei Nikolaevich, Olga Nikolaevna and Tatiana Nikolaevna. I kiss you and Anastasia Nikolaevna on the hand and ask God that you will be healthy and cheerful.

Now again I go to the Palace to dig into the books. God bless you! Mentally devoted P.V. P.

Maria's diary—

June 9 Sunday. Went 4 with Papa to a parade of the Equestrian Grenadier Regiment. Had breakfast 4 with Count Apraksin[47] and Olga Evgenievna[48] and Mama on the sofa. In the afternoon we with Papa, Mama and Aunt Olga [went] to the "Alexandria"[49] where we had tea. Arrived in Kronshtadt and went to the "Standart." At dinner sat with Zelenetzky and Sablin.

June 10 Monday. In the morning we 4 went to the consecration of the Navy Cathedral in Kronshtadt with Papa. At breakfast sat with Nilov and Babitzyn. In the afternoon was on the deck and in the cabin. Had tea 4 with Papa, the ladies and officers. Sat with Pi and Nastenka. Had dinner with Mama.

47. Count Peter Nikolaevich Apraksin, Empress Alexandra's secretary.
48. Possibly Butsova.
49. A palace and park in Peterhof.

June 13 Thursday. In the morning went to the Lily of Valley island with Trina, Nastenka and L.A.B. and Aunt Olga was there. At breakfast sat with Zelenetzky and Kuzminsky. In the afternoon took a walk on "patio" with Papa, Aunt Olga, the ladies and officers. Had tea 4 with them. At dinner sat with Schetatveli and Anurkov. In the evening played with Anya, Nastenka, Pi, L.M., K.A. N. and Arsenoev.

June 14 Friday. In the morning we 5 with Papa and Aunt Olga went to *moleben*. At breakfast sat with Nilov. In the afternoon went ashore with Papa, Aunt Olga, the ladies and officers, played tennis, I with Anastasia and Aunt Olga ran around barefoot. Had tea 4 with [illeg.]. At dinner sat with Papa and Nilov. In the evening sat 4 with Pi, Kolya and Nastenka. [Dried flower] Rose from a bouquet from Yalta.[50]

June 15 Saturday. In the morning stayed on the yacht. At breakfast sat with Nilov and Saltanov. In the afternoon went ashore played tennis and swung on giant steps. Had tea 4 with [illeg.]. Read with Trina. At dinner sat with Babitzyn and Rodionov. In the evening talked with Pi and Nastenka.

June 16 Sunday. In the morning 5 with Papa went to *obednya* on the deck. At breakfast sat with Nilov and Sangovich. In the afternoon sat with Mama and Kiki on the yacht. Had tea 4 with Papa, Aunt Olga, the ladies and officers. Had dinner with Anastasia and Alexei.

June 17 Monday. In the morning stayed on the yacht. At breakfast sat with Papa and Nilov. In the afternoon went ashore played tennis with *baiblo popi* [?] and swung on giant steps[51] with Papa, Aunt Olga, the ladies and officers. Had tea 4 with the same. Read with Trina. Had dinner with Mama.

50. Maria would often press flowers given to her on special occasions between her diary pages to dry.

51. Giant steps: A number of swings with harnesses are secured to a pole by long ropes, and everyone swings around, taking giant strides.

June 20 Thursday. In the morning stayed on the yacht. At breakfast sat with Nilov and in the afternoon went ashore, played tennis I with Zelenetzky, Anastasia and Arsenoev. Had tea 4 with Papa, Aunt Olga, ladies and officers who were on the shore. Read with Anastasia and Trina. Had dinner with Mama.

Maria to Maria Vishnyakova[52]—

21 June 1913
My dear Mary!
How are you? We are all well. Alexei goes to the shore every day in the morning and afternoon. Before he goes in the morning, he has electric treatment and swings his leg. Anastasia and I say prayers with him morning and evening. Anastasia says prayers with him and reads the Gospel.
Every day in the afternoon, we 4 with Papa and Aunt Olga go ashore and play tennis, swing on the gigantic steps and learn how to walk on stilts. Now at 6:30 we 4, Papa, Aunt Olga, the ladies and officers are going for a picnic dinner, the commander is also going with us. Anastasia kisses you and will write to you soon. Alexei is having supper and drinks tea with the boys in turn. Goodbye. I kiss you very, very firmly and hug you,
Maria

Maria's diary—

June 23 Sunday. In the morning 4 with Papa went to *obednya* on deck. At breakfast sat with Papa and Prince Vyazemsky.[53] In the afternoon went ashore played tennis with Arsenoev, and L.A.V. Had tea 4 with Papa, Aunt Olga, ladies and officers. Went 4 with Papa, Aunt Olga, ladies and officers from the yacht on [illeg.] and team on "patio." At first there was a show, the sailors performed. Then dancing, then supper, I sat with Pi. Then there was a [illeg.] and dancing again, after which we left which was 12 o'cl.

52. Nanny to the Imperial children.
53. Prince Peter Pavlovich Vyazemsky (1854-1931).

July 3 Wednesday. In the morning went swimming with Tatiana and Shura.[54] At breakfast sat with Zelenkin and Vysotsky. Went to tennis, I played with Papa, Tatiana and Pi. Had tea 4 with those who were at the shore. At dinner sat with Papa and Butakov. Departed to Revel[55] with Raid Standart at 3 o'cl.

July 5 Friday. In the morning swam with Tatiana and Shura. At breakfast sat with Papa and Zelenetsky. In the afternoon went to tennis, I played S.T., Anastasia and Nastenka. Had tea 4 with Papa, the ladies and officers who were at the shore. Talked 4 with Kolya, Mimka[56] and S.T. Read with Trina. Had dinner with Mama.

July 10 Wednesday. Rode with Anya and Shura. At breakfast sat with Papa and Nilov. In the afternoon sat on deck with Mama and Kiki. Had tea 4 with the ladies and officers who were at the shore. At dinner sat with Schepochka and Kiki.[57] We 4 with Mama and Papa went to the navigator's cabin and played bingo, it was really nice.

July 12 Friday. In the morning left from Raid Standart to Kronshtadt. At breakfast sat with Papa and Nilov. In the afternoon talked with Ippolit, Pi and Kolya. Left the yacht to the "Alexandria" and [headed] to Peterhof. It was very boring and sad. Had tea 5 with Mama and Papa. Ran around the garden. Had dinner with Anastasia and Alexei.

July 15 Monday. In the morning watched a film. The yacht was leaving for Crimea. Had a Russian lesson. Had breakfast 5 with Papa and Mama on the sofa. In the afternoon played tennis 4 with Papa and Anya. Had tea 4 with Papa and Mama. Read with Trina. Had dinner with Anastasia and Alexei.

July 21 Sunday. In the morning 4 went to *obednya* with Papa and Aunt Ella. Had breakfast with Papa, Aunt Ella and Aunt Irene. In

54. Alexandra "Shura" Tegleva, the imperial governess.
55. Modern Tallinn (Estonia).
56. Grand Duchess Olga Alexandrovna's beloved old nanny.
57. "Kiki" was a nickname for N.P. Sablin.

the afternoon took a walk with Papa and rode in boats. Had tea 4 with Papa, Mama, Aunt Ella and Aunt Irene.[58] Had dinner 4 with Papa, Aunt Ella and Aunt Irene.

July 22 Monday. In the morning went to *obednya* 4 with Papa. At breakfast sat with Dedulin and empty [seat]. In the afternoon 4 played tennis with Papa, Anya, Mishka and S.T.SH. Had tea 4 with Papa, Mama, Aunt Ella and Aunt Irene. Had dinner with Papa, Aunt Ella and Aunt Irene. In the evening took a walk in Peterhof with Papa.

July 29 Monday. In the morning 4 went horseback riding. Had God's Law and Russian language lessons. Had breakfast 5 with Mama on the sofa. In the afternoon played tennis with Nastenka. Had tea 4 with Mama and Aunt Irene. Read with Trina. Had dinned 4 with Aunt Irene and Mama on the sofa. In the evening played cards.

July 30 Tuesday. In the morning 4 went to *obednya* with Papa and Aunt Irene. At breakfast sat with Nilov and empty space. In the afternoon sat with Mama and Aunt Irene. Had tea 4 with Mama, Papa, Aunt Irene. Anastasia and I went to Aunt Irene's farm. Had dinner with Anastasia and Alexei.

July 31 Wednesday. In the morning took walk with Aunt Irene and Lori. Had breakfast 3 little ones with Aunt Irene and Mama on the sofa. In the afternoon drove to Krasnoe Selo with Aunt Irene and Lori. There was a review of the 8th Voznesensky Uhlan [regiment] and 3rd Elizavetgradsky Hussar regiment. Returned with Aunt Irene and Lori.[59] Had dinner with Aunt Irene and Mama on the sofa.

August 1 Thursday. In the morning read with Trina. Had breakfast 4 with Papa and Aunt Irene. In the afternoon 4 with Papa and Aunt Irene went to the engraving factory. Had tea with Mama, Papa and Aunt Irene. Anastasia and I went to Aunt Irene's. Had dinner with Anastasia.

58. Irene of Prussia, Maria's maternal aunt.
59. Lori Yertsen.

August 3 Saturday. Had music and God's Law lessons. Had breakfast 4 with Papa, Aunt Miechen,[60] Aunt Ducky,[61] Aunt Irene and Uncle Kirill. In the afternoon 4 went with Papa and Aunt Irene to see the maneuvers at Krasnoe [Selo].[62] Had tea with Aunt Irene there. Returned home 4 with Aunt Irene. Had dinner 4 with Aunt Irene and Mama on the sofa. Played cards.

August 4 Sunday. In the morning 4 went to *obednya*. Had breakfast 5 with Aunt Irene and Mama on the sofa. In the afternoon 4 played tennis with Nastenka and Lori. Went to Aunt Mops's with Aunt Irene. Had tea 4 with Mama and Aunt Irene. Rode around 4 with Aunt Irene. Had dinner with Anastasia and Alexei.

August 6 Tuesday. 4 went to *obednya*. Had breakfast 5 with Nastenka and Mama on the sofa. In the afternoon 5 with Papa and Uncle Kirill went to the "Alexandria" and the "Rabotnik." Had tea 4 with Mama and Papa. Read with Trina. Had dinner 4 with Mama on the sofa. [written in pencil:] I had a headache and temperature was 38.6.

August 7 Wednesday. I have temp. 39.3. Went to the train. Was lying down in bed. Temp. 39.7. Drank broth. Shura read to me. Very bad stomach ache. Temp. . . . [entry ends]

August 10 Saturday. In the morning was lying down on the sofa. Had breakfast in bed, Mama on the sofa.

August 11 Sunday. In the morning was lying down on the sofa at Mama's. Had breakfast with Mama [crossed out]. Stayed on sofa, sat with Mama and Kiki and had tea with them. Sat with Babitzyn and Kozhevnikov. Had dinner with Anastasia and Mama on the sofa.

August 14 Wednesday. In the morning departed Sevastopol to Yalta. At breakfast sat with Grinvaldom and Prince Trubetzkoy. Arrived

60. Grand Duchess Maria Pavlovna the Elder.
61. Grand Duchess Victoria Melita, wife of Grand Duke Kirill Vladimirovich.
62. Military town next to Tsarskoe Selo.

in Yalta, went to our house. There was a *moleben*. Had tea 4 with Papa, Mama and Aunt Olga. Went to *vsenoshnaya*. Had dinner 4 with Papa, Aunt Olga and Mama on the sofa.

August 17 Saturday. In the morning swam with Papa and Aunt Olga. Went to molebna at the "Standart" 5 with Papa and Aunt Olga. At breakfast sat with Nilov and Zlebov. Then [we] danced, it was very merry. Had tea 4 with Mama, Papa and Aunt Olga. Went 4 to *vsenoshnaya*. At dinner sat with Prince Trubetzkoy and Iyurikovsky.

August 19 Monday. In the morning went swimming with Papa and Aunt Olga. At breakfast sat with Dedulin and Mordvinov.[63] In the afternoon 4 took a walk to Oreanda with Papa and Aunt Olga. Had tea 4 with Mama, Papa and Aunt Olga. Had dinner with Anastasia and Alexei.

August 20 Tuesday. In the morning 4 with Papa and Aunt Olga took a walk and went swimming. At breakfast sat with Drenteln and Dedulin. In the afternoon took a drive with Papa, Aunt Olga and the suite to Aitetri and Eagle's Landing. Had tea 4 with Papa, Mama and Aunt Olga. Had dinner with Anastasia and Alexei.

August 23 Friday. In the morning went to Yalta with Anastasia and Aunt Olga. Had breakfast with Mama. In the afternoon sat with Mama on the balcony. Had tea 4 with Mama, Papa and Aunt Olga. With Aunt Olga took a ride to the Apraksins. Had dinner with Anastasia and Alexei. Had an ear-ache, temp. 38.1.[64]

August 24 Saturday. In the morning temp 37, stayed in bed. Had breakfast there too. In the afternoon sat [crossed off] was lying down with Mama. Temp. 36.7. Had tea alone, sat with Aunt Olga. Temp. 37.3. Had dinner alone.

---

63. Anatoly Mordvinov, adjutant wing of Nicholas II.
64. Maria got ill with an ear infection.

August 25 Sunday. In the morning was lying down on the sofa. Had breakfast alone. In the afternoon sat at Mama's and was lying down on the sofa. Had tea alone. Played cards with Shura. Had dinner alone.

August 26 Monday. In the morning was lying down in bed. Had breakfast with Mama. Was lying down, Mama, Kiki and Anya came to see me. Had tea alone. Played cards with Liza and Shura. Had dinner alone. In the morning temp. 36.9. In the afternoon 36.3. Evening 37.1.

August 27 Tuesday. In the morning stayed in bed. Had breakfast with Mama and Alexei. Trina, Shura and Liza sat with me. Had tea alone. Played cards. Had dinner alone. In the morning temp. 36.3, afternoon 36.9, evening 36.5.

August 28 Wednesday. In the morning stayed in bed. Had breakfast with Mama. In the afternoon sat [crossed out] was lying down. Shura and Trina read. Had tea alone. Had dinner alone. In the morning temp. 36.3, afternoon 36.6, evening 37.1.

August 29 Thursday. In the morning stayed in bed. Had breakfast with Mama and Alexei. In the afternoon was lying down, Shura and Trina read. Had tea alone. Had dinner alone. In the morning temp. 36.6, afternoon 36.4, evening 37.

Maria to Maria Vishnyakova—

Livadia. 30 August 1913
My dear Mary,
How are you? Thank you very much for the postcard with the picture of the Caucasus. Aunt Olga is leaving us today and Papa with the suite have gone in motors to Bakchisarai[65] to see her off. She greets you very much. I didn't go because yesterday when I got up I had ear-ache. Alexei is well. He has already had 4 mud baths. I took a photo of him when he was being treated with the mud and

---

65. Town in Crimea.

will glue in an album for you. Alexei's leg stretched 175 degrees and the leg is almost straight.[66]
Goodbye for now. Kissing you firmly,
Maria

Maria's diary—
August 30 Friday. Got up in the morning. Went to [illeg.] for *obednya*. Had breakfast with Mama on the sofa. In the afternoon went to tennis 4 with Papa, Mama and Aunt Olga, Anya, Zelenetzky, Kiki, Kolya and Pi were there. Had tea at tennis [court]. Had dinner 4 with Papa, Aunt Olga, Mordvinov and Mama on the sofa. In the morning 36.3, evening 36.8

August 31 Saturday. In the morning walked to the beach. Had breakfast with Mama on the sofa. In the afternoon took a walk with Anya. Had tea with Mama, Kiki and Anya. Went to *vsenoshnaya* at the [illeg.]. Had dinner 4 with Papa and Mama on the sofa. In the morning 36.5, evening 36.5.

September 2 Monday. In the morning walked right with Papa to the beach house. At breakfast sat with Sukhomlinov. Two officers from my regiment were there. In the afternoon played tennis 4 with Papa, Anya, Kiki, Kolya, Pi and Petrovsky. Had tea with them at home. Went to Irina's and played with [. . .] grandson. Had dinner with Anastasia and Alexei.

September 3 Tuesday. In the morning walked to the beach with Papa. At breakfast sat with Nilov and Drenteln. In the afternoon played tennis 4 with Papa, Mama, Anya, Kiki, Kolya and Petrovsky were there. Had tea during tennis. Played with grandchildren at Trina's and read in French. Had dinner with Anastasia and Vyazemsky.

September 6 Friday. In the morning went to Yalta with Trina. At breakfast sat with the Frenchman and Dedulin. In the afternoon

---

66. Alexei had therapy to straighten his leg due to a very serious hemophilia incident the previous year.

played tennis 4 with Papa, Mama, Anya, Kiki, Pi, Butakov and Petrovsky were there. Had tea at tennis. Read in French. Had dinner with Anastasia and Alexei.

September 11 Wednesday. Had lessons in the morning then went to Yalta with Trina. Had breakfast 5 with Mama on the sofa. In the afternoon chose things for the bazaar[67] 4 with Mama, ladies of the suite, Kiki, Kolya and [illeg.] were there. Had tea with same. Went to Trina's played with granddaughter. Had dinner 4 with Mama on the sofa.

September 16 Monday. In the morning took a walk with Papa. Had breakfast with Anastasia and Alexei and Mama on the sofa. In the afternoon Anastasia and I went to the beach with Mama in a small carriage. Had tea with same. Went to Yalta with Trina. Read in French. Had dinner with Anastasia and Alexei with Mama on the sofa.

Pyotr Petrov to Maria—

Tsarskoe Selo

September 18, 1913. My dear, good Maria Nikolaevna!

Finally, you've managed to "break the seal of silence" and please me with a letter. I understand very well that there are always a lot of reasons for delaying the answer to letters, and I am not in any way blaming you. Thank God that even a runny nose with complications has passed. Take care, especially in rainy weather. My ears have been suffering for 20 years because of colds that did not heal well and that I did not take care of! I seem to have written to you that there is an excellent protective agent invented by the English. I'll bring it and show it, and then we'll consult with Evgeny Sergeyevich.[68] This is the "Glaseptic" spray from Parke Dewiset Co, London.

My canary died on the third day. This is the second one. Now there are only dogs left, because Ivan Ivanovich the cat prefers to live in the garden, and I rarely see him. My garden is noticeably empty,

---

67. Annual charity bazaar where imperial family members sold their own handmade items for local charities.

68. Evgeny Sergeyevich Botkin, one of the imperial physicians.

and the young trees of the Hungarian lilac wilt miserably. He took off with rowan berries and made jam. Little by little, autumn approaches, and by the day of my departure (on the 1st day), it will get colder.

How I would like to be there and buy something at the bazaar on the 22nd. I wrote to Olga Nikolaevna that I might buy some of your needlework, and Peter A. Zhilik would pay for me. I ask you not to forget my request. Bitte, bitte, ayez la bonte! (please, please be so kind) Congratulate Alexei Nikolaevich and give him the attached card. He, of course, will know who is sitting at the monument. Greet your sisters and Trina, bow to everyone who remembers me. I write separately to Anastasia Nikolaevna. God bless you! Cordially faithful

P. V. P.

Maria's diary—

September 22 Sunday. In the morning went to a church consecration with Papa. Had breakfast 5 with Papa and Mama on the sofa. In the afternoon 5 with Mama went to the bazaar. Had dinner, I sat with Zelenetzky and Vikt. 4 in total were at the bazaar.

September 23 Monday. In the morning read with Trina. At breakfast sat with Apraksin and Nilov. In the afternoon 4 went to the bazaar. Had dinner with Papa and Mama on the sofa. Then again went to the bazaar.

October 3 Thursday. Had lessons in the morning. Went to Yalta with Trina. Had breakfast 5 with Mama. Played tennis 4 with Papa, Mama, Anya, Kiki and Kolya were there. Had tea with [illeg.] and Papa. Read in French. Had dinner with Anastasia and Alexei.

October 8 Tuesday. In the morning had lessons and were with Trina. At breakfast sat with Petrov and Nilov. In the afternoon played tennis 4 with Papa. Mama, Anya, Kiki and Kolya were there. Has tea 4 with Papa, Mama, Aunt Ksenia, Uncle Sandro and Irina. Read in Russian. Had dinner with Anastasia and Alexei.

October 12 Saturday. In the morning had lessons and went to the beach. At breakfast sat with Kasso and [blank space]. In the afternoon played tennis 4 with Papa. Mama, Anya, Kiki and Pi were there. Had tea at home. Went to *vsenoshnaya* 4 with Papa. At dinner sat with Dedulin and Nilov.

October 16 Wednesday. In the morning sat by the sea and had lessons. Had breakfast 5 with Mama on the sofa. In the afternoon 4 played tennis, Mama, Anya, Kiki, Kolya, Zborovsky and Shurik were there. Had tea with Papa at home and in between read in French and in Russian. Had dinner with Anastasia and Alexei.

October 21 Monday. In the morning everyone took communion. Had breakfast 5 with Papa and Mama on the sofa. In the afternoon drove to Ai Todor with Anastasia and there [we] played and had tea. Went to *vsenoshnaya*. Had dinner 4 with Papa and Mama on the sofa.

October 27 Sunday. In the morning went to *obednya* with Papa. At breakfast sat with Dumbadze and Knyazhevich. In the afternoon took a walk with Papa, Kiki, Kolya, Pi and Mama in a small carriage. Everyone had tea at home and also Aunt Ksenia. Read with Trina. Had dinner with Papa and Mama on the sofa.

Countess Emma Fredericks to Maria—
I thank you from my soul. [Context unknown.]
Emma Fredericks
30 October 1913

Maria's diary—
31 Thursday. Had lessons in the morning. At breakfast sat with Orlov and Nilov. In the afternoon played tennis, Papa, Mama, Pi, Shurik, Zborovsky, Butakov and Anya were there. Had tea at home. Read in French. At dinner in the saloon, [I sat] with Kolya and [illeg.]. After dinner there was cinema, it was very merry.

November 3 Sunday. In the morning I was lying down and had breakfast lying down. In the afternoon stayed home. Had tea 4 with Mama, Papa, Kolya, Pi, Shurik, Zborovsky and Anya. At dinner on the yacht sat with Komarov and Nilov. After dinner sat, danced and had awfully lot of fun.

November 5 Tuesday. In the morning had lessons. At breakfast sat with Papa and the Governor. In the afternoon pasted in albums with Mama, Kolya, Anya, Kiki, Pi and Stolitza. Had tea at home. Had dinner with Anastasia and Alexei.

November 7 Thursday. In the morning 4 with Papa toured the ship "Peter the Great" and stopped by the yacht. At breakfast sat with Uncle Georgiy and Komarov. In the afternoon played tennis 4 with Papa; Mama, Anya, Kiki, Pi, Shurik and Zborovsky were there. Had tea at home. Read in Russian. Had dinner with Anastasia.

November 10 Sunday. In the morning 4 with Papa to *obednya*. At breakfast sat with Nilov and Komarov. In the afternoon went to Kharax with Anastasia and Trina. Had tea there and played hide and seek. Had dinner with Anastasia and Alexei.

November 20 Wednesday. In the morning went to Kastritsky's[69] and had a lesson. At breakfast sat with Vetkin and Nilov. In the afternoon 4 played tennis, Papa, Mama, Anya, Kiki, Kolya, Shurik, Zborovsky and Sumarkov were there. Had tea at home. Went 4 to *vsenoshnaya*. Had dinner 4 with Papa and Mama on the sofa.

November 22 Friday. In the morning went to Kastritsky's and had lessons. At breakfast sat with Prince Trubetskoy and Nilov. In the afternoon played tennis, Papa, Mama, Anya, Kiki, Kolya, Shurik, Zborovsky and Sumarkov were there. Had tea at home. Read in French and Russian. Had dinner with Anastasia and Alexei.

November 26 Tuesday. In the morning 5 [went] with Papa and Mama to a parade. At breakfast sat with Kachalov and Count

69. Imperial dentist.

T[illeg.]. In the afternoon 4 took a walk with Papa, Anya, Kiki, Kolya, Babitzyn, Shurik[70] and Mama in a carriage. Had tea at home. Read in French. Had dinner with Alexei and Anastasia. Had our hair washed.

December 5 Thursday. Had lessons in the morning. At breakfast sat with Nilov and Prince Trubetskoy. In the afternoon 4 played at home, Mama, Papa, Anya, Kiki, Shurik, Zborovsky, Nevirovsky and Dmitri were there. Had tea at home. Went 4 to *vsenoshnaya*. Had dinner 4 with Papa, Dmitri and Mama on the sofa.

December 14 Saturday. In the morning went to Yalta and lessons. At breakfast on "Kichkum" sat with Christopher.[71] In the afternoon 4 took a walk with Papa, Kiki, Pi, Shurik, Zborovsky and Mama in a carriage. Had tea at home and also Dmitri. Read in French and Russian. Had dinner with Nastenka and Mama on the sofa.

December 17 Tuesday. In the morning arrived in Sevastopol. At breakfast sat with Nilov and Komarov. In the afternoon sat and talked with Pi, Kolya and Kotenok. Had tea 4 with Mama, Papa, ladies and officers. Sat with Kolya and looked at the train. There was a prayer service on the deck and then we left the yacht to the train and it departed. It was very boring. At dinner sat with Nilov and Papa.

December 19 Thursday. In the morning 5 sat with Mama. At breakfast sat with Papa and Nilov. Read with Trina. Had tea 4 with Papa and the suite. Arrived in Tsarskoe Selo. Had dinner 4 with Papa, Mama, Grandmama, Aunt Ksenia, Aunt Olga, Irina and Dmitri.

December 21 Saturday. In the morning 4 skated. Had breakfast 5 with Papa, Mama, Aunt Olga, Uncle Boris,[72] Count Fredericks, Count Sheremetiev,[73] Anastasia and Alexei. Had tea 4 with Papa, Mama and Aunt Olga. Went to *vsenoshnaya* 4 with Papa and Aunt

70. Nickname of a member of the imperial family's entourage.
71. Prince Christopher of Greece.
72. Grand Duke Boris Mikhailovich.
73. Count Alexander Dmitrievich Sheremetiev, a Russian composer.

Olga. Had dinner 4 with Papa, Aunt Olga and Mama on the sofa.

December 23 Monday. In the morning took a walk 4 with Trina. Had breakfast 5 with Papa, Mama and Mordvinov. In the afternoon set up for *yolka*.[74] Had tea 4 with Papa and Mama. Had dinner with Anastasia and Alexei.

December 24 Tuesday. In the morning 4 went to *obednya* with Papa and Mama. Had breakfast 5 with Papa and Mama. In the afternoon gave out firs to all ladies and got some ourselves. Had tea 4 with Papa, Mama and Anya. Went 4 with Papa to Grandmama's for *yolka* and *vsenoshnaya* and had dinner. Aunt Olga, Uncle Petya, Aunt Ksenia, Uncle Sandro and the children were there.

December 25 Wednesday. In the morning 5 went to *obednya* with Papa. Had breakfast 5 with Papa, Mama and Aunt Olga. Had tea 4 with Mama and Papa. Had dinner 4 with Papa and Mama on the sofa, also Aunt Olga.

December 26 Thursday. Had breakfast 5 with Papa, Mama and [illeg.]. In the afternoon 5 went to convoy yolka with Papa and Aunt Olga, later the Cossacks danced *lezginka*.[75] Had tea 4 with Papa and Mama. Had dinner with Anastasia and Alexei.

December 27 Friday. In the morning 4 with Nastenka to the yolka at nanny school. Had breakfast 5 with Papa, Mama and Uncle Kostya. In the afternoon 4 took a walk. Had tea with Alexei and Anastasia. Went to Trina's. Had dinner with Anastasia and Alexei.

Louise Battenberg[76] to Maria—
Dec 28th 1913. Dear Marie,
Thank you so much for the very nice glass you and Anastasia sent me. I like it very much and shall use it on my wash hand-stand. I

---

74. Christmas party, literally means "fir tree."

75. Traditional Chechen dance.

76. Maria's first cousin, daughter of Princess Victoria (Empress Alexandra's sister), and Prince Louis of Battenberg. In 1917 the family name was anglicized to Mountbatten and she became known as Lady Louise Mountbatten. She married Crown Prince Gustav Adolf of Sweden in 1923, becoming Queen Louise of Sweden in 1950. Queen Louise died on March 7, 1965.

hope you will have a very happy Xmas. I expect you will feel very cold now after nice sunny Crimea. Our winter has not been at all cold yet and mostly fine. I suppose you will be going to the theatre Xmas time. I love going. Yesterday, Papa, Dick and I went to see a very pretty operetta called "Gipsy love" at Windsor. The day before Dick and I went to a very good cinematograph performance. I probably shall not know you again when I see you, you look so very big on the photos.

Lots of love from your very loving cousin
Louise

Maria's diary—

December 29 Sunday. In the morning 4 took a walk. Had breakfast 5 with Papa, Mama and Aunt Mavra. Went to Grandmama's for officers' yolka and had tea 4 with Grandmama, Aunt Olga and Aunt Ksenia. Had dinner 4 with Papa and Mama on the sofa.

December 31 Tuesday. In the morning 4 took a walk. Had breakfast 5 with Papa, Mama and Ioann. In the afternoon with Anastasia and Mama went to Znamenie and to the Sobor. Had tea 4 with Papa, Mama and Anya. Went to Trina's. Had dinner 4 with Papa and Mama on the sofa.

1914

Catherine Schneider to Maria—
Dear Maria Nikolaevna! I congratulate you with the New Year 1914. All the best.
Your Trina

Irène of Prussia to Maria—
Kiel Jan 3rd 1914
My darling Marie
Merry Xmas to you all. I hope you will like the [illeg.] + the book I sent you. Mama can perhaps read it to you. I thought the pictures might please you! We have so little snow here that we cannot sledge. I hope . . . to skate. There was a frightful storm some days so that the boats from the ships could scarcely land + had holes knocked into them. I have had a lot of letters and cards to send off + present—I always wonder how Mama manages it all. I wonder what you . . . .

Helmine[1] to Maria—
Hadersleben 4 Jan 1914
Dear Grand Duchess Marie,
I wish you a Merry Christmas and a Happy New Year. Thank you very much for your card. My little Wilhelm-Heinrich is toddling and talking now and is at a nice age.
Heartfelt greetings, your Helmine

1. Wilhelmine von Oertzen, lady in waiting to Empress Alexandra's sister, Irène of Prussia.

Maria to Alexandra Feodorovna [in English]—
21 Feb 1914
God bless you my dear Mama sweet. I ask you very much pardon
and hope that I will get soon better. Slep wel +
M

Princess Margaretha of Sweden[2] to Maria [in English]—
Dear Marie
Thank you very much for your card. How are you all? We are all
well. On the card you see our country house. Much love from your
loving Margaretha. Please write soon. Stockholm 24.2.1914

Maria to Alexandra Feodorovna—
March 2 1914
I thank you so very much my dear Mama darling that you aloud
[allowed] us to go to Anya. I [illeg.] myself today. I kiss you very
tenderly and bless.
Maria
Did you not get to tired were they not sweet and dear [illeg.] today?
Kiss Papa lovingly from me

Princess Nina Georgievna[3] to Maria—
13th March 1914
Dear Maria, thank you very much for the letter which made me
very happy. Papa, Mama, Ksenia and Nana kiss you. I kiss you,
Nina

Maria to Alexandra Feodorovna—
Christ Has Risen! My beloved Mama, are you well? I wish you a
wonderful holiday. Kiss you affectionately.
Maria
God bless you Mama darling. Sleep well. Have lots of nice dreams
and dont be to lonly. Anastasia and I kiss ever so tenderly. Your lov-

---

2. Princess Margaretha of Sweden was a member of the Swedish royal family and Princess of Denmark
by marriage.
3. Princess Nina was the elder daughter of Grand Duke Georgiy Mikhailovich.

ing Maria +
29 Apr 1914

Authors' note: On July 19, 1914, Germany declared war on Russia. The next day Maria and her family traveled to St Petersburg to appear to the cheering crowds in Palace Square in front of the Winter Palace. Maria's sister, Tatiana, described the event in her diary:

"Masses of people on their knees cheering and blessing Papa and Mama. All the relatives went to the Nikolaevsky Hall which was full of military officers. There was a *moleben*, Batushka was there in the middle and read Papa's declaration of war manifesto. Then Papa said a few kind words to them, and they yelled terribly [loud]. It was wonderful. There were many of our Yakhtinsky and Guard-Equipage officers. Saw N.P. and were even able to greet him. [I] was so happy, then Papa and Mama bowed to the people on the balcony on the square. Thousands and thousands of [people] standing [there]. Then back again walking among the huge crowd. On the one side were the simple people, on the other officers. Ours were [there] too. Returned at 7 1/2. Had dinner [we] 2 with Papa and Mama. [Our] spirits [were] lifted greatly."[4]

During the following few months, the imperial family reached the peak of its popularity with the Russian people on all social levels. Each member of the imperial family got involved in the war effort, including the two youngest grand duchesses. Maria and Anastasia were too young to train as military nurses like their older sisters, but they became patronesses of the Feodorovsky Infirmary, located near the Alexander Palace.

Maria to Nicholas II—

20th September. My dear darling Papa! I am writing to you from downstairs. Mafia[5] and Dmitri, who had dinner with us, are sitting here. We went to *vsenoshnaya* and I prayed for you a lot. Batushka took advantage of your absence and made a speech after *vsenosh-*

---

4. Helen Azar and Nicholas B. A. Nicholson, *Tatiana Romanov: Daughter of the Last Tsar, Diaries and Letters, 1913–1918*.

5. Grand Duchess Maria Pavlovna, the younger sister of Grand Duke Dmitri and first cousin to the tsar.

naya. During *vsenoshnaya* it was extremely lonesome that you were not there. I kiss you affectionately and + 2, sleep well and have nice dreams. Your loving Maria.

21st September. I congratulate you, my darling Papa, with victory. This morning we 4 went to *obednya* with Mama. Our *Batushka* and deacon Shavelsky did the service. [We] had breakfast alone, then went to the train with the wounded. Went to Anya's and had tea with her. From there [we] went to the Grand Palace infirmary, Mama, Olga and Tatiana left to do dressing changes. Anya and I walked around all the rooms, where the soldiers were, and spoke with almost each one. Then Mama, Anya and I went home, as Mama had to receive the Sisters of Mercy who are leaving for the front. After that we went to the small infirmary, where your Sharp-shooter is [a patient]. There Mama and the sisters changed dressings again, and Anastasia and I went to [see] the officers. I played some game with Popov. After the dressings, the sisters and Mama also played with the officers, so we only returned at dinner time. Had dinner 4 with Mama. Alexei is fine thank God. I kiss you affection-ately, my very own darling. Your awfully loving, very own Maria. Next time definitely take me with you; or else I will jump into the train myself, because I am so lonesome without you. Sleep well. + MN

24th September. My dear Papa darling! I just returned from Anya's, where Nikolai Pavlovich was [too]. This afternoon Anastasia and I went to our infirmary. 15 people arrived to us on Shulenburg's last train. Unfortunately, I have to end, as it is now morning and I have to go to my lesson. I kiss you affectionately, my darling, and love you. Regards to Sasha and Nilov. Yours always daughter Maria. For-give me for such a boring and short letter.

22 October. My darling Papa dear! I just got a telegram from the regiment. "On this day of regimental holiday the Kazan Dragoons of His Imperial Majesty, raising prayers for the dear health of their beloved Chief, faithfully offer their congratulations and announce a greeting to the 'chief leader' Lord Emperor and our August Chief."

I will go to tea now, and then to *obednya*. Will pray for you and your regiment especially. We already went to *obednya* and had breakfast. I received a telegram from the regimental ladies, who asked for the infirmary which they founded to be under my patronage. Olga and Tatiana went to Petrograd. Anya and I, with Mama, will review the train-warehouse here on the vetka. Regards to Nikolai Pavlovich and Sasha. I kiss your affectionately. Your loving, Kazansha. May God keep you. +

23 October. My golden Papa! I'm so sorry that I did not have time to write today. Yesterday afternoon I was with Anastasia and Nastenka at the nanny school, and the children had tea, and I fed them porridge with the nannies, and was reminded of you when the porridge dribbled down their chins and we cleaned their chins with spoons. Today we went to our infirmary, there were many serious head wounds and one in the stomach. Today they all wrote letters home, and a few Siberians could not, so the other wounded helped them.

24 October. Just had breakfast. In the morning at 9 o'clock and 50 minutes went to *Obednya*. Now I will go to our infirmary with Anastasia, and then to the warehouse. Mama went to Petrograd with the sisters. Tatiana will have a committee there and Mama will go to her warehouse. It is very lonesome without you. Regards to Sasha and Nikolai Pavlovich. I kiss your whole body affectionately. I have not seen Demenkov.[6] May God be with you. Your always loving Kazansha.

25 October. My dear Papa darling! I am terribly sorry that I did not have time to write to you. This morning [I had] the obnoxious lessons, as always. Then [we] had breakfast. In the afternoon we went to 4 infirmaries in Pavlovsk with Mama and Aunt Mavra,[7] and saw a Cossack who was wounded by a Saxon swine (i.e., their equerry). I am writing so badly, because [I am using] Mama's quill. Just now

6. Nikolai Dmitrievich Demenkov, imperial officer who became Maria's favorite and romantic interest.
7. Grand Duchess Elizaveta Mavrikievna, wife of Grand Duke Konstantin Konstantinovich.

I washed up, and Liza is combing my hair. Also, today we went to the consecration of Svodny Regiment's infirmary. It is located in the building where the church used to be. A dining room was set up in that room, and there *moleben* was held right there. Where we used to leave our coats is now a room for dressings. Demenkov, my darling, of course was not there. After *vsenoshnaya* tonight we went to the infirmary, where Iedigarov was [admitted]. I kiss you affectionately, my golden one. Your devoted and loving Kazanetz. Big regards from me to Sasha and Kolya. Grigori was just here. He will remain in Petrograd until you get back. God be with you. +

29 October. My golden Papa! This morning, we have lessons, as always. Alexei has time to write to you today, as he will not have a lesson with Pyotr Vasilyevich. Yesterday evening at half past ten Mama went to the train. Before that Malama[8] was here, he was very sweet. Today all snow melted and the weather is very spring-like, only the grass is not green. Right now, it is drizzling a bit. The sisters rode with Anya, Olya[9] and Resin. In the afternoon, Anastasia and I will probably go to our infirmary. We have this one soldier there who does not say anything, but is awfully sweet. For some reason he loves bracelets and played with one of mine for a long time. We have three soldiers who cannot write at all. One of them learned to read a little with us. We have four officers. One is tall, [he] stinks and is afraid of dressings, and has a wife. Another is fat and not too smart. The third, a regiment commander, always has a bunch of visitors, and the fourth is leaving today it seems. Nikolaev just arrived here from the Svodny Regiment, [he] was wounded, and we are going there now. I kiss you very affectionately and love you. Your Kazanetz. May God keep you. +

30 October. My very own darling Papa! This morning Alexei's train arrived. Mama was there with Olga, Anastasia and Alexei. In the afternoon Olga and Tatiana will change dressings again, while Mama will stay home. Mama arrived yesterday at six o'clock. After dinner

8. Dmitri Malama was an imperial officer who was the favorite of Grand Duchess Tatiana Nikolaevna.

9. Probably Olga Butsova.

we 4 went to the infirmary with Anya, where Iedigarov[10] [is]. They
were all very sweet. Anastasia and I returned at half past nine. When
Olga was speaking to someone for too long, Iedigarov would start
coughing loudly, so that she would turn and go to their room. Anastasia and I don't know what we will do this afternoon. I have a cold.
Yesterday when we came to our infirmary, suddenly masses of people started coming out of the infirmary (that is the Svodny Regiment officers) and among them was my Demenkov. We got terribly
frightened and walked very quietly, so that they would not turn
around. Saw Nikolaev, [his hair] got rather gray. He told us a lot of
interesting things. In the morning had lessons as usual. Regards to
Kolya and Sashka. I firmly shake your hand, in order not to give
you my cold. Your Kazanetz. I wrote this letter before breakfast, but
Mama still has not returned from the dressings. May God keep you.
+

31 October. My darling Papa! The sisters will take this letter with
them. Yesterday afternoon we walked, then went to the Grand
Palace[11] infirmary. They already admitted eight officers there. Today
we will probably go to our infirmary. I don't know if the new
wounded arrived here with yesterday's train or not. The other day I
saw my Svodny Regiment sailor from "Ioann Zlatoust" at the gate,
and I said hello to him. Ah! I hope that I will see my Demenkov at
vsenoshnaya, but I'm afraid that [I will] not, as we are probably going
to be standing in the prayer room, and we are too embarrassed to
stand in church alone, and walk up to the New Testament. Ortipo[12]
is so sweet, and grew bigger in my opinion. Right now, I will have
an English lesson, how tiresome. I kiss you, your wife, and your two
daughters affectionately, and tell the oldest that I will try to call her
on the telephone, and if I talk with anyone interesting, I will send
her a telegram. Your very own Kazanetz. May God keep you. +

Maria to Alexandra Feodorovna [in English]—

10. One of the wounded officers, patient at imperial infirmary.
11. Grand Palace, a.k.a. Catherine Palace.
12. Ortipo was a French bulldog given to Tatiana by Dmitri Malama, who most likely purchased the
puppy from a litter bred by Felix Yusupov.

For Mama dear Oct 31 1914
My beloved Mother
I am so glad for you that you will see Papa dear. I or Anastasia will
say praise [prayers] with Baby. I hope you will sleep well and be
quite alrait for Grodno and Dvinsk. I hope I will see sumbody interesting tomorrow in church, but I am afraid not becouse we will
be in the *molebna*. My very tenderly kisses to you and sisters. Your
loving M. God bless you +

Maria to Nicholas II—

19 November. My darling Papa! Today I am the one writing to you,
as Olga and Tatiana just went to Petrograd for the charities.[13] I had
lessons in the morning. Mama rode in the train with Olga, Alexei
and Anastasia. Yesterday I was at the Grand Palace with Mama and
the sisters, to see the wounded officers and saw that young officer
who had a big bed sore on his back. He has a very sweet face. We
signed his cards, and now he is waiting for you to return and maybe
sign for him too. Right now, it is two o'clock. Mama is lying on the
sofa and writing you a letter, while Anastasia—to Aunt Olga. At
2.30 Anastasia and I will go to our infirmary. Probably new [pa-
tients] also arrived there. At tea I always sit in your chair. Mama got
a letter from you before breakfast. Later she will go to the Grand
Palace for dressings of two officers. Alexei is upstairs resting after
breakfast. Tomorrow Chakhov is going back to the front. I am so
happy that it's a holiday on Friday, so that we will not have lessons,
and this is very pleasant. Today during the arithmetic lesson the
teacher bent down to see if I wrote something correctly, and broke
the chair leg with his weight, and almost fell on me. Well so long,
goodbye my Darling. I kiss you affectionately and love you. Your
Kazanetz. May God keep you + Regards to Sasha and Kolya and
tell the latter to behave.

22 November. My very own darling Papa! Mama left with the sisters
last night at 9 o'clock. Malama had tea with us as he is returning to
the regiment. Iedigarov left the infirmary yesterday [he went] to

---

13. The two elder grand duchesses were patrons and chairs of charities for the families of officers at
the front.

Petrograd[14] for a couple of days to [see] his wife, and then to the regiment. Mama will arrive tomorrow morning at 9 o'clock, and her train with Loman[15] will already be at the station. So, Anastasia, Alexei and I will go meet her and go directly to the train with the wounded. We are getting 3 new officers at our infirmary. Now I will stop by Isa's, who has fever and stomach ache, which was why she did not go with Mama. Well so long, goodbye, my darling. May God keep you. +

Your always loving *Kazanetz*. Regards to your companions.

26 November. My sweet and dear Papa! The other day I wrote you a letter, but tore it up, as the courier already left. I have been going to my infirmary every day. The last train brought some rather seriously wounded [patients]. One of them came to us with a torn lip. Aunt Ella is now here with us, she tells us a lot of interesting things about her journey. May God keep you. Your very own Kazanetz.

30 November. My golden Papa! Mama is now lying on the sofa and resting. This morning all of us, 5 with Mama went to *obednya* and then to change dressings, and Alexei also watched and counted how many he was present at. After breakfast we took [photographs] with the wounded officers at the Grand Palace. From there we went to the Invalid House, and there, Mama gave out St George's medals to several lower ranks. Mama is very tired, and therefore she will not write to you today. We will now have tea with Uncle Pavel. Yesterday at *vsenoshnaya* I saw my darling Demenkov, while Shvedov was at the meeting. So, both Olga and I were very happy. Yesterday afternoon we went to the local infirmary, where Mama also awarded medals. Today after tea Mama will receive the officers, her two Crimeans, one from my regiment and the other from Olga's. I kiss you affectionately, your always loving Kazanetz. May God keep you.+

Regards to Kolya and Sasha.

---

14. After the war broke out, St. Petersburg was renamed Petrograd to sound more Russian and less German.

15. Dmitri N. Loman, colonel of the Life-Guard Pavlovsky Regiment, churchwarden of Feodorovsky Cathedral.

Maria to Alexandra Feodorovna—

2nd December 1914. Ts.S.
My beloved Mama dear!
Thank you so much for the sweet note and the telegram. We studied
in the morning, and I walked with Shura. Anastasia still has no real
Becker.[16]
Now we had a lesson from P. V. He read Turgenev to us.
VN cut out the eyes of the commander of the Shirvan regiment.
Firmly kiss you and love you.
Your daughter
Maria
God bless you +

Maria to Tatiana—

2nd December, 1914
Tatiana my darling! I thank you very much for the note and the
wishes. Although I have not yet seen my husband[17] but at least saw
him in a dream. Today we will go to the Grand Palace. And I hope
that Provotorov, i.e. your husband, will tell us masses of [illeg.]. It
is so boring without you. I hope that I will still see N.D. Your poor
husband Provotorov is leaving from the grand palace to the Koko-
revsky house. Farewell, I kiss you affectionately. Your Maria. Did
Anya come to see you yesterday or not? I have a temperature of 36.9
today. Tell Papa that I kiss him affectionately. What are you doing?
My head doesn't ache anymore. I had tea and broth. Olga Tatiana
and Anastasia wrote me letters.
Kiss you affectionately
From Maria

Maria to Alexandra Feodorovna—

3 Dec 1914
Mama my dear
I congratulate you and Papa very much. I am going to the ware-

16. "Becker" is how they referred to their periods.
17. This may be referring to some sort of a traditional reading of fortune, where a girl would see the
face of her future husband.

house now, and after with Madame Zizi[18] to you at the infirmary. Kissing you firmly, Loving you, Your
Maria
God protect you +

3 December, 1914
Mama my dear, I send you and Papa big congratulations. Just now we are going to the warehouse and then to your infirmary with Madame Zizi. I kiss you affectionately. Your loving Maria.
May God keep you +

Maria to Tatiana—
4th December 1914. T.S. My darling Tatiana! I was not terribly envious of you being in Moscow. Yesterday at the infirmary we ran into the same Mordvinov who came to visit the Nizhegorodtzy. Yesterday Karamazov asked to send his regards to you all and that his name should stand first and he bows the lowest of all. Yesterday when they sang something rather weak in French we guffawed and suddenly Vest [illeg.] and says, isn't it lovely, this one is my favorite song. I made a pleasant smile and did not respond, but Rudnev made a gaffe saying that we were not listening. After which Vest. left soon. I kiss you affectionately, your Dragun [Dragoon].

13th December, 1914
My dear darling Mama. I thank you very much for your letter. I feel so badly that you cannot come over but of course it is better for you to stay. I think I will be able to get up tomorrow. I kiss you very very affectionately and hope that you will feel better. May God bless you. Your loving Maria.

14 December, 1914.
My precious Mama, wishing you a good night and that tomorrow you feel well. My throat still hurts when I swallow, and I still have a compress on my head. May God keep you +

18. Nickname of Countess Elizaveta Naryshkina.

14th December 1914
My Mama darling, I thank you so very much for your dear letter. I am so sorry that your heart is still No.2. I hope your cold is better.—My temperature now is 37,1.—and my throat acks [aches] less than yesterday. Am so sorry not to see you today, but sertenely its better for you to rest. 1000 kisses from your own loving Marie

14 Dec 1914
My Golden Mama
I wish you a good night so that you feel well tomorrow. My throat is still sore when I swallow and I still have a compress on my head. God protect you +
Your loving and firmly kissing daughter
Maria

[In English] 15th Dec. 1914
My darling Mama! How are you today? I hope that you feel better, after your rest. Ostragorsky told that I will gets up tomorrow, but that I may not go out of the room as I must have still the compres on. He will come in the morning. He told that the налеты[19] are gon but that the t[h]roat is still red and that the железы[20] are still распухли.[21] I kiss you so very much. Your own loving Marie

16 Dec 1914
My dear and good Mama,
It is such a pity that I won't see you today again. I hope I can go downstairs tomorrow. I will stay in bed until 10 and then come down to see you after I get up. Kissing you firmly, and loving you, Your Maria

16th December, 1914
My darling and dear Mama! I feel so badly that I will not see you again today. I hope that tomorrow I will be able to go downstairs already. I will be lying down until 10 and then Ostrovsky[22] will

19. Rashes.
20. Lymph nodes.
21. Swollen.
22. One of the imperial physicians.

come and after that I will get up. I kiss your affectionately and love you. Your Maria.

[In English] 17th December. 1914
My Mama darling! I wish you good night and to see all sorts of nice people in your dream and to sleep wel. I don't no [know] most I have tomorrow lessons or not. Did you get this evening from Papa knews? [news]—I was so glad to sea you today. I love and kiss you with all my heart. Your own Maria [In Russian] May God keep you +

18 Dec 1914
My golden Mama.
I wish you a good night and hope that you feel good tomorrow. My throat still hurts when I swallow and I still have compress on my head. God bless you. +
Your loving and firmly kissing daughter Maria.

Victoria of Battenberg to Maria [in English]—

Dear Marie,
I hope I shall see you all again in the New Year, when the war is over, + for a little longer than in this year. Dick is beginning to drive our motor quite well, unluckily for us he goes to Dartmouth when these holidays are over, it would have been nice if he could have remained on at Osborne a bit longer.
Ever your loving Auntie Victoria

Maria to Alexandra Feodorovna [in English]—

Mama my darling,
I wish you a happy Xmas and hope that God will send you again strength to go to the hospital. Sleep well. Your own loving daughter Maria
I love and kiss you most tenderly.

Maria to Olga Kleinmichel Voronova[23]—

---

23. Daughter of one of the ladies in waiting, friend to the young grand duchesses, later married Pavel Voronov, a favorite officer and love interest of Olga Nikolaevna (prior to his marriage).

25 Dec 1914
My dear Olga!
Thank you for your dear letter and greetings. I congratulate you heartily and wish you all the best and that you may spend the holidays joyfully. I suppose it must be very lonely to spend your first Christmas without your husband. Anastasia thanks you and Tata very much for the letter. Olga and Tatiana have gone to the infirmary again today to do dressings. I congratulate your husband on his birthday with all my heart and wish him all that is good and bright. Anastasia is running around the room and setting up all her presents. I kiss and hug you firmly.
Loving you,
Your
Maria

29 Dec 1914
My dear and sweet Olga!
Thank you very much for your letter. How are you living—on your own or with one of your sisters? We are going to Christmas parties every day at the infirmaries. Today we were at Mama's Christmas Party at the Nanny School. There are lots of extra children there now, such awfully sweet darlings. We gave them all presents and they were so happy with them and each one showed their nanny what they got. They are so appetizing. There are some really little ones there, some are only two weeks old. I love little children so awfully much, play with them and carry them in my arms. Do you love babies? Olga and Tatiana have been at the dressings since 10 o'clock already. Anastasia is sitting here in the room and is reading a new book which she got for Christmas. I kiss you firmly my darling Olga and love you.
Your
Maria
Anastasia also kisses you very affectionately. If you will write, send regards to your husband from me.

1915

Maria to Olga Kleinmichel Voronova—

1 Jan 1915

My dear Olga!

I thank you very much for your dear letter. I hope this year brings you much happiness and joy. Just now, my sisters have gone for a walk, but I have stayed home because I have a cold. Later on, Anastasia and I will go to our infirmary. We have been going there almost daily. All the soldiers are such darlings, and so patient, it is really amazing. Your brother must have told you lots of interesting things. And Tata, does he continue going for dressings or did he stop? Goodbye for now, my dear Olga. I kiss you firmly. Loving you,

Yours

Maria

Princess Margaretha of Sweden to Maria [in English]—

Fridhem Sweden

Dear Marie, I wish you a very happy Xmas and new year from your loving cousin Margaretha. 1 Jan 1915

Maria to Maria Vishnyakova

My dear Mary,

How are you? Such an awful thing happened with poor Anya. Her left leg is broken in two places and she has cracked her malar bones. Her right leg and back have all been crushed. She was under the rubble. Today she hurts awfully over her whole body and around her right eye is some swelling. She is at the Palace Hospital in the officers' barracks where the sisters work.

Well, how are your wounded? Baby is well. Kissing you firmly,
Your Maria
4 January 1915

Nicholas II to Maria—
Stavka[1]
7 March 1915
Dear Marie,
Thank you heartily for your letters, which give me great joy. Chemodurov got me all these new postcards here in the mail. I am glad that you successfully bathed in the large bath. Every day I walk with the gentlemen of the suite. Yesterday I traveled with them for 24 versts to the Skobelevsky camp, where the 4th building is in summer. Beautiful forest and river; there are many officers' houses and the names of those who lived there are written on the plates. I firmly hug you, my Kazan.
Your Papa

Maria to Alexandra Feodorovna [in English]—
Mama deary! I thank you so much for your letter. I am so sorry that you must be today in bed. I hope your heart will be better tomorrow. I kiss you very much.
Your loving Maria
March 11 1915

Princess Margaretha to Maria [in English]—
Darling Marie, Thank you so very much for your card! Here is a new foto of my brother. Much love fr. your loving cousin. Margaretha. PS Write very soon!!! Stockholm 14/3.15 [14 March, 1915]

Maria to Nicholas II—
5 April. My golden Papa! I am now sitting near Mama, at her feet

1. Military headquarters in Mogilev.

lies Shvybzik. Anastasia is drawing. Olga and Tatiana left for the infirmary to [see] Vartanov. When they return, we will go to *Obednya*. Yesterday after you left, we went home, and then to our infirmary, all 4. The concert was very successful. Delazari was very sweet, and told several funny stories. Then one lady in a *sarafan*[2] danced a Russian [dance] (she was rather finicky). My Demenkov was very charming, and introduced all the performers to us. The little Shvybzik[3] just made a "governor"[4] on Mama's carpet, and Anastasia is now training him. Today we will see Rodionov and Kozhevnikov. The weather here today is not bad. 15 degrees in the sun. We will take a walk this afternoon there will probably be no one interesting in the guard room. Today none of the sisters will write to you as they will not have enough time. The courier is leaving at 5 o'clock, an awfully inconvenient time. Such a pity that Ilyinsky went with you and not Popov, as you will be in Odessa. So awfully tiresome that you are not here, we could have broken the ice together today. Yesterday Anastasia already found two crocuses and a snowdrop under the balcony, not where they were planted, but where they grow on their own. The bell is tolling at "Znamenie"[5] now and it is time for me to put on my hat. I kiss you affectionately, my angel, and love you terribly. Your very own Kazanetz. May God keep you. + Happy 8th April. Regards to Kolya. O., T., A., A. kiss you. I hope that someone good will be at the church, most likely Shvedov.

8 April. My sweet good Papa darling! Mama was terribly happy to receive the cross from you, and she is constantly wearing it today. She was lying down on the balcony for the first time today. Anastasia and I rode our bicycles for a bit around the house. The guard on duty today is not very interesting. In the morning it was 20 degrees in the sun. In the afternoon, I walked with Anastasia and Shura, and then went to our infirmary. Nikolaev has a toe abscess on his right foot, and they had to remove the nail, so now he has to stay in bed for a few days. [. . .] I am so happy for you, that you

---

2. Traditional Russian peasant dress.
3. Shvybzik was Anastasia's little pet Pomeranian.
4. Probably referring to the dog's "accident" on the floor.
5. Our Lady of Znamenie (the Sign), a church near Catherine Palace frequented by the imperial family.

will see Aunt Olga. Do you remember when Tatiana Andreevna[6] was here and asked for you to come over, back then you didn't think that you would be there so soon. Right now, I am sitting near Mama's bed, where she is staying, while Olga and Tatiana are reading. Alexei wanted to sleep in your spot today and told Mama that he wants to pretend that he is the husband. Yesterday he gorged on black crackers and in the evening, he was sent directly to Derevenko.[7] Olga and Tatiana were in Petrograd today, Olga at the charities, and Tatiana at the committee[8] and [she] took pleasure in dear Neidegart.[9] After dinner I played kolorito with Mama. Now she is reading some English book. Yesterday Kozhevnikov and Rodionov and Kublitsky were at Anya's for tea. Before that they stopped by to bid farewell to Mama, as they were leaving that evening. They were wearing the same shirts as yours. It is so lonesome here without you. I kiss you affectionately, and squeeze you in hugs and love you. Your Kazanetz. Big regards to Kolya. May the Lord keep you. + [. . .]

Grand Duke Michael Alexandrovich[10] to Maria—
H.I.H
Grand Duchess
Maria Nikolaevna
From MA
April 14, 1915.
My dear Marie,
I heartily thank you for the Easter card, which I received only now and was very touched by your sweet attention. I hope you are all well and pass the time well. I kiss you, my dear goddaughter, and send my greetings to Papa, Mama, your sisters and Alexei.
Loving you
Uncle Mimi

---

6. Tatiana Andreevna Groove was a nurse at imperial infirmary.

7. One of the imperial physicians.

8. Tatiana was the chair of the Temporary Relief of War Sufferers Committee, which assisted refugees from areas occupied by the enemy.

9. One of the infirmary patients.

10. Grand Duke Michael Alexandrovich, youngest brother of the tsar.

Maria to Nicholas II—

18 April. Papa, my dear darling! Well, how are you doing, can you? I am so happy I saw your glorious Plastuns.[11] We are doing the same as always. Today we went to *vsenoshnaya*. Batushka Kibardin did the service while the soldiers sang like angels, so nicely. At the church, there was no one interesting to me, except for our wounded. We just finished dinner. Alexei came to Mama's to pray. The sisters are dismantling the flowers that were sent by the Yanovs from Livadia. Wisteria and others. While that page was drying, I read Aunt Olga's letter to our Olga. I put Shvybzik on my lap, but he wished to be on the floor. [. . .]. Mama is sending Anastasia to bed, while she is in despair [because she] cannot find Shvybzik who is missing in action, everyone is shouting and calling him but he does not come, the bastard. Finally, we found him after 10 minutes, we were all looking for him under the sofas. Finally, Mama decided to bark and Shvybzik barked in response, and it turned out that he was sitting under the sofa at Mama's, and he was pulled out with joint effort. I gently kiss the bump on Kotov's forehead and curtsy to darling Litvinov and Chemodurov.[12] Shura is furiously kissing the heel of your left hind leg in her mind. Personally, I embrace and kiss you tenderly. Your faithful and devoted Kazanetz. May God keep you. +. Regards from me to Kolya.

Continuing this letter in the morning at 8 o'clock. I just opened the window curtains and to my joy saw that it is 19 degrees in the sun. Alexei came to our bedroom, and now he is lying on my bed and playing with Anastasia and Shvybzik. The sisters are still sleeping, Shvybzik is squealing, probably he wants to see the Governor-General. He has already done that, and Anastasia ran in with the little shovel from the fireplace and picked it up. Well, goodbye, my darling Papa. The sisters and Alexei kiss you.

13 June. My golden Papa darling! Last night we were at Anya's, [and] Nikolai Dmitrievich,[13] Alexander Konstantinovich[14] and Vikt.

11. Nicholas II's plastun regiment.
12. The tsar's lackey.
13. Demenkov.
14. Shvedov.

Erastovich[15] and Skvortsov were all there. It was very nice, we played "Dobchinsky-Bobchinsky"[16] and the Charades. Yesterday afternoon Anastasia and I played tennis. Of course, I lost as usual, all three sets. Today we will probably walk to the Grand Palace. The other day we went to the nanny school and squeezed the little children who were already going to bed. We were also at Mama's warehouse,[17] where they rolled bandages, and Anastasia and I had to wear white coats and kerchiefs like everyone else, so that we would both not be too embarrassed. Now we are sitting on the balcony. Anya is now going to [see] Grotov at Krasnoe Selo in the motor. Tatiana went horseback riding, I also wanted to go but have a cold, so did not go. Anastasia, Olga and I were just at the Red Cross infirmary and at the Grand Palace. Today Mama will receive the detachment of British medical motor cars. Well, so long, good-bye, my darling. May the Lord keep you. + I love you very much and kiss you. Your Kazanetz. Regards to Sasha and Kolya.

Princess Margaretha to Maria [in English]—
[4 June] 4/6 1915
Dear Marie, I thank you so very much for your kind letter. Now we are here in the country and have a lovely time. Where are you? I have put up my hair too and you did it so much earlier. Much love to you all from us. Many kisses from your loving cousin Margaretha
Please write soon.

Maria to Olga Kleinmichel Voronova—
15 June, 1915
My dear Olga! I thank you so much for the congratulations and good wishes and your husband as well. The other day one of the officers who was a patient here at Tsarskoe Selo went to Odessa to a *liman*.[18] Right now our weather is warmer and all our wounded

15. Zborovsky.

16. A game where players pass a counter around under the table. At the call of "Dobchinsky Bobchinsky" all must place their hands on the table and the players guess who has the counter.

17. Warehouse where infirmary supplies were kept.

18. Shallow, very salty beach, common in Odessa area.

sit in the sun in the mornings and during the day. They set up tennis here at our [infirmary] and we play sometimes. Regards to your husband and I kiss you affectionately. Your loving Maria.

Maria to Nicholas II—

15 June. My biggest darling Papa! Awfully big thanks to you for your sweet and long letter. I thank you once again for the wonderful gifts. Yesterday morning we went to *Obednya*, then had breakfast on the balcony. In the afternoon, Mama and Anya rode in a carriage, while we 4 in little equipages, which one can drive oneself, I was riding with Tatiana, while Olga with Anastasia. We took the same road that we did with you in the evening in the motor to Pavlovsk. Georgiy crashed his little motor into Mama's equipage, but did not wreck anything. We were riding behind [them] and laughing very hard. Later we had tea with Mama and of course Uncle Pavel, because it was a holiday. The Uncle sang as usual ti-ta-to and then said that he needs to talk to Mama alone, which always happens after he sings at tea. We then got up and went to Anya's and stayed there. Sat on her balcony, and then played in her room. The day was nice in general, but bad because you weren't here. I thank you so much again my darling, love and kiss you affectionately. May Christ be with you. Your Kazanetz. Regards to Sasha and Kolya. I only played tennis once with Anastasia. Anastasia kisses you. She is lying around on the balcony on Mama's sofa and drinking coffee.

19 June. My golden Papa darling! This afternoon I saw a few children swimming in the river and I, much like you, wanted to go swimming too. Alexei is line fishing almost daily now at the pond near the elephant. I forgot to tell you that today we 4 were at Mama's Invalid House and saw the two Cossacks from that Kuban regiment that used to be here. One [of them] was old with a beard, both very sweet. They brought two new officers to our infirmary, from the 5th Siberian Infantry Regiment, one heavily [wounded]. Your letter from Dushkinsk is sitting here at night on the table, and every evening I am happy to [see] it. May God keep you. I kiss you affectionately, same as I love you. Your Kazanetz.

Maria to Olga Kleinmichel Voronova—
24 July 1915
My dear Olga!
With all my heart, I thank you and your husband for the congratulations and good wishes. It must be very strange for your husband and the officers to be in Sevastopol without the yacht. There was a little concert today at Anastasia's and my infirmary. It was arranged by N.D. Demenkov. Do you remember him? He performed with you in Princess Baryatinsky's[19] play in Yalta. Our concert was held in a tent in front of the infirmary. Our infirmary isn't big, just 38 soldiers in all and 10 officers. There is an Officer from my regiment there. Your husband saw him at lunch one time in Livadia. His name is Karpov. We go to our infirmary almost every day and sit with the wounded outside in the fresh air, and with those with serious wounds—indoors. Goodbye for now, my dear. We all kiss you firmly and send our greetings to your husband.
Your loving
Maria
God protect you.

Maria to Alexandra Feodorovna [in English]—
God bless you Mama my deary in those hevy moments. Perhaps this Virgin will give you strength. Your Maria
Aug 22 1915

Maria to Nicholas II—
26 August. My golden Papa darling! I went to *obednya* and *moleben* with Mama and Anastasia, the Batushka gave a wonderful sermon. It all lasted 1 hour 45 minutes. Olga and Tatiana went to Petrograd and then they will have tea at Grandmama's on Yelagin.[20] I was just at our infirmary with Anastasia. It's so nice that everyone now knows that you replaced Uncle Nikolasha,[21] and now you probably feel a lot more peaceful. Well, so long, goodbye, my angel. May Christ be with you. + Your Kazanetz.

19. Catherine Alexandrovna, daughter of Emperor Alexander II by his second marriage to Catherine Dolgorukova.
20. Yelagin Palace, on Yelagin Island off Petrograd, another residence of the dowager empress.
21. Grand Duke Nikolai Nikolaevich.

Nicholas II to Maria—

Mogilev. 12 September, 1915. My sweet Marie, I thank you so much for your letters, which always make me laugh, from what you write as well as the amount of mistakes in them. I am happy for you, that N.D. is staying in Tsarskoe Selo, but because of that he lost his job at "The Worker." Have you recently been to Peterhof with Mama? I love to reminisce about our trips there on holidays during the summer. Here on the Dnieper,[22] I have from the beginning wanted to row in a boat, but have not been able to do it for some reason, only was able to cross the river twice on a ferry, along with the motors. I have very little time and therefore must end this letter. I give you a big hug my dear Kazanetz. May Christ be with you! Your Papa.

Maria to Nicholas II—

15 September. My golden Papa darling! I squeeze you in a hug and kiss you for your dear letter, which I was not expecting to get. We just finished breakfast. I will go walking with Olga and Anastasia. Hope to walk by the guard room, in case N.D. is there. In the morning we had lessons. These last couple of days we went to *Obednya* at the lower church, as the sisters went to the infirmary right after *Obednya*. Therefore, of course N.D. was specifically at the upstairs church, and Anya saw him. Rather weak: "Go to sleep, the achievements of fame, everyone, sleep forever." These days Alexei is building a fire again. We walk occasionally, but usually in the afternoons we go to the infirmary. Yesterday we went to the Nanny School and squeezed the children. There is this one refugee child, she is only two years old. Her mother died. She is so cute, but speaks Russian badly and calls her nanny Mama. My medical train brought her. These days almost all the medical trains pick up refugees if they have room. Right now, we are having tea. Took a very successful walk. N.D. was on duty and we talked with him very nicely through the window. We walked to the Caprice[23] and walked up the stairs. You know [a diagram drawing]. And then, when we got up there, Olga took her parasol and attacked one of the windows viciously,

22. River near Mogilev.
23. A decorative structure in Alexander Park, built by Catherine the Great.

and broke 3 glass panels, then gave me the parasol, and I broke a window too and Anastasia [did] too. It is probably so pleasant for you to have Uncle Misha there with you. Tell him that I kiss him lots. Are you still playing kosti? Tomorrow Aunt Ksenia and Uncle Sandro will have breakfast with us. Olga is reading a newspaper now, while Mama is talking to Anya. Our weather is rotten. Right now, it is foggy. Well, goodbye for now, my dear darling. May Christ be with you. + Your Kazanetz. Regards to Kolya and Sasha. I kiss you and Dmitri.

3 October. My golden Papa! Well this time I think you don't feel as empty. I am so happy for you, that you saw the 21st Corp. We are the same here: ride with Mama in the afternoons, and visit the infirmaries. This one officer transferred to our infirmary from the Red Cross, his name is Shakh-Nazarov. He is very appetizing, dark with a moustache, and in general I approve of him. He was a patient in Pskov before, at Maria's infirmary. We just had tea. In the afternoon we rode around with Mama and Anya. Olga and Tatiana are cleaning the instruments now, before *vsenoshnaya*. This evening Grigori[24] will be at Anya's. Yesterday morning [we] talked to N.D. through the window. Today I will probably not see him, as we will not be at *Vsenoshnaya* in the Sobor. I hope that Mama will not bring us to the consecration tomorrow, as there will be so many people and relatives, and so little room, it will be stuffy and one cannot pray. Well I must end now, as I will be trying on some dress, [which is] awfully tiresome. Well, goodbye my Papa, darling. I kiss you affectionately, like I love you. Your Kazanetz. May Christ be with you. + Regards to Kolya. We saw Uncle Pavel's wife taking a walk.

Maria to Alexei—

Ts. S. 3 Oct 1915
My sweet darling Alexei!
I congratulate you with all my heart, so awfully sorry that we cannot see each other on this day. Yesterday, I went for a walk with Shura in the morning. We were walking past the Chinese village when suddenly we saw the wife of Vladimir Nikolaevich and Kolya. She

24. Rasputin.

recognised Shura and called out, "Hello, Alexandra Alexandrovna!" We went to the caprice and greeted them. Kolya held Hina and the [Nikolaevich's] wife Brom.[25] We talked with them for a little bit and then went home. There was no watchman at the gate and we had to climb over. We went past the white tower and saw Sergei who was pushing Dunya in a cart, but when I went over, they ran off home. Today I went for a drive with Mama and Ania, Mama in the front and we 4 behind. When we were at Pavlovsk, we stood up as we were going along the whole time so that we were falling down and laughing. Olga fell on me then grabbed my head and pulled the tassel off my hat.

It's time to go to church. I kiss you firmly.

Maria.

Maria to Nicholas II—

7 October. My Papa darling! I am writing out of turn, as Tatiana did not have a chance [to write] because of Petrograd. We, with Anastasia, deigned to visit the warehouse and roll the bandages, then went to our infirmary. A young officer from my regiment was supposed to arrive there, [he was] wounded in the leg in the 25th September attack. He said that lately the regiment has all been on horseback. He is really young, 18 and a half years old. He was presented to me on the 1st of June with two other officers, when he graduated from the Nikolaevsky Cavalier School. We only just consecrated the cemetery church with Mama, and already two officers died at our infirmary and the Grand Palace infirmary. I must end now as they came in to see if we have a letter for you. I love you very much and kiss you and Baby. + Kazanetz. Regards to Kolya.

31 October, 1915. I am writing to you from the bedroom. Just had tea, the sisters are still sitting at Mama's. This morning [I] had lessons, and in the afternoon rode with Nastenka. Went to our infirmary with Anastasia, and she took [pictures] of our wounded officers. Two of them have St George's crosses. The snow is almost all gone, it is so strange to see grass again, and it seems as though Nature made a mistake and thinks that it is Spring already. In the

25. Hina and Brom were presumably the names of pet dogs.

morning I walked with Shura, [we] walked by the guard room, but did not see anyone, hopefully will see them tonight at *vsenoshnaya*. Probably Dmitri is doing lots of foolish things and talks [foolishly] too, kiss him for me. The other day an Englishwoman had breakfast with us, she came to Petrograd to establish an English infirmary in Dmitri's house. We are not really doing anything interesting. I will think of you at *Vsenoshnaya*, how you are now standing at church, and will pray for you. Nothing more to write, therefore I will end. I kiss you affectionately, like I love you. Your Kazanetz. May Christ be with you. + Regards to all of yours and Kolya.

13 November, 1915. My dear Sweet Papa! Heartfelt wishes for Grandmama's birthday and the wedding anniversary. We had tea at Grandmama's, and I think will go see her again tomorrow. She is very happy with her trip to Kiev and told us that she visited some infirmary every day. Right now [we] will go riding with Nastenka. Then Anastasia and I will go to our infirmary. Yesterday they brought 7 lower ranks there from the train. Rather seriously wounded, we have not seen them yet. Anastasia is sitting next to me, reading something. I have not seen Nik. Dm. It is rather boring for 2 weeks already. Since they had put a sofa in the sisters' bedroom, it became much cozier, I kiss you and Alexei affectionately. Your Kazanetz. Regards to all. Our arithmetic teacher is healthy again and is coming to [teach] us again.

1 December. My dear golden Papa! Right now, I am sitting on the floor in Mama's study, while she is lying on the couch. Anya is sitting in your arm chair, while the sisters are sitting on chairs and working. We just attended the *panikhida*[26] for Sonia.[27] Her little housemaid Ustinia was crying terribly. Tomorrow Olga and Tatiana will go to Petrograd, the former for charities, and the latter for a committee. I kiss you and Alexei very affectionately. Your very own Kazanetz.

---

26. A memorial service for the dead.
27. Princess Sonia Orbeliani died from a chronic debilitating illness.

Boatswain Andrei Derevenko[28] to Maria—

Good greetings, Your Imperial Highness. I bow to you and the Grand Duchesses. We are all fine. We take walks in the little garden with His I.[mperial] H.[ighness], in the mud and are engaged in marching, I have fulfilled your order and now it will be ready the 2nd of December. Saw off my old senior adjutant officer N. P. Sablin of the 2nd, I am sorry for him, but N. P. was very pleased and cheerful, the rest is all good the weather is changeable. Today 2 is degr. of frost, yesterday, His I.[mperial] M.[ajesty] E[mperor] H.[eir] Ts[arevich] had a haircut and a bath, I was completely doused and he was naughty and sat by the dirty Dnieper water, did not want to leave, he often remembers his Shot,[29] shake Artepko's[30] paw and ears from us. I bow to Alexandra Alexandrovna,[31] Elizaveta Nikolaevna,[32] Anna Yakovlevna.[33] Boatswain A Derevenko, Nagorny, Kotov and little Naidachin thank you for the regards. Your Imperial Highness's Loyal Servant Boatswain A. Derevenko
Kotov, Nagorny and Naidachin send a bow to you
1915, 1st December

Maria to Nicholas II—

30 December. May the Lord bless the crest of this new year! I hope this year will bring you, my dear Papa, many happy days. It is so tiresome that we will not see you on the first day of the New Year. In general, it is always very boring for us without you. Well, I will finish writing now, or else your imperial eyes will start hurting from reading on this red paper. May Christ be with you. + My dear, I squeeze you tightly in my hug. Your Kazanetz.

28. Derevenko was Tsesarevich Alexei's *dyadka*, "sailor uncle," who took care of him.
29. Alexei's pet dog.
30. Artepko was a dog.
31. Tegleva.
32. Maid Liza Erlsberg.
33. Maid Anna Yakovlevna Utkina.

Nicholas and Alexandra with their children in 1899. Alexandra is holding Maria, Tatiana is on Nicholas's lap, and Olga in the front. (*Russian State Archives* [*GARF*])

Empress Alexandra with her three eldest daughters, Maria, Olga and Tatiana, around 1900. (*GARF*)

Grand Duchess Maria Nikolaevna, 1904. (*GARF*)

Maria at her lessons. (*GARF*)

Summer 1912 on the *Standart*. Left to right: Maria, Olga, Alexei, Anya Vyrubova, Tatiana, and Anastasia Hendrikova. Grand Duchess Anastasia in front. (*GARF*)

Watching the games on the Finnish skerries with the suite, 1912. Anastasia is far left and Maria on the right. (*GARF*)

Maria and Olga aboard the *Standart*, 1912. (*GARF*)

The Imperial Family in Moscow for the tercentennary of Romanov rule, 1913. (*GARF*)

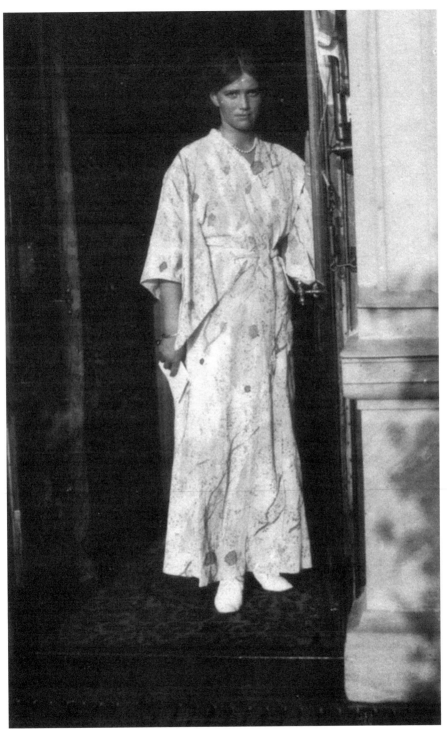

Maria in a kimono-style dressing gown, summer 1914. (*GARF*)

Empress Alexandra, Olga, and Tatiana as nurses, with Maria, Anastasia, and Alexei visiting the wounded and posing with nurses at the Palace infirmary, 1914. (*GARF*)

Maria (on the right) and one of her sisters in the Alexander Park, summer 1917. (*GARF*)

Maria, Nicholas II, and Olga with soldiers and guards at Tsarskoe 1917. (*GARF*)

Olga, Tatiana, Anastasia, and Maria, summer 1917, Alexander Park, Tsarskoe Selo. (*GARF*)

Maria, Olga, Anastasia, and Tatiana along with their dogs, Jimmy and Ortipo, during their imprisonment at Tsarskoe Selo, spring 1917. (*GARF*)

Nicholas II sitting with the convalescing Maria after his return to Tsarskoe Selo as a prisoner, spring 1917. (*GARF*)

1916

Letter to Grand Duchess Maria Nikolaevna—
[January 1916]
Your Imperial Highness.
I send to Your Imperial Highness my sincere thanks to your heartfelt care for me on the occasion of the death of my husband Alexander, and from his home at Mamonka, I send to Your Imperial Highness my heartfelt and sincere gratitude for your high and gracious care in our great sorrow, that we have received royal mercy and we fall down at your feet.
Kuznetsova

Maria's diary [title page: "Book of Memories, 1916"]—
-23 AM -16PM
January 1 Friday
4 at *obednya* in the morning. Breakfast 5 and Mama lying in bed ♥2. Was at our hospital with A in the day. Had tea 4 with Anya by Mama in bed. Read. Dinner 4. After dinner Mama went to the study and lay down on the sofa. Anya was there. Lilies-of-the-Valley from Kiki.

-20 AM -11 PM
January 2 Saturday
In the morning was at *obednya* with A. Breakfast 5. Mama stayed in bed. During the day, 4 went to the G[rand] P[alace]. and went

for a ride in a motorcar. Had tea 4 with Anya at Mama's. 4 went to the *vsenoshnaya*, dined. In the evening Mama lay down on the sofa. Anya came.

-5AM -3PM
January 3 Sunday
In the morning 4 at *obednya*. Breakfast 5. Mama lay in bed all day. In the day 4 went for a troika ride with Nastenka. 4 went to Koko-revsky Infirmary. Later went to our Infirmary with A. Had tea 4 with Anya at Mama's. I read. Dinner 4. Mama lay on the sofa. Kiki and Anya were there. Before that with O, A and A in Mama's big sitting room played with toy revolvers in the dark.

Alexandra Feodorovna to Nicholas II—

January 3 1916
. . . the Children are eating next door, chattering and firing away with their toy pistols . . .

Nicholas II to Maria—

I.[imperial] Headquarters. 3 January, 1916. Sweet Marie, I thank you for the little letter on red paper, which Teternikov brought to me just before the New Year. I am very touched by your consider-ation. Regrettably I don't have gymnastics here and have no one to squeeze, not even you. Today I found a shovel in the garden and worked in the snow really well. While I walk, I look at those driving and walking by, and sometimes see very funny things! I squeeze you in a tight hug. Your Papa.

Maria's diary—

-12AM -17PM
January 4 Monday
In the morning were at the Palace Hospital. Breakfast 5. Mama lying down all day. In the day went with O and T to the G[rand] P[alace]. Went for a drive in a motor and got stuck in the snow and had to be dug out. Had tea 4 with Anya at Mama's.

Maria to Nicholas II—

4 January. My golden Papa! I am writing to you in the morning. Anastasia is sitting on the sofa near the fireplace and drawing something. We completely changed our room, the cots are back in their old place, while the screen went elsewhere, I won't be able to describe to you very well where everything is. You will see for yourself when you get back, which I hope will be very soon. This morning at 9 o'clock [we were] at the Grand Palace infirmary, we haven't been there for a terribly long time. And yesterday we went to the Kokorevsky infirmary, your three Yerevantzy are patients there. Day before yesterday we were laughing awfully hard. The old Aunt Olga called our Olga, in order for her to ask this one soldier from the Svodny regiment to come over and visit her patient from the same regiment. Well, Olga immediately called the guard room, the guard on duty turned out to be Kulyukin, and he asks: "who is on the telephone?" She answers "Olga Nikolaevna." "Which Olga Nikolaevna?"—"Olga Nikolaevna, don't you know?" The one who lives above you."—"I don't understand anything"—"Grand Duchess Olga Nikolaevna, do you hear me?"—and starts to guffaw madly, so he got hurt and said: "Young lady, this is a service telephone, and practical jokes are not appropriate here," and hung up. Olga left. Then in 5 minutes, Tatiana comes over and makes a call; he recognized her, and she told him everything. Yesterday at *obednya* Kulyukin comes over and asks Resin to apologize to Olga for him, but that he wasn't expecting that she would call so he thought that someone was playing a practical joke. Because Mama stays in bed, we have breakfast and dinner alone. Well, so long, goodbye. Right now, I need to go to breakfast. I squeeze you tightly in a hug and love you. Your Kazanetz. Regards to everyone who is with you.

Maria's diary—

5 January. In the morning went to church with O[lga], T[atiana] and Al[eksei]. Mama is in bed. In the afternoon walked around the city with T. and Isa. Had tea with O., T. and Anya near Mama. Went to *vsenoshnaya* with O., T. and Alexei. Had dinner 3 and Mama [was] on the couch. Anastasia was in bed as she has a cold, she has high fever. Got a letter from Darling Papa.

-4AM -2PM
January 6 Wednesday
Was at *obednya* in the morning with T and O. Went for a walk by myself, sat with A. Breakfast with O, T and Al. Mama lay in bed all day. Went for a troika ride with O, T and Isa. Had tea with O, T and Anya at Mama's. Olga read to us as servants. Anastasia has bronchitis and she stayed in bed. Dinner 3 and Mama on the sofa. Kiki and Anya.

Maria to Nicholas II—

6 January. My very own dear Papa! I am awfully grateful to you for your dear little letter. I was not expecting it. Right now, Anastasia is lying down and having breakfast, Olga and Tatiana were with me at the lower church for *Obednya* at 9 o'clock, then the sisters and Alexei went to the infirmary, and I went to take a walk. Today it is 4 degrees, so it is nice to walk. Such a pity that I could not visit you, we could have shoveled snow together.—Such a pity that I am not a boy. Bad things keep happening to us when we ride in the motor. There is so much snow that we drive off to the side of the road and get stuck in the snow and the hetmans dig us out with shovels. This already happened three times, [it is] rather tiresome and it feels like the motor is turning over to its side. Today we will probably drive to the Grand Palace. Anastasia is already awfully tired of staying in bed, it is particularly tiresome on a holiday. The other day we saw little Olga from the Crimea at Trina's. She was the one who ducked down a lot when we played tennis, remember. Now she lives in Petrograd and studies at the Smolny Institute, and is terribly happy, as she is waiting impatiently for the day when the school break ends. Well so long, goodbye my darling Papa. I squeeze and hug you very very tightly in my mind, like I love you. Your very own, Kazanetz. Regards to all. May God keep you. +

Maria's diary—

+2AM +1PM
January 7 Thursday
In the morning lessons—German, English, French and History. Breakfast with O, T, Anya and Mama on the sofa. In the day I was

at our infirmary. After with O and T at the G[rand] P[alace] and at Mme Zizi's. Went for a troika ride with Isa. Tea with Mama, O, T and Anya. Had music [lesson] I prepared my lessons. Dinner 3 with Mama on the sofa. Kiki was there. Got a gramophone. A and A have temperatures and they were lying down.

+2AM +1PM
January 8 Friday
Lessons in the morning, Russian, English and Batushka. Was at Znamenie because they had colds and are in bed. Breakfast 3 with Mama on the sofa. Was at our infirmary in the day. Went 3 for a troika ride with Shura. Had tea 3 with Mama. A and A in bed. Had music [lesson]. Dinner 3 and Mama on the sofa. Was at Anya's.

+2AM +2PM
January 9 Saturday.
Lessons in the morning, German, French and Batushka [religion]. Breakfast 3 and Mama on the sofa. Was at our infirmary in the day. 3 went for a troika ride with Isa. Had tea 3 with Mama and A and A in bed. 3 at All Night Vigil. Dinner 3 and Mama on the sofa. Was at Anya's. She is still lying down.

0AM -3PM
January 10 Sunday
In the morning went 3 to Liturgy. Had breakfast 3 with Isa with Mama on her sofa. In the afternoon was with T at the G[rand] P[alace]. 3 with Isa at the Convoy Hospital. Afterwards went for a troika ride. Tea 3 with Mama but A and Al in bed. Played cabala with A. Dinner 3 and Mama on the sofa.

+2AM +2PM
January 11 Monday
In the morning history and Russian lessons. Sat with Mama on the balcony. Breakfast 3 with Mama on the sofa. In the afternoon 3 went to the G[rand] P[alace]. 3 had a troika ride with Isa. Was at our Infirmary. Tea 3 with Mama and A in bed. Had music and English lessons. Dinner 3 with Anya, Kiki and Mama on the sofa.

0 AM -9PM
January 14 Thursday
In the morning German, English, French and History lessons. Breakfast 5 with O.E, Papa, Fedorova and Mama on the sofa. With O to the G[rand]] P[alace]. 3 went for a troika ride with Isa. Tea 4 with Mama and Anya. Had music [lesson]. Read and did my homework. Dinner 4 with Anya, Kiki, and Mama on the sofa. Played Hide and Seek 5 in the dark.

+1 AM -5PM
January 15 Friday
In the morning lessons—German and Batushka [religion]. Breakfast 5. Mama lay down all day. In the afternoon 3 went for a troika ride with Isa. Was at our Infirmary. Tea 4 with Anya by Mama's bed. Had music [lesson] and prepared my homework. Dinner 4. Mama lay on the sofa for a bit. Anya was here.

+2AM -3PM
January 16 Saturday
In the morning German lessons, Batushka [religion] and French. Breakfast 5 and Mama on the sofa. Went for a drive 4 with Isa during the day and after that a concert at the G[rand] P[alace]. Tea 4 with Mama and Anya. 4 went to the *vsenoshnaya*. Dinner 4 with Anya, Mama on the sofa. Said goodbye to Kiki who is going to the war.

+1AM 0PM
January 17 Sunday
At *obednya* in the morning. We went to meet Papa. Breakfast 5 with Papa and Mama on the sofa. In the afternoon went to our infirmary with A. Went for a walk with O and Papa. Tea 4 with Papa, Mama and Anya. Went to Trina's. Dinner 4 with Papa and Mama on the sofa. Played in the dark. Papa read us a very interesting English book "A Millionaire Girl."

0 AM ___PM
January 18 Monday

Lessons in the morning—arithmetic, history and Russian. Went for a drive with Shura. Breakfast 5 with Papa and Mama on the sofa. Went 4 to the G[rand] P[alace] in the day. Went for a walk with Papa. Had tea with T and A in the children's room. Had English and music lessons. Dinner 3 with Papa, and Mama on the sofa. Anya was here. Papa read some more.

0 AM -2PM

January 19 Tuesday

In the morning German, English, French and History lessons. Breakfast 5 with Papa, Gavriil and U[ncle] Sergei. Mama was in a different room. Went for a walk in the afternoon with A and Papa. Went to our infirmary with A. Had tea with Mama, A and Anya. Had music [lesson]. Did my homework. Dinner 3 with Papa, Gavriil and Mama on the sofa. Kolya and Anya were here.

0 AM -1PM

January 20 Wednesday

In the morning Russian, history, arithmetic and religion lessons. Breakfast 5 with Papa, Sandor and Kazakevich. Went for a walk in the day with Papa and A. Went to the G[rand] P[alace] with T and A. Tea 4 with Papa and Mama. Had music and French lessons. Dinner 3 with Papa and Mama was on the sofa. Anya was here. Papa continued reading again.

0 AM 0 PM

January 22 Friday

Had lessons in the morning. Went for a ride with Shura. Breakfast 5 with Papa and Mama on the sofa. Was at the G[rand] P[alace] in the day with O and A. Went for a walk with Papa, T and A. Was at our infirmary with A. Tea with Papa, Mama and O. Had music [lesson]. Dinner 3 with Papa and Mama on the sofa. Anya was here. Papa read.

+1 AM -4 PM

January 23 Saturday

Lessons in the morning. Breakfast 5 with Papa, C[ount] Fredericks and Mama on the sofa. Went with A to our infirmary in the day. 4 went for a troika ride with Nastenka. 4 were at a concert at the G[rand] P[alace] infirmary. Had tea at home. 4 at the *vsenoshnaya* with Papa. Dinner [with] the same, and Mama on the sofa. Anya was here. Papa read.

-6 AM 0 PM
January 24 Sunday
In the morning 4 with Papa went to A[unt] Xenia's in Petrograd to *obednya* and breakfast. Buvgrik, A[unt] Ella and her suite were there. Went back home with Papa and A. Went to our infirmary with A. Tea 4 with Papa, Mama, Kolya and Anya. Went for a drive with A and Shura. Dinner 3 with Papa and Mama on the sofa. Anya was here. Papa read.

-1 AM +1 PM
January 25 Monday
Had lessons in the morning. Went for a ride with Shura. Breakfast 5 with Papa, Vilkitsky and Mama on the sofa Was at the G[rand] P[alace] during the day with O and A. Went for a walk with Papa, A and T. Went to our infirmary with A. Tea in the children's [room] with T and A. Had English and music lessons. Prepared my homework. Dinner 3 with Papa and Mama on the sofa. Anya was here. Papa read some more.

-1 PM
January 26 Tuesday
Lessons in the morning. Breakfast 5 with Papa and Mama on the sofa. A and I went to our infirmary in the day and were photographed there. Went for a walk with Papa and A. Tea with Papa, Mama and Anya. Had music [lesson]. Did my homework. Dinner 3 with Papa and Mama on the sofa. Grigori and Anya were here. Papa read.

-3
January 28 Thursday
Had lessons. Breakfast 5 with Papa, Mama and A[unt] Miechen. A

and I went to our infirmary in the afternoon. Went skiing with A. Went with A to the G[rand] P[alace]. Tea with Papa, Mama, O and T. Had music [lesson]. Went for a drive with A and Shura. Dinner 4 with Papa and Mama on the sofa. Saw Papa off—he went to Stavka in Mogilev.

-2
29 January
Lessons in the morning. Went for a ride with Shura. Breakfast 5 with Mama on the sofa. A and I went to our infirmary in the day. 4 went for a troika ride with Isa. Tea 4 with Mama and Anya. Prepared my homework. Had music [lesson]. Dinner 4 with Mama on the sofa. Anya was here.

-2
January 30 Saturday
In the morning had lessons. Breakfast 5 with Mama on the sofa. Went with A in the day to the G[rand] P[alace]. 4 went for a troika ride with Isa. Tea 4 with Mama and Anya. 4 were at the *vsenoshnaya*. Dinner 4 and Mama on the sofa. Kolya and Anya were here.

-5
January 31 Sunday
5 at *obednya*. Breakfast 5 with Mama on the sofa. Went to our infirmary with A. Went for a troika ride 4 with Nastenka. Tea 4 with Mama. Went 5 to a concert at the infirmary with Kolya at Anya's. 4 went for a drive with Shura. Dinner 4 with Mama on the sofa. Anya was here.

1 February Monday.
Had lessons in the morning. Rode with Shura. Breakfast 5 with Mama on the couch. Went to our infirmary with A. Rode in the troika with Nastenka. Had tea 4 with Mama and Anya. Went 5 to *Vsenoshnaya*. Had dinner and Mama on the couch. Anya was here.

2 February Tuesday.
Went to the lower church for *Obednya* with T. Breakfast 5. Mama

was in bed all day with a tooth abscess. In the afternoon 4 went to the G.[rand] P.[alace]. Rode in the troika with Nastenka. Had tea 4 with Mama and Anya. Rode with T., A. and Shura. Had dinner 4, Mama was lying on a sofa for a bit. Anya was here.

Maria to Nicholas II—

2 February. My dear Papa! I just returned from *Obednya*, I was at the lower church with Tatiana, as she now went to change dressings. And Olga, Anastasia and Alexei are going to church now. Mama is in bed, her cheek hurts terribly. I don't know what we will do today, probably nothing special. Anya wanted to invite us, with Irina Tolstaya, but Irina is playing the balalaika somewhere today. I am sure that Nikolai Dmitrievich will go to the upper church, because I will not be there, and I am angry in advance. I have not seen him for more than three weeks now. Tomorrow the sisters are going to Petrograd to accept charities. Today we need to go to the Grand Palace as we have not been [there] for two days already. I don't really know what to do before breakfast. Everyone is at church, so [there is] no one to walk or ride with. Maybe Mama will let me walk alone, I will go ask her. Well, so long, goodbye, my darling. I mentally squeeze you tightly in a hug and kiss you. Your Kazanetz. May God keep you. + Regards to all.

Maria's diary—

3 February. Had lessons in the morning. Breakfast 5 and Mama on the couch. Went to our infirmary with Anya. Rode with A. and Shura. Had tea with Mama and A. and Anya. Did homework. Had a French reading [lesson]. Had dinner 4 with Mama on the couch. Anya was here. Our [army] took [the town of] Erzerum.

+1
February 4 Thursday
Had lessons. Went for a walk with Shura. Breakfast 5 and Mama on the sofa. Went with A to our infirmary. 4 went for a drive with Nastenka. Tea 4 with Mama and Anya. Had music [lesson]. Went for a drive with A and Shura. Dinner 4 and Mama on the sofa in the children's [room] because Al. has a sore arm. Anya was here.

-7
6 February Saturday
Had lessons in the morning. Breakfast 4 and Mama on the sofa. Was
at our infirmary with A. Went for a drive 4 with Nastenka. The same
were at the G[rand] P[alace] for a concert. Tea 4 with Mama and Al.
He is lying down. Went 4 to the *Vsenoshnaya*. Dinner 4 in the children's [room] and Mama on the sofa. Anya was here.

-2
7 February Sunday
4 at *Obednya* in the morning. Breakfast 5 and Mama on the sofa.
Went for a troika ride 4 with Isa. Went with A to our infirmary. Tea
4 with Mama and D. Pavllom. Went for a ride 4 with Shura. Dinner
4 with Mama on the sofa. Anya was here, read to us a foreign [pub-
lication]. Papa saw the 1st Siberian Corps.

-7
8 February Monday
Lessons in the morning. We met Papa. Went for a drive with Shura.
Breakfast 5 with Papa and Mama on the sofa. Went for a walk with
Papa and A. Went with A to our infirmary. Tea with A in the children's [room]. Had an English and a music lesson. Prepared my
homework. Dinner 4 with Papa and Mama on the sofa. Anya [illeg.]

-4
9 February Tuesday
Had lessons in the morning. Breakfast 5 with Papa and Mama on
the sofa. Had lessons in the afternoon. Were 4 at the G[rand]
P[alace]. Went for a troika ride 4 with Isa. 4 had tea with Mama
and Anya. I had a music lesson. We were at a concert at Zhilik's[1] at
the gymnasium. Dinner 4 with Papa and Mama on the sofa. Anya
was here. Pasted albums with Papa.

-7
10 February Wednesday
Had lessons. Breakfast 5 with Papa and Mama on the sofa. Went

1. Nickname for Pierre Gilliard.

to our infirmary with A. Went for a troika ride with O, A and Isa. Tea with Papa and Mama. Saw Papa off to Stavka. Had music and French lessons. Dinner 4 and Mama on the sofa. Anya was here. She read us a foreign [publication].

-8

11 February Thursday
Had lessons. Breakfast 5 and Mama on the sofa. Went with A to our infirmary. 4 went for a ride in the troika with Isa. Tea 4 with Mama and Anya. 4 at the stockrooms. Had music [lesson]. Went for a ride with A and Shura. Dinner 4 and Mama on the sofa. Anya was here. Read.

-4

12 February Friday
Had lessons. Went for a ride with Shura. Breakfast 5 with Maria and Mama on the sofa. Went with A to our infirmary. Shakh-Nazarov has broken his leg again. 4 went for a troika ride with Isa. Tea 4 with Mama. Before that we were at the G[rand] P[alace]. Prepared my homework, had music [lesson]. Dinner 4 and Mama on the sofa. Anya, Lili Dehn and her husband were here.

-9

13 February Saturday
Had lessons. Breakfast 5 with Isa and Mama on the sofa. In the day I went to our infirmary with A. Went for a drive 4 with Isa. Tea 4 with Mama and Anya. 4 went to the *Vsenoshnaya*. Dinner with the same and Mama on the sofa. Anya was here.

-3

14 February Sunday
4 went to *Obednya*. Breakfast 5 and Mama on the sofa. Went to our infirmary with A. After that with A and A to Anya's infirmary for a concert. My Kolya was there, De Lazari, Morfres, Sasha M and others. Tea 4 with Mama and Anya. Got my homework ready. Dinner 4 and Mama on the sofa. Anya was here. We read.

-6
15 February Monday
Had lessons. Breakfast 5 with Mama and Isa. Went with A to our infirmary. 5 went to the G[rand] P[alace] for a concert. Tea 4 with Mama and Anya. Had music [lesson]. Prepared my homework. Dinner 4 and Mama on the sofa. Alexander Tevlov and Anya were here.

-3
16 February Tuesday
Had lessons. Breakfast 5 and Mama on the sofa. I had a Russian lesson in the day. Was at our infirmary with A. Tea 4 with Mama and Anya. Had music [lesson]. Prepared my homework. Dinner 4 and Mama on the sofa. Anya was here. We read.

-6
17 February Wednesday
Had lessons. Breakfast 5 with Maria, Dmitri and Mama on the sofa. In the day went to the G[rand] P[alace] with A and T. Went for a drive 4 with Nastenka and stopped by the Man'zovski Infirmary. Went with A to our infirmary. Sat with Sh.N. Tea 4 with Mama and Anya. Had music and French lessons. Dinner 4 and Mama on the sofa. Anya was here. Read.

-5
18 February Thursday
Had lessons. Welcomed Papa back. Breakfast 5 with Papa and Mama on the sofa. Went for a walk with Papa and the sailors. Papa made a white snow hill. Went with A to our infirmary. Tea 4 with Papa and Mama. Had music [lesson]. Went for a troika ride with A, A and Shura. Dinner 4 with Papa and Mama on the sofa. Papa read "The woman in the car." Anya was here.

-2
19 February Friday
Went with Olga on foot to the infirmary with A and Shura. Went for a drive with A and Shura. Went to our Infirmary with A. Sat with Sh. N. Breakfast 5. Papa and Mama on the sofa. Had a bath.

Went with A and T to the G[rand] P[alace]. Had tea and dinner 4 with Papa and Mama. Went to a concert with O, A and T at the [illeg.]

20 February Saturday.
Rode with A. and Shura. Walked-skipped with A. Breakfast 5 with Papa and Mama and 2 Englishmen. In the afternoon built the tower 4 with Papa and the sailors. Went to our infirmary with A. Sat with Sh.[akh]-N.[Nazarov]. Had tea with Papa, Mama and Uncle Pavel. Went to *Vsenoshnaya* 4 with Papa. Had dinner with the same with Mama on the couch. Papa read, Anya was here.

21 February Sunday.
In the morning went to *Obednya* 5 with Papa. Breakfast with same, Mordvinov and Mama on the sofa. 4 went to the Grand Palace. Walked, built the tower 4 with Papa and Mordvinov. Had tea 4 with Papa and Mama. Had a cinematograph in English. Dinner 4 with Papa, Mordvinov and Mama on the couch. Papa read. Anya was here.

22 February Monday.
Had lessons. Then went to church 5 with Papa. Breakfast with same, with Vikitsky and Mama on the couch. In the afternoon went to our infirmary with A. Sat with Sh.N. Walked 5 with Papa, built and jumped off the tower. Had tea in the playroom. Had an English lesson. Went to church 5 with Papa and Mama. Had dinner with same except Al. Papa read, Anya was here.

23 February Tuesday.
Had lessons. Went to church 5 with Papa. Breakfast with same, with Count Sheremetiev and Mama on the couch. Built the tower, and jumped from it. Had tea in the playroom. Had music. Went to church 5 with Papa and Mama. Had dinner 4 with Papa, Count Sheremetiev and Mama on the couch. Papa read, Anya was here.

24 February Wednesday.
Had lessons in the morning. Went to church 5 with Papa. Breakfast

with same, with Kazakevich and Mama on the couch. In the afternoon went to our infirmary with A. This husband and wife [couple] were there, sat with M.Z.G. and A.V.K. Built the tower. Had tea with Papa, Mama, O., A., and Alek. Went to church 5 with Papa and Mama. Dinner with same except Al.[eksei]. Grigori[2] and Anya were here.

25 February Thursday.
Lessons as usual. Went to church 5 with Papa. Breakfast with same and Mama on the couch. Built the tower. Went to our infirmary with A., sat with Sh.N. Had tea with Papa, Mama and O. and A. Went to church 5 with Papa and Mama. Had dinner with same except Al. Papa read. Anya was here.

26 February Friday.
Had lessons. Then to church 4 with Mama. Breakfast 5 with Mama on the couch. Went to the Grand Palace with A. Built the tower. Had tea 4 with Papa and Mama. Confessed. Went to church 5 with Papa and Mama. Had dinner 4 with Papa, Silaev and Mama on the couch.

27 February Saturday.
Received communion with the entire family. Then had tea. Rode in a troika 4 with Isa. Breakfast 5 with Papa, Count Fredericks, and Mama on the couch. In the afternoon went to our infirmary with A. Sat with Sh.N. Built the tower. Had tea 4 with Papa and Mama. Went 4 to *Vsenoshnaya*. Dinner 4 with Papa and Mama on the couch. Anya was here.

28 February Sunday.
Went to *Obednya* 5 with Papa and Mama, breakfast with same and Kashin. Rode in the troika 4 with Isa. Walked. Had tea with Papa, Mama and Dmitri. Saw a cinematograph about the French war. Rode 4 with Shura. Dinner 4 with Papa and Mama on the couch. Papa read "In White Raiment." Anya was here.

2. Rasputin.

29 February Monday.
Had lessons. Breakfast 5 with Papa, Uncle Georgi and Ioann. In the afternoon went to our infirmary with A. Sat with M.Z. Baron, Ton, and A.V. Walked and built the tower. Had tea with A. and T. in the playroom. Had English and music lessons. Did homework. Dinner 3 with Papa, Ioann and Dmitri. Papa read, Anya was here. Mama has neuralgia, and she stayed in bed almost the entire day.

-3
1 March Tuesday
Had lessons. Breakfast with A and A. Was with A at the G[rand] P[alace] and our infirmary. Sat with everyone for a bit, Shibaev cut, [illeg.]
Tea with Papa, Mama and O. Had music [lesson]. Went for a troika ride with A and Shura. Dinner 4 with Papa and Mama on the sofa. Papa read to us. Anya was here.

2 March Wednesday
Had lessons. Saw Papa off. Went to the cemetery with A. and T., got stuck in the snow, and there was so much snow at the cemetery that we sunk almost to our waist. Breakfast 5. Rode in the troika with Isa, went to the tower. Had tea 4 with Mama and Anya. Had music and French lessons. Before tea went to our infirmary with A., sat with everyone. M.Z.[3] sat. Dinner 3 and Mama on the couch. Anya was here.

0
3 March Thursday
Had lessons. Breakfast 5 with Mama on the sofa. 4 went for a troika ride with Nastenka.
Went with A to our infirmary and sat with M. Z. A. V. Pap and Shibaev. Tea 4 with Mama and Anya. Had music [lesson]. Went for a drive with Shura. Dinner 4 and Mama on the sofa. Kiki and Anya were here.

---

3. Perhaps Madame Zizi (nickname for Elizaveta Alexeyevna Naryshkina, Mistress of the Robes).

Maria to Nicholas II—

3 March. My sweet and dear Papa! Yesterday after we saw you off, Tatiana, Anastasia and I went to the cemetery in a motor. We drove there for an unusually long time because the roads are so bad. We arrived there and went to the officers' graves, there was nothing there yet, and too much snow, then I wanted to visit the graves of our patients from the lower ranks. There was a big pile of snow on the side of the road, so I was able to climb up with great difficulty on my knees and jump down from it. Down there the snow turned out to be above the knees, and although I was wearing long boots, I was already wet so I decided to continue ahead. Nearby I found one grave with the surname Mishenko, this was the name of our patient; I laid down some flowers there and walked ahead, and suddenly I saw the same surname again, I looked up at the board, [to see] which regiment he was from, and it turned out that he was one of our patients [too], but not the same one. So, I laid down the flowers for him and was just starting to walk away when I fell on my back, and was lying there for almost a minute not knowing how to get up, there was so much snow that I could not reach the ground with my hand for leverage. I finally got up and walked ahead. Earlier Tatiana and Anastasia said they were going to go to another cemetery, to Sonia Orbeliani's [grave] and that they will return for me. But instead they sent a man in charge of the graveyard to help me. He crawled over to me with great difficulty and we went to look for another grave together. We searched and searched and could not understand at all what happened to it. It turned out that it was closer to the fence and that we should have climbed over a ditch. He stood in the ditch and said to me "I will carry you over," I said "no," he said "let's try." Of course, he put me down not on the other side but right in the middle of the ditch. And so, we are both standing in the ditch, up to our bellies in snow, and dying from laughter. It was hard for him to climb out, as the ditch was deep, and for me too. So, he climbed out somehow and stretched his hands out to me. Of course, I slid back down into the ditch on my stomach about three times, but finally climbed out. And we performed all this with flowers in our hands. Then we couldn't fit through between the crosses for a while, as we were both wearing our coats.

But in the end, I did find the grave. Finally, we were able to leave the cemetery. Tatiana and Anastasia were already waiting for me on the road. I felt half-dead from heat and dampness. We climbed into the motors and drove away. I took off one boot to shake out the snow. At this same time, we ran into a wagon. We were driving rather fast. We just swerved to the side a little, when Lapin's steering wheel spun [out of control] and our front tires slid into a snow bank, and scarily [we] turned on to our side, I jumped out wearing one boot and put the other one back on out on the road. What could we do, no one was there anymore and it was already 1 o'clock 10 minutes. Then we 3 decided to walk home on foot, but luckily at this moment some squadron was walking back from shooting practice and they dug out the motor, while we walked almost all the way to the shooting gallery. The motor caught up to us and we got home safely. But the road was so bad the entire time that we were certain that the motor would break. Across from the Cuirassier Cathedral. And we were tossed up so high that Tatiana almost hit her head on the roof. In the afternoon during our troika ride we almost pushed over another sleigh. So, after all this, we went to our infirmary, and we were certain that we will fall into a ditch or something else will happen to us again. [We] went to the tower yesterday. The sailors were all very sweet and worked hard. You were very much missed there. [. . .] In the evening Anya finished reading "Our People Abroad" to us. Olga went to bed early of course. And you are probably enjoying the English book. Grandmama sent the book "Olive," and Mama sent her another one. Well, farewell my darling. May Christ be with you. + Your Kazanetz. I kiss you affectionately and squeeze you a lot and for a long time. Titanis titanis. Dukchik. Dukchik.

Maria's diary—

-2

4 March Friday

Had lessons. Breakfast 5 and Mama on the sofa. Before that I went for a drive with A and Shura. Went with A to the G[rand] P[alace]. 4 went for a troika ride with Nastenka. Was on the tower. Tea 4 with Mama and Anya. Had music [lesson]. Dinner 4 and Mama on the sofa. Anya was here.

-2
5 March Saturday
Had lessons. Breakfast 5 with Mama on the sofa. Went with A to our infirmary. Sat with M. Z., A. V and Shibaev. 4 went for a troika ride with Isa. Went to the tower with T and worked with Sidor there. Tea 4 with Mama and Anya. Went with T and A to church. Dinner 4 and Mama on the sofa. Anya was here.

-3
6 March Sunday
5 at Liturgy. Breakfasted the same with Isa and Mama on the sofa. In the day 4 were at the G[rand] P[alace]. Went for a troika ride 4 with Trina. Was at our infirmary with A. Played halma with M.Z. and A.V. Tea 4 with Mama. Was with T, A and A at Anya's at the infirmary where also was Magician Ivan and I. Tolstaya. Went for a drive with A, T and Shura. Dinner 4 and Mama on the sofa.

-11
8 March Tuesday
Had lessons. Breakfast 5 and Mama on the sofa. Had a Russian lesson. Went for a ride with Shura. Went to the G[rand] P[alace] 5 for a variety concert. Tea 4 with Mama and Anya. Had music [lesson]. Went for a troika ride with O, A and Shura. Dinner 4 and Mama on the sofa. Anya was here.

-8
9 March Wednesday
Had lessons. Breakfast 5 with Isa and Mama on the sofa. In the day I went to our infirmary with A. Played tiles [illeg.] Went for a drive with Shura. Tea with Mama, A and Titi Dehn.[4] Had lessons—music and French. Dinner 3 and Mama on the sofa. Anya was here.

Maria to Nicholas II—
9 March. My dear darling Papa! Today is Spring already, but it's 7 [degrees] below here and snow with wind. Completely unacceptable. [I] just finished breakfast. Olga and Tatiana are going to Petrograd for charities and committee, and will have tea at

---

4. Alexander Dehn, toddler son of Lili Dehn.

Grandmama's, and will also stop by Aunt Ksenia's who feels terrible and does not leave the house. I will now go to our infirmary with A. Nikolai Dmitrievich said goodbye to Mama. Before that, the regiment had a farewell party for him in the evening at 7 o'clock, which only ended at 5 in the morning, so Resin looked rather sad, and when he was leaving the room [he] almost knocked over a vase with flowers, and his voice was not very nice either. But N.D. himself was very charming. I have not seen him since then, and don't even expect to anymore. Right now, Anastasia is sitting here and playing the balalaika. Well so long, my dear. I kiss you affectionately and apologize for a boring letter. Your Kazanetz. May Christ be with you. +

Maria's diary—
-7
10 March Thursday
Had lessons. Breakfast 5 and Mama on the sofa. In the day went for a troika ride with A, O and Trina. 4 went to the tower. Tea 4 with Mama and Anya. Had music [lesson]. Went for a ride with A and Shura. Dinner 4 and Mama on the sofa. Anya came over, was sewing, I quarreled and left.

-6
11 March Friday
Had lessons. I went for a ride with Shura. Breakfast 5 and Mama on the sofa. In the day went with A to the Grand Palace. 4 went to the tower. Tea 4 with Mama and Anya. Went for a ride with Shura. Had music [lesson]. Dinner 3 with Kiki and Mama on the sofa. Anya was here. I rang Ivan several times but he wasn't at home.

+1
12 March Saturday
Went for a ride with Shura. Had lessons. Said goodbye to Ivan on the telephone. Breakfast 5 and Mama on the sofa. I met with Ivan. Was with A at our infirmary and played T.d.b. 4 with Tata at the tower. Tea 4 with Mama, Anya and Titi. Played with them in order. 4 at the *Vsenoshnaya* and the bringing down of the Cross. Dinner the same [people] and Mama on the sofa. There was a big telling off.

-2
13 March Sunday
5 to *Obednya*. Breakfasted the same and Mama on the sofa. In the day 4 went for a troika ride with Isa. Received the same at my train which arrived [illeg.] with wounded. A and I went to our infirmary, sat with Sh, N and AV. Tea 4 with Mama. Went for a drive 4 with Shura. Dinner 4 and Mama on the sofa. Anya was over.

+1
14 March Monday
Had lessons. Went for a ride with Shura. Breakfast 5, Igor and Mama on the sofa. In the day, A and I were at our infirmary and stopped by to see Poopse's[5] sister An P in the room. Went with A to the tower. Tea 4 with Mama and Anya and Alya.[6] Had lessons— English and music. Went for a ride with A and Shura. Dinner 3 and Mama on the sofa. Anya was here.

Maria to Nicholas II—
14 March. My golden Papa! Oh well, Nikolai Dmitrievich left on Saturday. I spoke with him on the telephone. He was awfully happy to be leaving. Do you remember I sewed him a shirt, so I asked him, and he said that it fits him very well. Yesterday 3 medical trains arrived here, one of them is mine, and we went there and saw about 300 soldiers and 8 officers. I am writing to you from Orchie's[7] room. Mama is lying on the couch, and Vladimir Nikolaevich is doing electrotherapy on her. I just rode around with Shura. Igor will have breakfast with us. In the afternoon I will go to our infirmary with Anastasia. They haven't brought the wounded there yet, but I think [they are] supposed to on Sunday. Yesterday Voikov was at church and from afar he looks a bit like Nikolai Dmitrievich, what swine, how dare he. And instead of Popov, I think Voronov will be in the regiment, as he is not completely healthy and needs to do something with his throat. We are really not doing anything interesting at all.

5. Literally translates as "baby doll," obviously a nickname.
6. Vyrubova's sister.
7. Mary Ann Orchard (1830-1906) was Empress Alexandra's childhood nanny.

When we have time, [we] ride around with Shura before dinner. It is so strange that it's still rather light outside at 6 o'clock. Well, farewell for now, my dear. I love you very very much, squeeze and kiss you. Your very own Kazanetz. May the Lord keep you. + Regards to all.

Maria's diary—

+1

15 March Tuesday

Had lessons. Breakfast 5 and Mama on the sofa. Had a Russian lesson. Was with O and A at the tower and jumped forcefully into the snow. Tea 4 with Mama and Anya. Had music [lesson]. Went for a troika ride with O, A and Shura. Dinner 4 and Mama on the sofa. Anya was here.

+2

16 March Wednesday

Had lessons. Breakfast 5 with Nastenka and Mama on the sofa. Was with A at our infirmary, Poopse was there and his wife and her sister. Went for a walk with A and Titi whose hair had been cut off. Tea with Mama, A, Titi and Anya. Had lessons—music and French. Dinner 4 and Mama on the sofa. Anya and Malama were here.

+1

17 March Thursday

Had lessons. Breakfast 5 and Mama on the sofa. Was with O and T at the G[rand] P[alace]. Had a *troika* ride 4 with Isa. Went with A to our infirmary, we stood on waste. Had tea 4 with Mama and U[ncle] Pavel. Had music [lesson]. Dinner 4 with Mama and Anya. Before that went for a drive with O, A and Shura.

+3

18 March Friday

Had lessons. Went for a walk with Isa and a ride with Shura. Breakfasted 5 and Mama on the sofa. Was with A at our infirmary. Went for a troika ride 4 with Isa. Tea 4 with Mama and Anya. Got my lessons ready. Had music [lesson]. Dinner 4 and Mama on the sofa.

In the evening Anya, Serg Vas, Al Iv Pi and Olga were here. We had tea with them.

19 March Saturday
Went for a walk with Trina. Had lessons. Breakfast 5 with Mama and Drobezgin. Went with A to our infirmary. Went for a ride 4 with Isa in a carriage. Tea 4 with Mama and Anya. Went for a drive with A and Shura. We met Papa. Dinner 4 with Papa and Mama on the sofa. Papa read "The white raiment." Anya was here.

20 March. Sunday Went to church with Papa and Mama. Had breakfast 5, Papa and Mama on the couch. 4 went to the Gr.[and] Pal.[ace]. Walked with Papa and Mama [rode] in an equipage. Broke the ice 4 with Papa. Had tea in the playroom. 5 went to Anya's concert at the infirmary, "Ivanov Pavel" and the magicians. Went to our infirmaries with A., 17 soldiers arrived from the train. Rode with A. and Shura. Had dinner 5 with Papa, Mama, Silaev and Anya. Papa read.

0
21 March Monday
Had lessons. I went for a ride with Shura. Breakfasted 5 with Papa, Dmitriev and Mama on the sofa. Broke up ice 4 with Papa and the sailors. Was with A at our infirmary. MN removed plaster casts. Tea 4 with Mama and Anya. Had music [lesson]. Went for a ride with A and Shura. Dinner 3 with Papa and Mama on the sofa. Anya was here. Papa finished the book. Mama was for the first time this year at the infirmary.

+3
22 March Tuesday
Had lessons. Breakfasted 4 with Papa, Mama and Igor. Went with A to our infirmary. Broke up ice 4 with papa and sailors. Tea with Papa, Mama and O. Had music [lesson]. Went for a ride with A and Shura. Dinner 3 with Papa, Igor and Mama on the sofa. Anya was here. Pasted albums with Papa.

+5
23 March Wednesday
Had lessons. Breakfast 4 with Papa, Mama and Kostya. Was with A at our infirmary. Broke up ice with Papa and the sailors. Tea with Papa, Mama, O and U[ncle] Pavel. Had music [lesson]. I prepared my lessons. Dinner 4 with Papa, Kostya and Mama on the sofa. Anya was here. Papa read "The Man Who Was Dead."

-4
24 March Thursday
Had lessons. Breakfast 5 with Papa, Mama and A[unt] Olga. In the day 4 broke ice with Papa, A[unt] Olga and the sailors. Tea 4 with Papa, Mama and A[unt] Olga. 5 went to the *Vsenoshnaya* with Papa and Mama. Dinner 4 with Papa and Mama on the sofa. Anya was over. Papa continued reading.

-4
25 March Friday
5 had breakfast with Papa, Mama and Dmitri. 4 went to the G[rand] P[alace]. We walked 4 and broke ice with Papa. Was with A at our infirmary. Tea 4 in the children's [room]. Went for a ride with A and Shura. Was with A at the Regimental Infirmary. Dinner 4 with Papa and Mama on the sofa. Anya was here. Papa read.

0
28 March Monday
Had lessons. Went for a ride with Shura. Breakfast 5 with Trina and Mama on the sofa. Was at our infirmary with A. Broke up ice 4 with the sailors, but Mama sat. Tea 4 with Mama and Anya. Had English and music lessons. Went for a ride with O, A and Shura. Dinner 3 with Mama on the sofa. Anya was here and she read.

29 March Tuesday
Had lessons. Breakfast 5 with Isa and Mama on the sofa. Had a lesson in the day. Went for a ride 4 with Mama and Anya. Had tea, the same people, and Tatiana Andreyevna. Had a music lesson. Went for a ride with A and Shura. Dinner 4 and Mama on the sofa. Anya was here and read on.

0

30 March Wednesday

Had lessons. Breakfast 5 with Mama on the sofa. Broke up ice with A and the sailors. Was with A at our infirmary. Tea 4 with Mama. Had a music lesson. Went for a drive with A and Shura. Dinner 4 with Mama, T Mathroy and Elena P.[8] Anya was here.

+3

31 March Thursday

Had lessons. Breakfast with A, Al, Trina and D N[9] in the children's [room]. Was with A at our infirmary. Broke up ice with A and the sailors. Was with A at the G[rand] P[alace]. Tea 4 with Mama and Anya. Had music [lesson]. Went for a drive 5. Dinner 4 and Mama on the sofa. Anya was here.

+3

1 April Friday

Had lessons. Went for a ride with Shura. Breakfasted 5 and Mama on the sofa. Was with A at our infirmary. After that 4 were at a concert at the Palace infirmary. They sang, narrated and played violins and cellos. Had music [lesson]. Went for a ride with A and Shura. Dinner 4 with Mama on the sofa. Anya was here. Chose eggs.

+2

2 April Saturday

Went for a ride with A and Shura. Had lessons. Went for a ride with Shura and managed it myself. Breakfast 5 and Mama on the sofa. Broke ice 4 with the sailors and Mama sat. Tea 4 with Mama and U[ncle] Pavel. Were 5 with Mama at the *Vsenoshnaya*. Dinner 4 and Mama on the sofa. Anya was here.

3 April Sunday

Went to church 5 with Mama, Aunt Olga and Christo[10] and had breakfast. Went 4 to the G[rand] P[alace]. Rode with Mama and Anya. Went to our infirmary. Had tea with Mama and Dmitri.

8. Grand Duchess Elena Pavlovna.

9. Possibly Dyadka Nagorny, Alexei's other "sailor uncle."

10. Prince Christopher of Greece.

Rode with Shura. Had dinner 4 and Mama on the couch. Anya was here. Read.

4 April Monday
Walked with Trina. Went to church 5 with Mama, breakfast with same. Rode 4 with Isa. Went to our infirmary with A, then went to [see] the construction of the new infirmary with Loman and Ev[geni] Al[ekseevich]. Had tea 4 with Mama and Anya. Went to church 5 with Mama. Had dinner 4 and Mama on the couch. Anya was here. Read.

5 April Tuesday
Rode with Shura. Went to church with Mama, had breakfast with same and Uncle Petya. Rode 4 with Isa. Went to our infirmary with A. Had tea 4 with Mama and Anya. Went to church 5 with Mama. Had dinner 4 and Mama on the couch. Anya was here—read again.

6 April Wednesday
Alexei's arm hurts, sat with him with A. at 5 in the morning. Went to the Gr. Pal. with A. Then went to church 4 with Mama., breakfast with same. Rode 4 with Trina, went to our infirmary with A. Went to look at the radiology machine, Loman's chancellery, and again to the construction [site]. Had tea and went to church 4 with Mama. Had dinner with same with Anya. Confessed before *Vsenoshnaya*.

Maria to Nicholas II—

7 April, Thursday. My darling sweet Papa! I ask for your forgiveness before confession. Olga wanted to send you a telegram for this occasion yesterday, but of course forgot. It was so sad to have communion without you and Alexei. The weather now is wonderful here. In the morning when we were driving to church it was foggy, but now it is wonderfully sunny and the sky is blue. Just finished breakfast and [we] will now go riding with Mama and Anya. We had breakfast upstairs in the playroom near Alexei. His arm is not hurting now. A lot of soldiers and Cossacks were at communion today, awfully appetizing hetmans. Of course, Batushka's entire fam-

ily was there. It's such a shame that you did not have communion at Stavka. Well, I must end. May Christ be with you. I kiss you affectionately. Your Kazanetz.

Maria's diary—
7 April Thursday
Received Communion 4 with Mama, while Al. [did] later, [his] arm was hurting. Had tea all together. Rode 4 with Isa. Had breakfast 4 with Mama, while Al [was] in bed. Rode 4 with Mama with Anya. Went to our infirmary with A. Had tea 4 with Mama and Anya. Went to 12 Gospels 4 with Mama, and had dinner with same. Anya was here.

8 April Friday
Rode with Anya and Shura. Went to our infirmary with A., sat with the sisters. Had breakfast 4 with Mama near Al. Went to the Shroud procession 4 with Mama. Had tea 4 with Mama and Anya. Played 4 with Zhilik. Went 4 with Mama to the Burial. Had dinner with same near Al. Anya was here. Made drawings.

9 April Saturday
Went to our infirmary with A. Went to church 4 with Mama. Had breakfast 5 and Mama on the couch, with Mama and Anya. Had tea with same and Kolya. Rode with A. and Shura. Had dinner 4 with Mama on the couch. Went to *zautrenya* 5 with Mama and had dinner. Broke the fast with Mama and Anya.

10 April Sunday
Easter. Christ's Resurrection. Went to *Khristovanie* with Mama. Had breakfast with same. Went to our infirmary with A. Exchanged Easter greetings with everyone. Then went to the Palace infirmary 4 with Mama and sat in the parlor. Had tea 4 with Mama and Anya. Rode with A. and Shura. Went 4 to church. Had dinner with the same and Mama on the couch. Anya was here.

Emma Fredericks to Maria—
Truly He is Risen! I thank you very much and kiss you, darling

Maria Nikolaevna
Emma Fredericks 1916

From OTMA and Alexandra to N.P. Sablin—

1916. Christ Has Risen! Sending wishes of all happiness for the bright holiday dear Nikolai Pavlovich. May God keep you +
Olga
Tatiana
Maria
Anastasia
Mistress [Alexandra]

Maria's diary—

11 April Monday
Went 4 to *Obednya* and the Procession of the Cross. Had breakfast 5 and Mama on the couch. The same went to Khristovanie at the Gr. Pal. infirmary, and upstairs for the officers and soldiers. Went to our infirmary with A. Had tea 4 with Mama and Anya. Alexei showed a cinematograph, rode 4 with Shura. Had dinner 4 with Mama on the couch. Anya was here.

12 April Tuesday
Went on Olga's train with A., O. and Isa. Walked with A. and Isa. Went to our infirmary with A., and sat outside in fresh air. Had breakfast 5 and Mama on the couch. Went 4 with Mama to Khristovanie at Matveyevsky infirmary and the Red Cross. Had tea with same and Dmitri. Everyone went to a concert at Anya's infirmary. Yu. Morfessi, Sasha Makarov and DeLazari, Orlov, etc, were there. Rode in the evening, and afternoon 4 with Nastenka. Had dinner 4 and Mama on the couch. Anya was here.

+7
13 April Wednesday
Went for a walk with O, A and Trina. Was with A at our infirmary. Got to know the pilots. Breakfast 5 and Mama on the sofa. 4 with Mama at Kokorevsky Lane. Met Papa. Broke up ice with the sailors. Tea 4 with Papa and Mama. Dinner with the same. 4 went for a

ride with Isa. Anya was over here. Papa read "The Man Who Was Dead."

+5
14 April Thursday
Went for a walk with O, An, Trina. Was with A at our infirmary and sat outside. Breakfast 5 with Papa, Mama, A[unt] Ksenia and Sandro. In the day we broke up ice with the sailors. Had tea with A in the children's [room]. Went for a ride with A and Trina. Sat with O and A on the balcony. Dinner 4 with Papa, Mama and Sandro. Papa read. Anya was here.

+2
20 April Wednesday
Had lessons. Was with A at our infirmary and sat in the dining room. Breakfast 5 with Papa, Mama, Gen[eral] Ivanov and Igor. Went for a walk 4 with Papa, Mama and Anya in a carriage. 5 with Papa and Mama were at a concert at Anya's infirmary. Tea with O., T., Mama and Papa. Had lessons, were at a concert put on by [Tsarskoe Selo] Real School. Dinner 3 with Papa, Igor and Mama on the sofa. Tried on hats. Anya was here. Papa read.

+8
21 April Thursday
Had lessons. Went for a walk with A and Trina to the guest court-yard. Was with A at the G[rand] P[alace]. Breakfasted with Papa, Mama, Zizi, Isa, C[oun]t Benkendorf, Petrovsky, Tatich, Iankovich, Iovanovach, and Spokoikov and Evraimov. Went for a walk 4 with Papa. Tried on [clothes]. Tea with Papa, Mama, O, T and U[ncle] Pavel. Had lessons. Went for a ride with Isa. Dinner 3 with Papa, Mama, Kiki and Anya. Looked at photographs.

+12
22 April Friday
Had lessons. Went for a ride with Shura. Breakfast 5 with Papa, Mama, A[unt]Olga, Christo and Ioann. Was with A at our infir-mary. Went for a walk 4 with Papa; Mama in a carriage. Went for

a drive 4 in an open motor. Tea 4 with Mama on the balcony. We were 5 at church with Mama. Dinner 4 with Papa, Ioann and Mama on the sofa. Went for a drive 3 with Papa and Mama in an open motor. Anya was here.

+4
27 April Wednesday
Had lessons. Had breakfast 5 with Anya and Mama on the sofa. Was with A at our infirmary. Went for a ride with A, two of us on bicycles. Tea 4 with Mama and Anya. Anya left for Evpatoria.[11] Had a lesson. Went for a ride with A and Trina. Dinner 3 with Mama on the sofa.

28 April Thurs
Had lessons. Was with A at our infirmary. Breakfasted 5 with Mama on the sofa. Went 4 with Mama to Petrograd to the English Infirmary set up at Dmitri's palace.[12] Tea at Grandma's with A[unt] Xenia. Went back home. Went for a ride with A and Trina. Dinner 4 with Mama on the sofa. We read.

+3
29 April Friday
Had lessons. Went for a ride with Shura. Played cards with Al and Zhilik. Breakfast 5 and Mama on the sofa. Was with A at our infirmary. Tea 4 with Mama. Had a lesson. Went for a ride with A and Nastenka. Dinner 3 and Mama on the sofa. We read.

+3
30 April Saturday
Had lessons. Went for a ride with A and Shura. Breakfast 5 and Mama on the sofa. In the day, I was with A at our infirmary. Tea 4 with Mama and Christo. We played with Teimuraz and Natalia.[13] Went 4 to the *Vsenoshnaya* and had dinner. Read at home.

11. Town in Crimea.

12. An infirmary staffed by British nurses was set up in Petrograd, at the palace of Grand Duke Dmitri Pavlovich.

13. Teimuraz and Natalia were the children of Princess Tatiana Konstantinovna and grandchildren of Grand Duke Konstantin Konstantinovich.

+1
1 May Sunday
Were 4 with Mama at Church. Breakfast 5 with Mama on the sofa. In the day 4 went for a ride with Trina. Was at our infirmary with A, and O and T came over with Mama. Tea 4 with Mama and U[ncle] Pavel. Went for a ride with A and Shura. Dinner 4 and Mama on the sofa. Went the same to the sisters at the infirmary.

+7
2 May Monday
Had lessons. Went for a ride with Shura. Breakfasted 5 and Mama on the sofa. Were 4 at the warehouse and after at the G[rand] P[alace]. Was with A at our infirmary. Tea 4. Had lessons. Went for a ride with T, A and Trina. Dinner 4 and Mama on the sofa. Were 5 with Mama at Anya's house where we saw Grigori. After that we went to the infirmary.

+7
3 May Tuesday
Had lessons. Went for a walk with A and Trina. Breakfast 5 with Mama, Zizi and Trina. In the day went with A and Mama to the cemetery. After that I went with A to our infirmary. Tea with Mama and A. Had a lesson. Had a fitting. Dinner 4 and Mama on the sofa. Were 5 and Mama at the sisters' infirmary.

4 May Wednesday
Said farewell with A at our infirmary. We left for Stavka. Breakfast 5 with Mama, Isa, Zolotarev, Resin and Anzarovsky. Had tea and dined with the same. Zhilin and Vl. Nik. D. played cards with O, Al and Zhilik. Mama read. Wrote letters. Dinner with the same [people].

5 May Thursday
Walked around at the [train] stations. Breakfast 4 with Isa, Resin, Zolotarev, Zhilik, V. N., and 2 engineers. Arrived in Mogilev. Went in motors across the Dnieper. 4 with Papa and Mama and the Suite, and walked. Had tea in the train with same. Went to *Vsenoshnaya*

4 with Papa and Mama. Had dinner at Stavka, sat with Uncle Boris and Uncle Sergei. Returned to the train.

6 May Friday
Went to Church 4 with Papa and Mama. There were greetings. At breakfast sat with Uncle Kirill and Igor. In the afternoon walked on the rails 5 with Papa. Had tea in the train. Everyone went to see a cinematograph. At dinner sat with Uncle Sergei and Uncle Boris. Returned to the train.

7 May Saturday
Walked around the train station. Wrote. At breakfast sat with Uncle Kirill and Igor. Walked. Saw 1 battalion. Left Mogilev. Everyone had tea with the suite. Played ball with A. At dinner sat with Nilov and Igor.[14] After tea saw 2 battalions at the station.

8 May Sunday
Grandma and A[unt] Olga came to the station at Kiev. Worked at Mama's. At breakfast, I sat with Nilov and Valya D.[15] We arrived at Vinnitsa and were at Mama's storehouse wagon, pharmacy and the infirmary. We all had tea at 18 1/2. At dinner, I sat with Nilov and Gr. Apraksin. Had tea with the suite.

+7
9 May Monday
Arrived at Bendery. We were met. After that there was a parade outside the town. We were at the infirmary 21 and at breakfast sat with Nilov and Brusilov and at dinner as well. We had a walk at the station. Tea with the suite. We arrived at Odessa. We were met at the station. We went to the cathedral and warehouse. Had tea. Went for a walk with the suite.

10 May Tuesday
We were at a parade.
Papa, Mama and Al planted trees. At breakfast sat with Brusilov

14. Prince Igor Konstantinovich, son of Grand Duke Konstantin.
15. Prince Vasily Dolgorukov.

and Nilov. Went to Mama's Kuyalnitsky [sanatorium] and Mama's Hajibeysky saw them making iodine. Had tea together with everyone. Went for a walk on the platform. At dinner sat with the same as before. Had tea.

+14
11 May Wednesday
I wrote. Went out at the station. At breakfast, I sat with Nilov and C[ount] Sheremetiev. Again [illeg.] and went for a walk of 3 versts along the rails. Had tea together. Played ball with A. At dinner sat with Voeikov and Resin. We are stopped at Popovo St[ation]. Went out and tore (white) [illeg.] Had tea.

+11
12 May Thursday
Arrived at Sevastopol. We were met on the pier. We went to the Romanovsky Institute. At breakfast, I sat with Nilov and Grigorovich, and the same at dinner. Went on two dreadnoughts—"Empress Catherine" and "Empress Maria" on which I saw Ivan. Went on all the decks etc. All had tea. Went on the pier. After tea went on the pier again.

+13
13 May Friday
Were 4 with Mama and Isa at the army and navy infirmaries and at the red cross. At breakfast, sat with Grigorovich and Nilov. Were 5 with Papa on a destroyer. Tea like always. Ivan came to Resin and we talked. At dinner I sat with U[ncle] Sandro and Nilov. Walked between the train and the pier. Had tea.

+13
14 May Saturday
Were all at the *Obednya* on the "Empress Maria." How awfully good it was. At breakfast I sat with Grigorovich and Mankovsky. We went to see the new naval housing and aviation. All had tea at 5:30. Played with stones. At dinner sat with Grigorovich and Pokrovsky. Played with candles. Had tea.

+14
15 May Sunday
Sat in the sun on the pier. Was at the *Obednya* at Vladimirsky cathedral. After that went to the view. At breakfast I sat with Grigorovich
and Nilov. Went to the Georgievsky monastery and on the way in-
spected a fort, were in the Church of Ioann the Warrior as well.
Had tea. Ivan and Mikhail[16] were here. At dinner sat with Grigorovich, and played like yesterday. Had tea.

Pyotr Petrov to Maria—

Tsarskoe Selo, May 15, 1916.

The most precious representative of the junior branch, my dear student Maria Nikolaevna. I even gasped in surprise, upon receiving
your postcard.

I understand perfectly well that you do not have enough time for
correspondence, and therefore I especially appreciate the dear remembrance and attention given to me. I do not know whether
Alexei Nikolaevich shows you my letters. If he doesn't, please ask
to look at them. They are written to Him, but they were meant for
all of you!

The Dnieper near Ekaterinoslav is immortalized by Pushkin in
"The Robber Brothers"! I'm sitting composing the summer schedule.

Two days we had warmth, but today it's cold again (+ 4R) and
gloomy. Do not go anywhere, not even to the park. Pen, pencil,
paper, book and. . . . loneliness—that's my lot! Greet Anastasia
Nikolaevna and the others. God bless you!

P. V.P.

Maria's diary—

+12
16 May Monday
We arrived at Evpatoria [Crimea]. We were at the cathedral, a mosque
and at a Karait temple. After that we were at a sanatorium which is
an infirmary. At breakfast sat with Nilov and Count Grabbe.[17] We

---

16. Children of Dr Derevenko, Kolya's brothers.
17. General Paul Grabbe.

went to Anya's dacha. Rita was there. Had tea, ran around barefoot in the water. At dinner sat with Nilov and Count Sheremetiev. Had a walk at Sarabuz station, Anya went back to her dacha.

+5
17 May Tuesday
We walked at the stations. Sat with Voiekov and Feodorov at breakfast. We arrived at Kursk and Papa and Al. went to Mogilev. We 4 with Mama to Ts S. Aunt Ella came to us. Had tea and dined with Resin, Ragonsin [illeg.] and Gardaev.

0
18 May Wednesday
Played ball. At breakfast sat with Resin. We arrived at Tsarskoe. Was with A at our infirmary. Had tea. Went to the sisters at the infirmary and was there for the *Vsenoshnaya*. Dinner 4 and Mama on the sofa. Before dinner unpacked.

+4
19 May Thursday
Were 4 with Mama at *Obednya* at the infirmary at the G[rand] P[alace]. Went for a walk with A and Trina. Breakfast 4 and Mama on the sofa. Was with A at our infirmary and we sat in the sun and went for a walk to the construction. Were 4 at the G[rand] P[alace]. Tea 4 and Mama. Went for a drive 4 with Isa. Dinner 4 and Iedigarov, and Mama on the sofa.

+10
20 May Friday
Had lessons. Went for a ride with A and Trina. Breakfast 4 with Trina and Mama on the sofa. In the day went for a drive 4 with Trina. Was with A at our infirmary and sat with AP, MZ and ME in the sun. Tea and dinner 4 with Mama. Had a lesson. Went for a ride with Isa, O and A. Talked with Iedigarov on the telephone.

+8
21 May Saturday
Had lessons. Went for a walk with A and Trina. Was at the sisters

at the infirmary, saw Iegidarov and Karangozov. Breakfasted 4, Zizi and Mama on the sofa. In the day went for a ride 4 with Nastenka. Was with A at our infirmary. Tea 4 and dinner, and were 4 at the *Vsenoshnaya* with Mama. Was at the sisters at the infirmary and sat with Pavlov and we did a puzzle. Had my hair washed.

+6
22 May Sunday
Were 4 with Mama at *Obednya*. Breakfasted the same with Isa and Nastenka. In the day went 4 with Mama to the G[rand] P[alace] and after that were at the F[edorovsky] Cathedral for a *moleben*, brought out St Nicholas the Wonderworker. Was with A at our infirmary. Tea and dinner 4 with Mama. Went for a drive 4 with Isa. We went to our infirmary—one of the soldiers had an operation because of a burst artery. Was at the sisters' infirmary and did a puzzle with Naterov, Nikiforov and Polyakov.

+10
23 May Monday
Had lessons. Went for a ride with Trina. Breakfast, tea and dinner 4 with Mama on the balcony. In the day I was with A at our infirmary. Went for a ride with Mama, O and A. Had a lesson. Went for a drive with A, T and Trina. Was at the sisters' infirmary. Did puzzles with Countess S Grekova, Nikiforov, Natarov and Doctor.

+14
24 May Tuesday
Had lessons. Went for a walk and a ride with A and Trina. Breakfast and dinner 4 with Mama on the balcony. In the day I went for a drive with O, A and Nastenka. Was with A at our infirmary. Tea 4 with Mama and U[ncle] Pavel on the balcony. Picked flowers, swung in the hammock and went for a ride 4 with Nastenka. Was at the sisters' infirmary. Did puzzles with Nikiforov, S Zvolyansky and Doctor.

+10
26 May Thursday
Had lessons. Went for a walk with Trina. Was at the sisters at the

infirmary, where we saw the Kob family. Breakfast and tea 4 with Mama on the balcony. Was with A at our infirmary and in the garden. Went for a drive 4 with Mama. Had lessons. Went for a ride with O, A and Isa. Dinner 4 and Mama. Went to the sisters' infirmary. Played *bloshki*[18] and did puzzles.

+9
27 May Friday
Had lessons. Went for a ride with Trina. Breakfast 4 with Mama on the balcony, tea and dinner the same. Was with A at our infirmary. An. P picked lilies-of-the-valley with us in the garden on the Children's Island. Had a lesson. Went for a drive with A and Nastenka. Was at the sisters' infirmary. Played *bloshki* with Countess S Grekova, Nestorov, Nikiforov and Hadzhivanov.

+12
28 May Saturday
Had lessons. Went for a drive with Trina. Breakfast 4 with Mama, B and Count Fredericks on the balcony. Was with A at our infirmary. Went to the construction of the new infirmary. Tea 4 on the balcony with Mama and Kiki. Were 4 with Mama at the *Vsenoshnaya* and dinner. Was at the sisters' infirmary and played *bloshki* with Countess S Volshina, Doctor, Nikiforov, Popanov, Matarov and Polyakov.

+15
29 May Sunday
Were 4 with Mama at *Obednya* and breakfasted and dined the same, on the balcony. Went 4 for a drive with Isa. Was with A at our infirmary. Tea 4 with Mama and Zizi on the balcony. Was at the sisters' infirmary and played *bloshki* with Countess, Bibi, S Grekova, S Volshina, Doctor, Popanov, Nikiforov and Natarov.

Letter from Maria to Nicholas II—
29 May. [At] The Feodorovsky Cathedral Imperial infirmary for the Wounded.

18. Tiddlywinks.

My dear Papa! I don't think I ever wrote to you on this paper before. Today it was hot here, but now [it is] not that [hot], as it rained a little. In the morning we went to *Obednya* and had breakfast on the balcony, also had tea with Zizi. She is leaving to her village tomorrow. I am all bitten up by some nasty beast, and therefore my entire body itches. It is extremely unpleasant, especially in public, when one wants to scratch. These days we go to the sisters' infirmary almost every evening. They clean the instruments and prepare materials for the next day. Anastasia plays table croquet with the wounded, while I play *bloshki* or put together a puzzle. This afternoon we rode around, and then went to our infirmary. Almost all the wounded are lying in the tent, only the heavily [wounded] ones are not allowed. Those who are able, walk to Catherine Park and sail around the lake in row boats. They really enjoy this and always ask the nurses to go with them. We go to our infirmary every day too, this is much better than the Grand Palace with Nurse Lyubushina. She of course noted that we got tan and all the nurses too. The other day we went to the Children's Island with Poopse's sister, and she weeded with us. There is so much decayed grass among the lilies of the valley that they are not growing well. We cleaned half, and will finish the other one in the next couple of days. I kiss you and Alexei affectionately. May God keep you. + Your Kazanetz.

Vasily Stepochkin[19] to Maria—
Your Imperial Highness!
I dare to appeal once again to Your Grace and deeply apologize for my courage in disturbing you. Devotional love prompts my writing. I wanted to express to you my most humble and sincere gratitude. I thank God for giving me the great happiness and joy of seeing your Imperial Highness and all of the August Family on May 16, the day of your visit—to us, grey warriors—where you honored me with Highly gracious questions and your wishes and greetings from the Infirmary. Your Most August Parent, our Beloved Supreme Leader and Sovereign, Emperor Nicholas II Alexandrovich and the

19. A wounded officer from infirmary.

Autocrat of All Russia, and the Matushka Tsaritsa blessed us with a Holy Icon of the Unmercenary and Miracle Worker Panteleimon the Healer on May 26 at 5 pm in the afternoon—such touching joy. I received your Highly Merciful news of May 19th.

At your feet, I lay the most humble and ardent feelings of infinite devotion and the deepest gratitude, for your highest affection and angelic gaze to me, the unworthy.

I am very sorry that, up to the present time, I still have no power to fulfil the oath of duty at the foremost positions at such a necessary and precious time, for the common good, but I thank God, my situation is improving, the mud is doing me good.

Since May 2, I have been serving as an overseer for the lower ranks, which is more fun for me. Your Imperial Highness, on the 5th of June is the Memorable and solemnly joyful birthday of Your Most August Sister, Her Imp. Highness Grand Duchess Anastasia Nikolaevna. I have the happiness to congratulate Your Imperial Highness with my sincere wishes for your complete happiness and long life, for joy and happiness for all of us Loyal ones. We were visited almost daily by Anna Al. Vyrubova, and last night I found out by chance that she was leaving for Tsarskoe Selo.

I dared to go to say goodbye and was honored to talk with her, she deigned to hand me a photograph card of you that is dear to me in my memory, and I am very grateful to her for her Motherly Affection. Your Imperial Highness, if you find the opportunity to convey my Warm Greetings and thanks to Dmitri Nikolaevich Loman and all the Staff of the brilliant Infantry Hospital N17 in Your Name—for their kind remembrance and affection, as well as to the servants and the wounded.

Happy to be Your Imperial Highness's Most Distinguished Servant and Pet,
Ensign Vasily Stepochkin
on May 30, 1916.
Evpatoria.
Very happy with the success of General Brusilov's army, this 22nd May, may the Lord God help them to completely destroy the Insidious enemy.

Maria's diary—

+8
30 May Monday
Were 4 with Mama to church for *Obednya* and went for a drive with
A and Trina. Breakfast 4 with Mama on the balcony, had tea too.
Were 4 at the G[rand] P[alace] then went with A to our infirmary,
was at V N's room. Went for a drive with A and Trina. Swung on
the hammock with A. Dinner 4 with Mama. Was at the sisters' infirmary. Played *bloshki* like yesterday.

+9
31 May Tuesday
Had lessons. Went for a drive with A and Trina. Breakfast, Dinner
and tea 4 with Mama on the balcony. Was with A at our infirmary.
Went for a drive with Mama, O and A. Swung on the hammock
with A. Had a lesson. Went for a drive with A and Trina. Was at
the sisters' infirmary and played *bloshki*.

1 June Wednesday
Had lessons. Russian, music, English and Batushka. Went to the
cemetery for Sonia's panikhida with Mama. Had breakfast 4 with
Mama on the balcony. Went to our infirmary with A., Rimma
Zborovskaya[20] came over, Vikt. Erastovich was wounded. Rode with
Mama. Had tea with Mama and A. and Anya. Rode with A and
Trina. Had dinner 4 with Mama. Went to the sisters' infirmary,
played *bloshki*.

+10
2 June Thursday
Had an English lesson. Went for a ride with A and Trina. Breakfast
4 with Mama on the balcony. Was at our infirmary with A during
the day.

+10
3 June Friday
Had lessons—Russian, music and English. Went for a drive with A

20. Sister of Viktor Erastovich.

and Trina. Breakfast 4 with Mama and Anya on the balcony. Was with O and A at the G[rand] P[alace]. After that I was with A at our infirmary. Tea 4 with Mama on the balcony. The same went for a drive. Went for a walk with T, A and Trina. Swung with A on the hammock. Dinner 4 with Mama. Was at the sisters' infirmary and played *bloshki*.

+6
4 June Saturday
Had lessons—English and Batushka. Rode on the hammock with A. Breakfast 4 with Mama, Anya, C[ount] Fredericks with Emma. Went for a ride 4, and Mama with Anya. Was with A at our infirmary. Tea 4 with Mama. Were 4 at the *Vsenoshnaya*. Dinner the same with Mama. Were 4 at the sisters' infirmary and played *bloshki*.

Letter from Maria to Nicholas II—
4 June. My golden Papa darling! I send you good wishes for Anastasia's birthday. I am writing you on this paper, as this is the last of it from our infirmary. If you would like, I can write to you on the infirmary postcards. It is raining every day here, but despite that we still walk and ride. Yesterday morning we had lessons, but only for an hour, so Shvybz and I were free and went riding with Trina. On the way we ran into an old woman who was selling lilies of the valley, and so we bought some from her. Had breakfast on the balcony although it was not really warm. Then we went to the Grand Palace. We planned on going riding afterwards, but it was raining very hard, so we didn't go. Shvybz and I went to our infirmary. Had tea on the balcony too then swung in the hammock. It is hanging between two trees behind the path by the balcony. The trees there are very strong. You probably heard that Viktor Erastovich and Skvortzov were wounded, while Shvedov has typhus. I am writing you in the morning, as I have a free hour. At 10 o'clock I will accompany the sisters and Mama to the infirmary. She seems to feel better, as she now goes to the infirmary earlier with the sisters. I am sending you, Alexei and the Suite a few pictures. I signed all of them, but not yours. I kiss you affectionately, like I love you. Your Kazanetz, may Christ be with you. +

Maria's diary—

5 June Sunday

Went to *Obednya* 4 with Mama. Had breakfast with same and Anya. Rode 4 with Mama. Sat with Nastenka and looked at albums. Went to the sisters' infirmary. Played *bloshki*.

+4

6 June Monday

Had lessons music, history and Russian. Went for a walk with Trina. Breakfast, tea and dinner 4 with Mama. Were at the Christening of Marina [daughter of sailor]. Was with A at our infirmary. Went for a drive with O, A and Nastenka. Was at the infirmary with the same and played *bloshki*.

+10

7 June Tuesday

Had lessons English and history. Went for a ride with A and Isa. Breakfast 4 with Mama, A[unt] Mavra, Vera and Georgi on the balcony. Was with A at our infirmary. Chatted with Katya Zborovskaya. Were 4 with Mama at the manege. There was a cinematograph The Capture of the Herzrome and Trapezoid. Tea 4 with Mama and Anya. Went for a drive with A and Zizi. Dinner 4 and Mama on the sofa. Were at the sisters' infirmary 4 played *bloshki*.

+6

8 June Wednesday

Had lessons. Breakfast 4 with Sashka and Mama on the sofa. Were 4 at the Gr[and] P[alace]. Went for a drive 4 and Mama with Anya. Was at our infirmary with A. Tea 4 with Mama and Anya. Played ping pong with A. Dinner 4 with Mama. Was at Anya's and we saw Tatiana and her aunt. Played *bloshki* and Dobchinsky-bobchinsky at the sisters' infirmary.

Authors' note: Maria had 9 June and 10 June back to front in her diary and had crossed out and rewrote the dates.

+6

~~10 June Friday~~ 9 June Thursday

Had lessons. Went for a drive with A and Trina. Breakfast 4 with Mama. Was with A at our infirmary. Played ping pong with A. Tea 4 with Mama, U[ncle] Pavel and Maria. Went for a walk with T, A and Isa. Returned home by cab. Dinner 4 with Mama. Were 4 at the sisters' infirmary and played dobchinsky-bobchinsky. Sat with Bogdanov.

Letter from Pierre Gilliard to Maria—

I hope, Madam and very dear pupil, that it is more beautiful in Tsarskoe Selo than it is here. If you knew how much it's raining here! Water, always water, nothing but water!! We will all be frogs soon if this continues. The "little corporal"[21] wants me to tell You that He is kissing You tenderly. He is a little sad these days thinking about Sevastopol and Evpatoria where He felt so good, where it was so beautiful.

I hope Her Majesty can read my letters easily. I write so fast, just minutes before lunch or before the walk. And since Alexis Nikolaevich is almost always beside me and I take care of him as much as my letters, I do not know what I write. I beg you very much to ask Her Majesty to forgive me for writing so badly, in view of the short time I have at my disposal. Another prayer, Marie Nikolaevna: I beg you to look after me when I return to Tsarskoe Selo. You are, Madam, as good, as sweet and as patient as Olga Nikolaevna, an angel, what, and I am sure that You will help me. With You as an ally, I do not fear anyone. Dr. Derevenko asks you to accept his most respectful greetings.

And I, Madam, beg you to believe me Your most humble and obedient servant.
Pierre Gilliard
Grand headquarters, this Thursday, June 9, 1916

Vasily Stepochkin to Maria—
The 10th of June 1916.
Evpatoria.
Her Majesty's Sanitorium

21. Alexei.

If possible, then I Humbly ask you to convey my greetings to the Personnel, the Servants and the wounded of the unforgettable Infirmary in Your Name, and the clergy of the Feodorovsky Cathedral and to Her Excellency Anna Alexandrovna. And after you—to our Mother.

Maria's diary—
~~9 June Thursday~~ 10 June Friday
Had lessons. Were 4 with Mama at *Obednya*. Went for a ride with A and Trina. Breakfasted 4 and Mama. We were at the warehouses. After that with A at our infirmary. Tea 4 with Mama and Dmitri. Walked 4 and rode with Derevenko and the children on the gigantic steps. Dinner 4 with Mama. 4 at the sisters' infirmary and played dobchik-bobchik. Sat with Bogdanov.

+9
11 June Saturday
Had lessons. Was with A at the G[rand] P[alace]. Breakfast 4 with Mama. With the same at a *panikhida*[22] for Isukov. Was with A at our infirmary. Vikt. Er. arrived with a hand injury and also Tolstoy. Tea 4 with Mama and Anya. Went for a drive 4 with Mama. Were 4 at the Autumn. Dinner 4 with Mama and were at the sisters' infirmary, played dobchinsky-bobchinsky and sat with others.

+8
12 June Sunday
Were 4 with Mama at *Obednya* and the same had breakfast along with Anya. Was with A at our infirmary. Mama and sisters were also here. Sat with Vikt. Er., Tolst., Sh. N., and Vikt Er's sister. Afterwards removed curtains with the sisters. Tea 4 with Mama on the balcony, and dinner the same. Went for a walk with T, A and Trina. Was at the sisters' infirmary. Sat with Zykov and played D.B. [Dobchinsky–Bobchinsky].

Maria to Nicholas II—

12 June. My Papa golden darling! Yesterday morning we had lessons, and during the last hour Shvybz and I were free, as Zhilik is

22. Requiem service for the dead.

not here. We took advantage of that and went to the Grand Palace. Then, after we returned home, we waited for Mama and the sisters for breakfast until 13.30. After breakfast we went to the panikhida for Zhukov and two other Cossacks. Then we returned home. Shvybz and I waited out the rain and went to our infirmary. On the way a motor caught up to us, it was going rather fast, we moved to the side of the road in order not to be sprayed with dirt. The motor passes and who do you think is in it? Loman? Nothing of the sort, who but Viktor Erastovich himself. He was riding next to Ensign Tolstov of the Tekinsky regiment, and across from them, with her back to the driver sat a sister of mercy who brought them from Poltava in a regular train. We got to the infirmary at the same time. The motor stopped. The sister of mercy came out and helped Viktor Erastovich. He came over so pitifully to greet us, it was a bit unnecessary. Of course, he was, as always, [wearing] his grey *cherkeska*,[23] but [it was] very battered, his little *papakha*[24] was also dirty. We greeted the nurse, she had an appetizingly tan face. "Well, I brought them to you,"—she said, smiling. Tolstov was wearing his uniform, a burgundy robe and a huge black *papakha*. Underneath his huge *papakha* he looked very small, wretched and thin. He is almost the same height as Viktor Erastovich. After that we entered the infirmary and went to the lower ranks' room. There is a woman patient there, a volunteer from my regiment. They offered her a separate room, but she did not want it, saying that she is the same soldier like everyone else. She looks like a boy, although she is 33 years old. While we were with the soldiers, Viktor Erastovich went home for 10 minutes, of course he stayed there for a half hour, because a lot of officers came over their flat. Viktor Erastovich came back to the infirmary while we were sitting in his room with Tolstov. He was tired from walking and therefore agreed to sit down right away. He told us a lot about the Hundred, and in general was the same as always. He sits hunched over as his back hurts him the most. The entry wound healed already but the exit wound on his back—did not, the bullet luckily did not touch the spine. Guess who I got a letter from? From Nikolai Dmitrievich. He sent me

23. A long caftan, tightened at the waist, without a collar and with a wedge-shaped neckline on the chest.
24. Quilted half-caftan and cape, of Tatar origin.

three pictures taken during their last landing. So terribly sweet, is it not? I squeeze you tightly, kiss and love you and Alexei. May God keep you. + Your Kazanetz.

Nicholas II to Maria—

Imperial Headquarters, 13 June, 1916. My dear Maria, I congratulate you with your 17th birthday and wish you all that is bright and good. I regret to be away. I thank you for the letters, reading them I often laughed at your stories. I am also grateful for the photographs of which I now have so many. The old album is full, will need to order a new one soon—but [there is] never enough time to paste them. I am happy that Vikt. Erast. already arrived at your infirmary. Tell Shvybzik that I share her joy in seeing him and following him if she deigns him with it. Recently I read in a command that three officers in your Kazansky regiment received St George's crosses for past heroism and a few others got Georg. Weapons. This is good. For ten days the weather has been nasty, cold and constant rain. Finally, today it is clear and warm and we will start eating in the tent again. Alexei, Nagorny and Muravnukin are on the giant steps or we play sort of a hide-and-seek. Well it is time to end. I embrace you tightly, my sweet Maria, and your sisters too. May Christ be with you. +. Your Papa.

Maria's diary—

+10

13 June Monday

Had lessons. Went for a walk with A and Trina. Breakfasted 4 and Mama on the balcony and had tea too. Was at our infirmary with A and sat with Vikt. Er., Tolst., and Sh. N. Dragged the things for the dressings into the new infirmary. Went for a ride 4 with Isa. Dinner 4 with Mama and Anya on the balcony. Was 4 at the sisters' infirmary and sat with Bogdanov, played D.B.

Vasily Stepochkin to Maria—

Tsarskoe Selo

Mistress of the Feodorovsky Infirmary N17

Her Imperial Highness
Grand Duchess
Maria Nikolaevna
Your Imperial Highness!
I am happy for my destiny through the providence of the Most-
High God, that He honored me to not only see you and all the
Most August Adorable Tsarist Family, but also to enjoy that Great
happiness and joy—to be under the direct highly favored patronage
from August 30, 1915 to March 7, 1916, and even now am under
the auspices of your most August Parent, for whom I thank God
Almighty every day! And I pray to Him to send you all the blessings
of the earth according to your generous wishes. Now it is a joyful
for me on this Highly Honorable and Memorable Day—The Ju-
bilee of Your Most Gracious Birth on this 14th June. Full of excite-
ment, joy and happiness with the coming day of your
birthday—with the most humble gratitude to you Your Imperial
Highness, I dare to ask Your Imperial Highness to accept from
me—congratulations and share the joy of your high birthday and
sincere and heartfelt wishes: sending you, and the whole of the August Family and all the reigning house—from the Omnipresent
God—full prosperity and longevity—for joy and consolation to us
Your loyal children.
Most gratefully grateful and boundlessly loyal to you.
Your Pet and Servant
Ensign
Vasily Stepochkin.

Nicholas II to Maria—
Stavka 13 June 1916
My dear Maria,
I congratulate you on the day of your 17th birthday and wish for
you all things bright and good. I am very sorry to be away from
you. Thank you for the letters. Reading them, I often laughed at
what you said in them.
I am also very grateful for the photos, of which I have accumulated
a great many. The old album is full, I will have to start a new one
soon—but I don't have enough time to glue them.

I am glad that Vikt. Erast. already arrived at your infirmary. Tell Shvybzik that I share her pleasure to see him and follow after him if she honors him with this.

Recently I read in the order that in your Kazan regiment three officers received the St. George Cross for their former exploits and several others received the Georg Weapon. Good.

For ten days here the weather was bad, cold and constantly rainy. Today it is finally clear and warm and we will start eating in the tent again.

Before dinner, I run with Alexei, Nagorny and Muravitsky on giant steps or play a kind of hide-and-seek.

Well, it's time to stop.

I hold you tight, my dear Maria, as well as all the sisters.

Christ is with you +.

Your Papa

Alexei to Maria—

Mogilev 13 June 1916
My dear Maria
Congratulations on your holiday.
Your Alexei

Maria's diary—

+10
14 June Tuesday
Was with A at our infirmary. We saw how the wounded were transferred to the new infirmary and were there. Breakfast 4 with Mama on the balcony and tea and dinner too. Were 4 at the new infirmary with Mama at its consecration and had tea there. Went for a drive 4, and Mama with Anya. Ran on the gigantic steps with Derevenko's children. Was with A at the new infirmary, there was a concert. The new infirmary is very pleasing. Was at the sisters' infirmary and played D.B.

Maria to Nicholas II—

14 June. I don't know how to thank you, my golden Papa for your

dear letter. Unfortunately, I cannot write a lot to you as I am very busy. In the morning we went to the infirmary and dragged all the wounded over to the new infirmary. We had breakfast just now and now we all must go to the consecration of the new infirmary. It is rather cozy. I kiss you and Alexei affectionately. May God keep you. Your Kazanetz.

Maria's diary—

+10
15 June Wednesday
Had lessons. Breakfast 4 with Mama and Anya on the balcony. Was with A at the G[rand] P[alace]. Went for a drive with Mama and A. Was with A at the new infirmary and sat with Vikt. Er., Sh. N., Tolstoy. Went by the old infirmary after tea on the balcony. Dinner 4 with Mama on the balcony. Was at the sisters' infirmary. Sat with Zykov and played D.B.

+11
16 June Thursday
Had lessons. Went for a ride with A and Trina. Breakfast, tea and dinner 4 with Mama on the balcony. Went horseback riding with T and A and Karzh. Was with A at our old and new infirmaries. Sat with Vikt. Er., Tolst., and Sh. N. Was also out in the fresh air. Were 4 at the sisters' infirmary. Sat with Bogdanov. Played D.B.

+10
17 June Friday
Had lessons. Went for a drive with A and Trina. Breakfasted and had tea 4 with Mama on the balcony. Was with A at the new infirmary and sat with Vikt. Er., Tolst., and Sh. N. We were at the cinematograph. Walked with A, T and Isa. Dinner 4 with Mama and Anya. Was at the sisters' infirmary. Sat with Zykov and played D.B.

Maria to Nicholas II—

17 June, 1916. My dear Papa! Right now, I am sitting on the balcony with Mama and Anya. We just finished breakfast. The rain storm is everywhere, and the thunder is very loud. I don't know

what we will do. These days Anastasia and I go to our new infirmary very often. It is awfully cozy. I hope that when you return you will come visit us [there]. Every evening we go to the sisters' infirmary, and there we play dobchinsky-bobchinsky. You cannot even imagine how Baron Taube bustles about and argues with Rita Khitrovo. They constantly exasperate each other. The lightning keeps flashing, and Anya crosses herself and says "Oy, please no, I don't want the storm." I will end my letter, as there is nothing more [to say]. I kiss you affectionately, and Alexei. Please thank Zhilik for the letter. May God keep you. + Your Kazanetz.

Maria's diary—

+13
18 June Saturday
Had lessons. Went for a walk with T and Trina. Went for a drive with A and Shura. Breakfast, dinner and tea 4 with Mama on the balcony. Was with A at our new infirmary. Sat with Vikt. Er. and Tolst. Were 4 at the *Vsenoshnaya*. After that were 4 at the sisters' infirmary. Played D.B.

+13
19 June Sunday
Were 4 at *Obednya* with Mama. Breakfasted the same with Anya on the balcony. Was with A at our new and old infirmaries. Sat with Vikt. Er., Tolst., and Sh. N. Tea 4 with Mama on the balcony. Dinner the same. Ran about with A and Derevenko's children. Was at the sisters' infirmary, sat with Zykov. Tolst[oy] was there. Played D.B.

A. Mordvinov to Maria—
19th of June, 1916.
Lashino Estate, Novgorod Province.
I have just now been sent your lovely telegram, and you cannot imagine, my beloved "tormentor," how sincerely and heartily pleased I was with your dear attention, and at the same time terribly upset that I could not use your sweet invitation and come to breakfast at 13 o'clock, on the 15th of June.

Believe me, it was a very, very big deprivation for me, all the more difficult, that I have not seen all of you so long, and for me, the last time was not enough!

Unexpectedly for myself, my departure to the village came out this way. The fact is that on the 14th of June is your birthday and my birthday. My family is already in the village, and I lived in Gatchina, alone, waiting for His Majesty's arrival. This day the morning was magnificent, absolutely not for the city but for the village, and my loneliness became even more dreary. I then suddenly decided to give myself a gift for this day, i.e. to go home, to the Novgorod province, so that at least the last minutes of my birthday I would not be alone.

I say "minutes," because I had a long way to go—from the railway station it was necessary to go 80 versts on the postal horses, and according to my calculations, I could be at home, at Lashino, about half an hour before midnight.

In fact, as always, it turned out that all my assumptions were wrong. One of the stations did not have enough horses, I was late, and only at one o'clock in the morning on the 15th, I came home. Of course, no one was expecting me. I got out of the equipage far from home, and quietly bypassing the servant appeared in my wife's room, who was reading and not yet asleep. The effect of my arrival was astounding and a surprise with the joy of meeting!

I'm thinking of staying here for another three or four days, as I was told that His Majesty is unlikely to arrive earlier than the 23rd or 24th of June, and maybe later, and then return to Gatchina.

All this time, I was often, very often, mentally with all of you, and sincerely sad that fate, for so long, did not give me the opportunity to see you all.

Thank you heartily therefore, once again, for your kind remembrance, for your sweet invitation and for not having forgotten me yet!

My warmest heartfelt greetings to all of you and 1000000000000 000 most sincere wishes.

Be healthy, joyful, happy, and have all your heart desires. Deeply and sincerely devoted to you

A. Mordvinov

Maria's diary—

+10
20 June Monday
Had lessons. Breakfast 4 with Mama and B Derevenko on the balcony. Was with A at our old and new infirmaries. Sat with Vikt. Er., Tolst., and Sh. N. Tea 4 with Mama and A[unt] Miechen. Played ping-pong with Shvybz. Dinner 4 with Mama on the balcony. Were 4 at the sisters' infirmary. Sat with Zykov and Natarov. We stopped by [illeg.].

+12
21 June Tuesday
Had lessons. Went for a drive with A and Trina. Was with A at the Gr[and] P[alace]. Breakfast and dinner 4 with Mama on the balcony. Was with A at our old and new infirmaries and sat with the same. Tea 4 with Mama, Vikt. Er., and Yuzik at Anya's on the balcony. Went for a drive with A, T and Isa. Was at the sisters' infirmary. Sat only for quite a little bit.

+12
22 June Wednesday
Had lessons. Breakfast, dinner and tea 4 with Mama on the balcony. Was with A at our old and new infirmaries and sat the same. Went for a drive with A and Trina. Was at the sisters' infirmary and sat at Sedov's and Zykov's and played some game.

Nicholas to Maria—

Telegram No 216. 20 words. Sent from Stavka. 1916 at 12 o'cl.50 min.
Received at Tsarskoe Selo 22 June, 1916 at 13 o'cl.28 min.
To G.D. Maria Nikolaevna
I CONGRATULATE YOU WITH NAME DAY MANY RE-GRETS THAT HAD NO TIME TO WRITE. HUGS TO YOU AND [YOUR] SISTERS.
PAPA

Maria's diary—

+14

23 June Thursday

Had a lesson. Went for a drive with A and Shvybz. Basked in the sun. Breakfast 4 with Mama and Nastenka on the balcony. In the day was at our old and new infirmaries with A. Sat with the same. Tea 4 with Mama. Swung 4 on the hammock and made a bonfire. Dinner 4 with Mama on the balcony. Were 4 at the sisters' infirmary, sat with all.

+15

24 June Friday

Had lessons. Basked with Shvybz in the sun. Breakfast 4 with Mama and Sashka on the balcony. Was with A at the old and new infirmaries. Tolst. had an operation. Went for a drive 4 with Mama and Anya. Tea with the same on the balcony. Was with A at the G[rand] P[alace]. Went for a drive with A and Trina. Dinner 4 with Mama on the balcony. Were at the sisters' infirmary and played croquet, sat with Zykov.

+13

25 June Saturday

Had lessons. Went for a drive with A and Trina. Breakfast 4 with Mama and C[ount] Fredericks on the balcony. Were at a thanksgiving *moleben*—the First Kuban Hundred returned from the war. Was with A at the old and new infirmaries and sat with the same. Tea 4 with Mama and Anya on the balcony. Were 4 at the *Vsenoshnaya*. Dinner 4 with Mama on the balcony. Were 4 at the sisters' infirmary. Played croquet and sat. The [illeg.] convoy arrived.

+14

26 June Sunday

Were 4 with Mama at *Obednya*. Breakfasted the same and Sandro on the balcony. Was with A at the old and new infirmaries. Sat with Vikt. Er., and Tolst. Went for a drive with Mama and Anya. Tea and Dinner 4 with Mama on the balcony. We lay on the grass. Went for a drive with A and Trina. Was at the sisters' infirmary. Played croquet sat with Zykov and others and we sang.

+16
27 June Monday
Had lessons and a bonfire. Breakfast 4 with Mama and C[ount] Apraksin on the balcony. Was with A at the new infirmary and sat as usual. Were 4 with Mama at the sisters at the infirmary, the local artillery played balalaika. Tea 4 with Mama on the balcony. Dinner the same and Anya. Was at the sisters' infirmary and played croquet and Dobchinsky-Bobchinsky on the balcony.

+14
28 June Tuesday
Had lessons and a bonfire. Breakfast 4 with Mama and Anya on the balcony. Was with A at the new infirmary, sat with the same and caught flies too. Tea 4 with Mama, Anya, Mila and Tata on the balcony. Went for a drive 4 with Trina. We met Shurik who has returned from Shpoln where he was injured. Dinner 4 with Mama on the balcony. Were 4 at the sisters' infirmary, played croquet and D.B.

29 June Wednesday
Went to *Obednya* 4 with Mama at the Palace infirmary. Had breakfast 4 with Mama, Isa on the balcony. Before that rode with Shvybzik[25] and Trina. Went to the new infirmary of the Svodny regiment No. 36 with A. Went to the new infirmary with A. Sat with Shurik too. Had tea with Shvybz and the same swung in a hammock. Rode with A. and Isa. Had dinner 4 with Mama on the balcony. Went to the sisters' infirmary. Played croquet and Dobchinsky-Bobchinsky.

+9
30 June Thursday
Had a lesson and a bonfire. Lay around in the sun and went for a drive with A and Trina. Breakfast 4 with Mama and U[ncle] Georgi

25. Shvybzik was the nickname of Anastasia, which in German means impish.

on the balcony. 4 Hundreds—Tatonov, Yuzik, Zerschikov and Skl-
yarov off to the war. Was with A at our infirmary. Sat with Vikt.
Er., and Sh. N. Tea 4 with Mama and Anya on the balcony. T. A
was here. Went for a drive with A and Trina. Dinner 4 with Mama
on the balcony. Were 4 at the sisters' infirmary. Sat with Tolst.
Played D. B.

1 July Friday
Had lessons. Rode with Anastasia and Trina. Breakfast 4 with Mama
and Isa on the balcony. In the afternoon went to our infirmary with
A. Sat as usual. Went 4 to the farewell molebna. The 4th Hundred
rode on vetka and they passed by us and we bid [our] farewells. Had
tea 4 with Mama on the balcony. Rode with A. and Trina. Had dinner 4 with Mama and Zhilik on the balcony. Went to the sisters'
infirmary. Played croquet and D.B.

+12
2 July Saturday
Had lessons. Went for a drive with O and Trina. Breakfast 4 with
Mama, Lolo and Dolgoruky on the balcony. Was with A at our new
infirmary, sat as usual. Was at the Manege at the cinematograph.
Tea and dinner 4 with Mama on the balcony. Went for a drive with
A and Shura. Were 4 at the sisters' infirmary and played croquet
and D.B.

3 July Sunday
Went to *Obednya* with Mama at the Pal. infirmary. Rode with A
and Trina. Had breakfast 4 with Mama and Anya on the balcony.
Went to our infirmary with Anya. Sat as usual. Had tea and dinner
4 with Mama on the balcony. Rode with A and Shura. Went to the
sisters' infirmary and played croquet and D.B.

+14
4 July Monday
Had lessons. Breakfast 4 with Mama and U[ncle] Petya on the balcony. Was at the new infirmary with A and sat like always. Tea 4
with Mama, Shurik and Vikt. Er. on the balcony. Went for a drive

with A and Trina. Dinner 4 with Mama on the balcony. Were at the sisters' infirmary and played croquet and D.B. on the balcony.

+16
5 July Tuesday
Had lessons. Went for a drive with Shvybz and Trina. Breakfasted 4 with Mama and Isa in the balcony. Was with A at the new infirmary, were photographed, sat (with the same) as always and Shurik. Tea 4 on the balcony. Were the same at the G[rand] P[alace]. Had my hair washed. Dinner 4 with Mama and Trina on the balcony. Were at the sisters' infirmary, sat with Gusev and Bogdanov, played D.B. on the balcony.

+20
6 July Wednesday
Was with A at the new infirmary and sat as we ought to. Were on the train and went to Mogilev. Dinner, breakfast and tea 4 with P.V.P., Anya, Isa, Ressin, Yaodarovsky, Galushkin and Ishkener. Went out for a walk with M Visher, Boly, Lihoslav and Rzhev. Nothing to do in the afternoon, so slept. Sat with P.V.P and smoked.

7 July Thursday
Arrived in Mogilev. Papa and Alexei came [to meet us]. Had breakfast all together. Rode in a motor across Dnieper to the other bank. Had tea in the train. Had dinner at Stavka on the balcony. Sat with Uncle Sergei and Father Shavelsky. Returned to the train and Papa too, and then he returned home and we went to bed.

+13
8 July Friday
Wrote. At breakfast sat with Fr. Shavelsky at Stavka on the balcony. Went in a motor and walked. All who walked had tea on the train. Wrote. Dinner on the train.

9 July Saturday
Wrote in the morning. Picked flowers in the field. Had breakfast at Stavka in a tent, sat with Uncle Sergei and Father Shavelsky. Rode

in a motor ferry upstream on Dnieper. Got off to walk. Went to *Vsenoshnaya*. Had dinner in the train. Walked near the train, shot from a revolver at Yulia [Isa's maid].

10 July Sunday

Went to *Obednya*. Walked with T., A., and Count Grabbe in the town garden. At breakfast at Stavka in a tent sat with Uncle Sergei[26] and Uncle Petya.[27] Rode in a motorboat downstream on Dnieper. Had tea in a tent. Went to a cinematograph. It was a drama and a funny [film]. Had dinner in the train. Syroboyarsky[28] and Lubimov were there—Talked with Gramatin.

11 July Monday

Went to molebna. At breakfast at Stavka in a tent [sat with] Uncle Boris and Konzerovsky. Went upstream on Dnieper in a motor, swam 4 with Isa 17 deg[rees]. Had tea at the 3rd Hundred Convoy camp. All the officers were there. The Cossacks danced, sang, and played various games. Had dinner in the train. Talked with Golushkin.

12 July Tuesday

Went to a monastery, venerated the Mogilev Mother of God [icon]. At breakfast at Stavka sat with Uncle Georgi and Nilov on the balcony. Rode in motors and walked on the highway. Had tea at Stavka. Returned to the train, bid farewell to darling Papa, Alexei and others and departed. Had dinner 4 with Isa, Anya, Golushkin, Resin and 2 engineers. Anya was reading Chekhov.

13 July Wednesday

Did not do anything. Had breakfast and dinner 4 with Isa, Anya, Golushkin, Resin and 2 engineers. Baked in the sun. Olga was reading Chekhov. Walked at the stations Bologoe, Tosno, M. Vishera. Arrived at Tsarskoe. Went to the new infirmary with Shvybz. Sat with Viktor Er. And Tolstov. Had tea 4 with Mama on the balcony. Unpacked.

26. Grand Duke Sergei Mikhailovich (1869-1918), Nicholas II's first cousin once removed.

27. Duke Peter of Oldenburg, first husband of Grand Duchess Olga Alexandrovna.

28. One of the imperial officers.

+9
14 July Thursday
Had a lesson. Went for a drive with A and Isa. Breakfast 4 with
Mama on the balcony. Was with T and A at the G[rand] P[alace]
and after that was with A at the new infirmary and sat like yesterday.
Tea and dinner 4 with Mama and Anya on the balcony. Went for a
drive with A and Isa. Was at the sisters' infirmary and sat with all
for a little while.

+11
15 July Friday
Had lessons. Went for a drive with A and Trina. Breakfasted 4 with
Mama on the balcony. Was with A at the new infirmary and sat as
usual. Went to O V Loman with [his] niece, Gusik, Nadia and her
son Roman. Had tea 4 with Mama on the balcony. Went for a drive
with A and Trina. Dinner 4 with Mama and Anya on the balcony.
Were 4 at the sisters' infirmary. Sat with everyone. They took
Volodya Yenlaev to his home.

+11
16 July Saturday
Had lessons. Went for a drive with A and Trina. Breakfast, tea and
dinner 4 with Mama on the balcony. Was at the new infirmary with
A and sat as usual and squashed flies. Went for a drive with A and
Trina. Was at the sisters' infirmary and sat and played ruble.

Maria to Nicholas II—
16 July. My dear Papa! You will tire your eyes while reading my
letter to Alexei, as I wrote to him on red paper. This morning we
are thinking of going riding with Shvybz and Trina. Yesterday afternoon we went to our infirmary, and then to Loman's farm, or
rather not his but his daughter's, who gave birth to a son, Roman,
two weeks ago, who will be christened by Mama on Sunday. The
baby of course was sleeping, and we only looked at him, and then
they showed us their rooms. They are very small but cozy. We
started going to the sisters' infirmary again in the evenings. I am
writing to you while waiting for the Batushka, who probably forgot

that he has a lesson with me, and is not coming. Shvybz is sitting across from me and drawing something in an album. We almost never ride with Mama during the day, because we are at our infirmary the entire time. It's time to end, I hear the Batushka's voice in the hallway. I kiss you affectionately. May Christ be with you. + Your loving Kazanetz.

Maria's diary—

+12
17/30 July Sunday
Were 4 with Mama at *Obednya* at the Pal. infirmary church. Went for a drive with A and Trina. Was with A at the G[rand] P[alace]. Breakfast and tea 4 with Mama on the balcony. The same at the Christening of Roman—son of Nadia Sirotishina. After that was with A at the new infirmary and sat with Vikt. Er. Played ping pong with A. Dinner 4 with Mama on the balcony. Were at the sisters' infirmary, sat and played ruble.

+9
18 July Monday
Had lessons. Went for a drive with A and Trina. Breakfast and dinner 4 with Mama on the balcony. Went for a drive 4 and Mama with Anya. Tea the same on the balcony. Was with A at the new infirmary. Sat with Tolst. Were 4 at the sisters' infirmary. Sat with Pav[el] Taube and Syroboyarsky and played ruble.

Nikolai Demenkov to Maria—

Linear ship "Empress Maria." 18 July, 1916. Sevastopol.
Your Imperial Highness Grand Duchess Maria Nikolaevna!
Loyally I dare to report a significant day in the life of our ship: on the 9th July we took first military shots at the cruiser "The Breslau," into which we ran at sea. We shot from 12 cannons, but unfortunately, we were not able to sink it, because having had speed privilege, it changing course at far distance from us and releasing white smoke screen, which merged with the clouds on the horizon,—it escaped. It shot a few explosives at us, which fell without reaching [their target]. Most amusing of all [is that], when the course we fol-

lowed while shooting at "Breslau" was outlined on a map, the result was the exact profile contour of "The Breslau's" commander, which I am enclosing here. We also added some tears on him, since we assumed that he did not have a sweet time being chased by us for the duration of three hours.

Currently the former commander of our regiment General Komarov is getting [medically] treated in Sevastopol. I was so happy when I met with him. Twice I invited the general to our ship.

I dare ask Your Imperial Highness to receive and pass on to Their Highnesses my sincere heartfelt regards.

I pray to the Lord God to grant health and happiness to Your Imperial Highness.

Your Imperial Highness' most loyal servant,

Lieutenant Demenkov.

Maria's diary—

19 July Tuesday

Went to *Obednya* downstairs 4 with Mama. Drew with A. Rode with A and Trina. Had breakfast and dinner 4 with Mama at the new infirmary. Sat with Tolst. and others. Had tea 4 with Mama and Anya on the balcony. Was lying down and drawing. Sat with Count Taube and Nikiforov, played ruble.

+9

20 July Wednesday

Had lessons. Breakfast and tea 4, dinner 4 with Mama on the balcony. Was at the G[rand] P[alace] in the day with A and after that was with A at the new infirmary. Sat with Vikt. Er and Tolst. Was at the sisters' infirmary and played ruble.

Maria to Nicholas II—

20 July. My golden Papa, almost forgot to write to you today, I must be confused. We will go to the dear Grand Palace with Shvybz now. The sisters are going to Petersburg, and after the Gr. Pal. we will go riding with Mama and Anya. An ensign from my regiment, Shtyrev, is a patient at our infirmary, he was wounded in the leg by an explosive bullet, but he can walk on crutches. He told [us] a lot about

the regiment. Today it is awfully cold and damp, but we still had breakfast on the balcony, albeit in our coats. The motor was supposed to be here already, and it just arrived so I will run. I kiss you affectionately and warmly and squeeze you. May God keep you. Your Kazanetz.

Letter from an admirer—

Dear Beloved Maria! And so now in the entire World, no one but Maria, like the Imperial Family, would recognize and enlighten, what is seen: One outlived God's Omnipotence, and in this is Everything, I am discomforted by a thousand rubles, but undoubtedly now I am free, as always: no and not necessary! Where is the liberty, if not at home and at the Palace and at the Palace trench: before you know it they'll murder, while one is physically deprived of liberty?! Let us assume, one is in debt, like a black Moore, 100 rubles for the father, if the war continues another year, on it is 200 rub., not one pair of socks, but completely free, as this is most important, and the rest will fall into place! Your Knight of Pure Heart Mikhail

20 July, 1916 All will be given to the sword, which is repulsive to Your Heart! Your Knight of Pure Heart Mikhail

Maria's diary—

+10

21 July Thursday

Had a lesson. Went for a drive with A and Trina. Breakfast 4 with Mama on the balcony. Was with A at the new infirmary and sat with Vikt. Er. Tea and dinner 4 with Mama and Anya. Was at the sisters' infirmary and played ruble.

Alexei to Maria—

Mogilev 21 July 1916

I congratulate you, my dear Dragoon, with your Angel Day. I can't wait for you to get here. I play with Makarov. PVP sends all of you his greetings. Papa kisses you. Stay well. Your Efreitor.[29]

29. Corporal.

Maria's diary—

+11

22 July Friday

Were 4 with Mama at *Obednya*. Breakfast the same on the balcony. Were 4 with Mama at a concert at the infirmary. Tea 4 with Mama and Uncle Niki. Wrote a telegraph. Dinner 4 with Mama and Anya. Was with A at the new infirmary and there was a play: "A Boyar Family Evening in the 17th Century." Was at the sisters' infirmary and played ruble.

Alexei to Maria—

Telegram No 210. 10 words. Sent from Stavka 13.2. 1916 at 8 o'cl.1 min.

Received at Tsarskoe Selo 22 July, 1916 at 8 o'cl.50 min.

TO THE GRAND DUCHESS MARIA NIKOLAEVNA HEARTFELT CONGRATULATIONS. THE LETTER WILL BE LATE

ALEXEI

Maria's diary—

+8

23 July Saturday

Had lessons. Went for a drive with A and Trina. Breakfast on the balcony, tea and dinner 4 with Mama. Was with A at the new infirmary and sat with Vikt. Er., Tolst., and Medvedev. Were 4 with Mama at the G[rand] P[alace] at a concert to which the wounded officers were taken from all the infirmaries. Were 4 at the *Vsenoshnaya*. After that went to the sisters' infirmary and played ruble.

24 July Sunday

Went to *Obednya* at the Pal. infirmary with Mama. Rode with A and Trina. Had breakfast and tea 4 with Mama on the balcony. Went to the new infirmary with A. Said goodbye to Syroboyarsky. Walked with A. T and Trina. Had dinner 4 with Mama and Anya. Went to the sisters' infirmary. Played ruble.

Maria to Nicholas II—

25 July. My dear Papa, I am so terribly happy to visit you and Alexei, after all you are so missed here. I have not packed yet, although not taking a lot of things with me, only the most necessary. I got a letter from N.D., will bring it with me and show it to you, [it] may be interesting for you. Yesterday we finally had a nice day, although not very hot but very pleasant, so a lot of the wounded were lying outside. They brought three officers to us, 2 Keksumentzy and then a Petrogradetz or a Muscovite. We saw them only for a few minutes as they just brought them in, and the doctor and Lazarev were with them. We had a very successful concert here at our infirmary on 22 July. Please thank P.V.P. for the letters. I will not have the chance to write to him. I kiss you and darling Alexei affectionately.

Maria's diary—

25 July Monday
Had lessons. Breakfast 4 with Mama on the balcony. Went to the Gr. Pal. then to the new infirmary with Shvybz., sat with Vikt. Er. and Tolst. Had tea 4 with Mama and Anya. Packed. Had dinner 4 with Mama. Went 4 to the sisters' infirmary, sat with Pavlov, Bogdanov and Kasyanov, played ruble. Before that went to Anya's, saw Alya and Grigori.

26 July Tuesday
Went to the new infirmary with A.—to say goodbye. Went on the train to Stavka. Had breakfast and tea and dinner 4 with Nastenka, Count Grabbe, Resin, Botkin, Shkuratov and 2 engineers. Walked at the stations Tosno, Bologoe, and M. Vishera. Played with Count Grabbe and Nastenka, read fortunes.

+11
27 July Wednesday
Arrived. Breakfast with Papa and Mama. Went for a drive with Papa, T, A, A, the suite and Cadets Makarov and Agayev. Had tea with the same. Went to the town garden and saw how the boys played different games. Dinner 4 with Mama and Papa.

28 July Thursday
Were lying down in the field. Ate breakfast in the tent, sat with
Uncle Georgi and Gen[eral] Alekseyev. Sailed on Dnieper on Desna.
Had tea in the train. Played various games with the village children.
Had dinner 4 with Mama and Papa. Walked.

+11
29 July Friday
Was at U[ncle] Georgi's dacha. At breakfast sat with Gen[eral]
Ruzsky and U[ncle] Sergei. Went up the Dnieper on the Desna
where the boys from the town garden played. Had tea on the train.
Played cards, Whose Soul Do You Want, Burners and Cat and
Mouse with the Children. Dinner 4, and Mama with Papa. Went
for a walk.

30 July Saturday
Went to *Obednya*. At breakfast sat with Uncle Kirill, Uncle Georgi.
Stayed on the train with Mama. Worked. Had tea all together.
Wrote. Had dinner 4 while Mama [ate] with Papa. Walked.

31 July Sunday
Went to *Obednya*. At breakfast sat with Uncle Sergei and Gen[eral]
Alekseyev. Everyone rode in a motor boat up the Dnieper, ran
around in the bushes. Had tea at Papa's. Went to a cinematograph
"The Chase After Gold" (drama), "The Heroic Act of Knight
Dupron," Sha-no-u, a love novella with a fight (comedy),
Tupyshkin's Whip too. Had dinner 4 while Mama with Papa.
Mordvinov was here and we were scaring him.

+12
1 August Monday
We wrote. At breakfast, I was with Voeikov and Stürmer. Went up
the Dnieper on a motor boat, walked and ran in the bushes. Tea at
Papa's. Wrote. Dinner 4 with Papa and Mama. Went for a walk.
Dmitri was here.

+11

2 August Tuesday
Wrote, sat and played in the sun with the children. Sat with Dmitri and U[ncle] Sergei at breakfast. Went up the Dnieper in a motor boat and came back on foot to the usual place and lay in the sun and ran in the bushes. Had tea at Papa's. Dinner 4; Papa with Mama. Mordvinov was here. We tormented him.

3 August Wednesday
Sat with the children and baked in the sun. Stopped into the church and venerated the Mogilev Mother of God. At breakfast sat with Nilov and Father Shavelsky. Rode in the motor boat up the Dnieper. Walked, lounged in the sun and [ran] around in the bushes. Had tea in the train. Said goodbye to Papa and Alexei. Everyone boarded the train and left for Ts.S. Had dinner with Nastenka, Resin, Dehn, Yuzik's brother, the engineers and Zhilik. Walked at the stations. Had tea.

+11
4 August Thursday
Sat at Mama's. Breakfast, dinner and tea 4 with Nastenka, Resin, 2 engineers, Dehn, Zhilik and Yuzik's brother. Got out at the stations M Vishera, Bologoye, and Tosno. Guessed with Shura. We arrived at Tsarskoe Selo. Was with A at the new infirmary. Anya was here.

+11
5 August Friday
Had a lesson. Went for a drive with A and Shura. Breakfast and dinner 4 with Mama on the balcony. Was at the new infirmary with A. Went for a drive 4, and Mama with Anya. They had a horse and came to us at the infirmary. Tea 4 with Mama and Anya on the balcony. Were at the *Vsenoshnaya*, and after at the sisters' infirmary and played *ruble*.[30]

6 August Saturday
Went to *Obednya* 4 with Mama. Rode with A and Isa. Had breakfast and dinner on the balcony. Went 4 to the G. P., then to the in-

---

30. A game named after Russian currency.

firmary with A. Had tea 4 with Mama and Anya on the balcony. Went to *Vsenoshnaya* 4 with mama. Went 4 to the sisters' infirmary. Played ruble. Before the infirmary stopped at Anya's and saw Alya and Grigori.

7 August Sunday
Went to *Obednya* at the Pal. infirmary with Mama. Rode with A and Trina. Had breakfast and dinner 4 with Mama on the balcony. Went 4 to the sisters' infirmary. Played ruble.

Maria to Nicholas II—

7 August, 1916. My dear darling Papa! Every time we return from Mogilev it seems harder and wanting so much more to return to Mogilev. Today we went to *Obednya* at the Palace infirmary, then the sisters and Mama stayed for the dressings while Shvybz and I went riding with Trina. [We] saw the train which arrived from Mogilev with the courier and envied him. Trina and Isa were sick the entire time and only recently got out of bed. We continue going to our infirmary. Because the Tsarskoe [Selo] one does not have enough beds for the officers, they will be enlarging our infirmary the soldiers will be transferred to the old infirmary, while the officers will be admitted to the new one in place of the soldiers. It will be a huge infirmary, instead of 12 officers there will be more than 36, and it will be scarier to visit them, such masses [of people]. Our wounded [patients] play tennis now, I don't understand how one of them—[plays] with his left hand, another was wounded in his neck and cannot turn it, but they still love it and play all day long, even those who never knew how to play before, they also play it, and ask us [to play] all the time, but we don't really have time. I kiss you darling and Alexei affectionately, as warmly as I love you. May Christ be with you + Your Kazanetz. Regards to Vasya and his wife. Also to P.V.P.

Maria's diary—

+13
8 August Monday
Was at *Obednya*. Mama had Communion. Had lessons. Went for a

walk with A and Trina. Breakfast 4 with Mama on the balcony. Was at the new infirmary with A. Tea 4 with Mama and Anya on the balcony. Olga read to me. Dinner 4 with Mama. Were at the sisters' infirmary and played ruble.

9 August Tuesday
Had a lesson. Went for a drive with A and Trina, after that was at the G[rand] P[alace] with A. Breakfast and dinner 4 with Mama on the balcony. Was at the new infirmary with Shvybz. Tea 4 with Mama and Anya on the balcony. Olga read to me. Were 4 at the sisters' infirmary. Krasnova sang accompanied by M Konrad. Played ruble.

+9
10 August Wednesday
Had lessons. Went for a drive with A and Trina. Breakfast 4 with Mama on the balcony. Was at the new infirmary with A. Played tennis with Tolst., Vasiliev, Bezobrazov, Zhilinsky and Tsekhanov. Tea 4 and dinner 4 with Mama. Olga read to me. Were 4 at the sisters' infirmary. Sat with Bar[on] Taube, after that sat at home with Mama.

+8
11 August Thursday
Went for a walk with Trina. Was with A at the new infirmary. Played tennis with Vasiliev, Chekhovsky, Zhilinsky and Tolstoy. Breakfast, tea and dinner 4 with Mama on the balcony. Were photographed by Funk.[31] Was with A and T at Alya's. We were at the sisters' infirmary and I played ruble.

+8
12 August Friday
Had a lesson. Went for a ride with A and Trina. Breakfast 4 with Mama and Isa on the balcony. Was at the new infirmary with Shvybz and played tennis with Vasiliev, Gezobrazov, Tolstoy,

31. Imperial photographer.

Chekhovsky and Zhilinsky. Tea and dinner 4 with Mama on the balcony. Was at the Derevenkos. A and S played. We went to the sisters' infirmary and played *ruble* and wrapped bandages as usual— 209 [the number of bandages wrapped].

+10
13 August Saturday
Had lessons. Went for a drive with A and Trina. Breakfast 4 with Mama on the balcony. Was at our new infirmary with A and saw Shura Pototsky [Poopse's brother]. Tea 4 with Mama and Dmitri on the balcony. I wrote. Dinner 4 with Mama. Were at the sisters' infirmary and played ruble and wrapped bandages. I stopped by Nekiforov.—263

14 August Sunday
Went to *Obednya* with Mama. Walked with A and Trina. Had breakfast and dinner 4 with Mama. Went to the new infirmary with A. Had tea 4 with Mama, Irina and Felix. Went 4 to *Vsenoshnaya*. Later [went] to the sisters' infirmary, played ruble.

15 August Monday
Went to *Obednya* 4 with Mama. Rode with A and Trina. Had breakfast 4 and dinner 4 with Mama. In the afternoon went to the new infirmary with A., saw Shura Pototsky. Had tea 4 with Mama and Aunt Miechen. Olga read to me. Went to the sisters' infirmary. Played ruble. Rolled bandages.

Maria to Nicholas II—
15 August. My dear kind Papa! Well it is the fourth day already that we have not played tennis due to awful cold and daily rain. This morning we went to *Obednya* at the Grotto church and then I rode with Trina and Shvybz. When we passed by the train station, I ran into Voeikov and Nilov in a motor. A train from Mogilev will arrive at Tsarskoe at 11.30. It must be so pleasant to have Nik.Pav. with you—The door and windows in our room are open and I am freezing, slowly but surely. Now I need to go to breakfast, but Mama will probably be late. When you are not here, they return terribly

late. The other day they returned at 13.40. Well I kiss you and Alexei affectionately. I apologize for this boring letter, but I know of nothing interesting. May God keep you. + Your Kazanetz. Regards to Kolya and Toto.

Maria's diary—

16 August Tuesday
Was at the new infirmary with A and played bones. Breakfast 4 with Mama, tea and dinner also. Were photographed 4 with Mama at the G[rand] P[alace]. After that we to Alya's, her husband was there. Trina's Olya was here. We were at the sisters' infirmary and played ruble. Olga played the piano and Kasyanov the violin.

+8
17 August Wednesday
Had lessons. Went for a drive with A and Trina. Breakfast and dinner 4 with Mama. In the day I went with A to the new infirmary. Shura Pototsky was there. Played tennis with Tolst. and Medvedev. Tea 4 with Mama and Lady Paget [the senior sister at Dmitr. Infirmary] We were at the sisters' infirmary and played ruble. Wrapped bandages—150.

+9
18 August Thursday
Went for a drive with A and Trina. Breakfast, tea and dinner 4 with Mama. Was with A at the new infirmary. We had a good chat with Tanya Silaeva. Played tennis with Tolst., Vasiliev, Bezobrazov, Zhilinsky and Shura. Was at the sisters' infirmary and played ruble. Wrapped bandages—350.

+8
19 August Friday
Had a lesson. Went for a walk with Trina. Breakfast and dinner 4 with Mama. Was with A at the new infirmary. Tea with C[oun]t Fredericks and Mama. Olga read to me. Were at the sisters' infirmary and played ruble. Folded 458. Sat with Nikorov and Zaraiba.

+6
20 August Saturday
Had lessons. Was at Alya's and her husband's. Had a fitting with
Shvybz. Breakfast 4 with Mama and M Zizi. Were 4 at the G[rand]
P[alace], after that I was with A at the new infirmary. Tea 4 with
Mama and Dmitri. The hairdresser was here. Was with T and A at
Vsenoshnaya. Dinner 4 with Mama. We went to the sisters' infir-
mary. Sat with Nikiforov and played ruble after that.

Pyotr Petrov to Maria—

Stavka
20 Aug. 1916.
I received your scarlet letter, dear Grandfather's Granddaughter,
and, taking guard, I answer in greeting: "Good health!"
His Majesty just went to the Headquarters (10 1/2), and Alexei
Nikolaevich and I, having already played in the tent, were seated
for correspondence. The morning was grey, but now it is squinting
and teasing, Phoebe peers out on her fiery chariot. After a thunderstorm, it became cool (+ 14 ° R). It's better, before it steamed it was
so awful.
Al. N. received the first letter from Agayev in Moscow. Lessons from
him have not yet begun.
We are waiting for Makarenko today or tomorrow.
It would be nice if you could bring your bilboquet[32] with you to
play with in the garden. We are waiting for you patiently and we
only want one thing: the sun! And to get warm well, and take pictures well! With the most devoted greetings to Her Majesty and the
Sisters and with bows to all who remember me, and also greetings
from S.I.G (Sig) [tutor Sydney Gibbes] I'm finishing here.
Your P.V. P.

Maria's diary—

21 August Sunday
Went to *Obednya* with Mama. Then bid farewells at our infirmary
with Shvybz. Boarded the train and went to Smolensk. Had break-

32. A toy with a ball on a string, which has to be caught in a cup or on a spike.

fast, tea and dinner 4 with Mama, Isa, Resin, Lavrov, Zhilik and 2 engineers. Zhilik read "Anand ee monde s'enuie" to us.

22 August Monday
Arrived in Smolensk, went to the cathedral and 4 infirmaries. Had breakfast with same as yesterday. Arrived in Mogilev. Everyone met us. Papa had tea with us on the train. Walked around the train. Had dinner 4 with Papa and Mama and Kiki. After dinner we sat in our [train car].

23 August Tuesday
Went to Molebna. Then had breakfast at Hotel "Bristol" with the staff officers. I sat with Uncle Boris and Count Benkendorf. In the afternoon, we went up the Dnieper. Ran around in the bushes. Had tea at Papa's. Went to a cinematograph, they showed the drama "Mystery of Nogorok" and others. Had dinner 4 while Mama [ate] with Papa and Igor. Mordvinov was here and we tormented him. Before dinner talked to Lavrov.

24 August Wednesday
In the morning [we] wrote and sat in the field with the children. At breakfast in the tent [I] sat with Uncle Georgi and Uncle Kirill. Went to the left bank in a ferry. 2nd half-Hundred and 3rd half-Hundred came there, officers Papasha, Ponkratov, Gramatin, Shkuropotsky, Kolesnikov and Ergushov. The Cossacks played various games, danced and sang, it was really nice. Then [we] crossed to the right side and ran around in the bushes there. On the way back [we] caught up with the Hundred that was walking along the bank and they rode along with us while "djigiting."[33] Had tea at Papa's on the train. Had dinner 4, while Papa [ate] with Mama. Tormented and scared Toto, played hide and seek.

+10
25 August Thursday
Sat with the children. At breakfast, I sat with U[ncle] Sergei and Nilov. Went to see some kind of new motor, then went down to

33. Georgian custom of doing acrobatic tricks while galloping on a horse.

the Dnieper and returned by boats. Tea in Papa's tent. Talked with Gramatin. Dinner 4, Mama with Papa. Kiki was here and Toto.[34] Played hide and seek in the dark, in the wagons with Gramatin too.

+11

26 August Friday

Sat with the children. At breakfast, sat with U[ncle] Georgi and Ezin. Walked along the Dnieper and ran among the bushes. Had tea upstairs at Papa's. Wrote. Dinner 4 with Mama, Papa, Igor and Anya. Mordvinov came. We sat and ran with him on the wood.

+9

27 August Saturday

Sat with the children. At breakfast, I sat with U[ncle] Georgi and Nilov. Went to the same place on the Dnieper. After that, Papa and I rowed with Count Grabbe at the wheel. Ran among the bushes. Had tea upstairs at Papa's. Were 4 with Mama at *Vsenoshnaya*. Dinner 4 with Papa, Mama, Anya and Mordvinov. Kiki and Dmitri were here and we played hide and seek with Mordvinov [officer], Kasilov, Pakchurenkin and Kazak on the wood.

28 August Sunday

Went to *Obednya*. At breakfast sat with Uncle Georgi[35] and Dmitri. Went up the Dnieper in a ferry. Later, Papa and I rowed, while Count Grabbe was behind the wheel. Had tea at Papa's. Talked with Gramatin. Had dinner 4 with Mama, Papa, Kiki and Anya. Dmitri was here.

+12

29 August Monday

Played with the children, threw them into a hole and pulled them out. We went to a monastery. At breakfast I sat with U[ncle] Sergei and Nilov. Went by motor to the bridge and from there returned up the Dnieper to Mogilev on a motor that stopped on the banks. Had tea with Papa. Were at *Vsenoshnaya*. Dinner 4 with Papa,

---

34. Mordvinov's nickname.

35. Grand Duke Georgi Mikhailovich, the tsar's first cousin once removed.

Mama, Anya, Igor and Dmitri. Kiki came over. Dmitri sat with us on the beam.

30 August Tuesday
Went to *Obednya*. At breakfast sat with Uncle Georgi and Dmitri. Went to the same place in motorboats. Children from the city garden were playing there. Returned during a rain storm. Had tea at Papa's. Went to [see] a cinematograph, the continuation of "Mystery of Nogorok" and others. Had dinner 4 with Papa and Mama, Dmitri, Anya and Kiki.

+8
31 August Wednesday
We tossed the children into the pit with Lavrov and Yergushev. At breakfast, I sat with U[ncle] Sergei and Voeikov. Went along the Dnieper and ran among the bushes. Tea at Papa's. Dinner 4 with Papa, Mama, U[ncle] Mimi and Kiki. Talked with Yergushev and Khodarovsky, learned to whistle through the fingers.

+5
1 September Thursday
Sat with U[ncle] Mimi and U[ncle] Sergei at breakfast. We went in motors to the woods where we walked and gathered mushrooms. Had tea at Papa's. Played with the children watching Gramatin and Khodarovsky. Dinner 4 with Mama, Papa, Dmitri, U[ncle] Mimi and Igor. Afterwards Igor left and we sat in the sitting room.

+8
2 September Friday
We were with Gramatin on the pathway and afterwards threw the children into the pit. Sat with Dmitri and U[ncle] Sergei at breakfast. Went in a motor and stopped at the Dnieper where we ran among the bushes. Had tea at Papa's. Played with the children. Dinner 4 with Papa, Mama, Dmitri, U[ncle] Mimi and Kiki. Looked at pictures.

+8
3 September Saturday

We threw the children into the pit. Lavrov led the game. At breakfast, I sat with U[ncle] Mimi and Nilov. Went by motorboat to the old place. Ran around in the bushes and ripped up yearlings. Had tea at Papa's. Were at *Vsenoshnaya*. Dinner 4 with Papa, Mama, Kiki and Dmitri. Looked at pictures. Passed the time awfully [well] with Dmitri.

4 September Sunday
Went to *Obednya*. Wrote to Zhilik. Papa was at Stavka. At breakfast sat with Dmitri and Uncle Sergei. Rode to the upper bridge in motors and walked. Had tea in the train. Said goodbye to Papa, Alexei, and the children whom we [playfully] pushed into a pit in the ground and left. Had dinner 4 with Isa, Kiki, Khodarovsky, Ergushev, and the engineer. P.V.P. read to us.

+3
5 September Monday
P.V.P. read to us. Breakfast and dinner 4 with Isa, Mama, Kiki, Khodarovsky, Ergushev, P.V.P. and engineers. P.V.P. read to us a lot and we smoked and ate fruit. We arrived at Ts[arskoe] S[elo]. Walked at the stations as usual. Were with ours at the infirmary. They brought 4 wounded Cossacks from the 4th Hundreds convoy— troopers Vasilenko, Petrenko, Barantsev and Cossack Nikishchenko.

6 September Tuesday
Went to Znamenie. Rode with O and Trina. Had breakfast with Mama and Isa. Went to our infirmary with A. Had tea with Mama and Uncle Pavel. Had a music lesson. Had dinner 4 with Mama and Anya. Went to the sisters' infirmary. Played ruble.

Letter from Maria to Alexei at Stavka—

Tsarskoe Selo. 6 Sept., 1916. My darling little soul, Alexei! You cannot even imagine how boring it is to be back at Tsarskoe. Today, when I first woke up I was really surprised to be back in my room. I saw you in my dream, as if we never left you. The head of the infirmary, Baron Kaulbars,[36] also wanted to be in the photo and sat

36. General Baron Kaulbars was a member of the Supreme Military Council of Russia.

on the little table which you [would normally] put near the bed, Of course the table couldn't hold him, one leg broke, and he fell, it was all very funny. I kiss you and dear Papa affectionately. Your sister, Maria. May God keep you.

Maria's diary—

7 September Wednesday
Had Russian language, history and arithmetic lessons. Went to Zolotarev's funeral service, his body was brought over and buried at the brethren cemetery. Had breakfast 4 with Mama, Silaev and Ravtopulo. Went to the G. P. with T and A. Rode 4 with Trina. Had tea 4 with Mama and Anya. Had dinner, went to *Vsenoshnaya* and to Anya's with Mama. Grigori and Alya were at Anya's.

Maria to Nicholas II—

8 September. My sweet and dear Papa, this morning we went to the early *Obednya* and then to our infirmary with Shvybz, the 4th Hundred Cossacks are such darlings and they talk so much that it makes it hard to leave. They tell [us] all about how it was and how they were driven around cities, when they were wounded. Such foolish people, they do not know that [they are] the Convoy, and referred to them as Cherkestzy and said that they are not Russian. They were terribly offended.—It was so sad yesterday at the funeral of poor Zolotarev. Now I will go riding with Mama, Shvybz and Anya, while Olga and Tatiana with Irina. Shegolev came to our infirmary, he has terrible dropsy and we drained one and half buckets of fluid from him. He lost a lot of weight and got old, we saw him today.— And what is Dmitri up to? Time to end. I kiss you and Alexei affectionately and warmly, like I love you. May God keep you. + Your Kazanetz

Maria's diary—

8 September Thursday
Went to *Obednya* 4 with Mama. Then played kosti with Shvybz at the new infirmary. Had breakfast 4 with Mama and dinner. Rode with Mama, Anya and A. Had tea with Mama, Anya and Kiki. Sat with Isa. Went 4 to the sisters' infirmary and played ruble.

+2

9 September Friday

Had Russian and religion lessons. Went for a ride with A and Trina. Breakfast and dinner 4 with Mama. Was at the new infirmary with O and A. We 4 went for a drive with Isa. Tea 4 with Mama and Anya. Had music [lesson]. O and T read to me. Were 4 at the sisters' infirmary. Talked with Boris R and played ruble.

+4

10 September Saturday

Had German and religion lessons. Went for a drive with Trina. Breakfast 4 with Mama and Anya. Was at the new infirmary with A. Had tea and had dinner 4 with Mama. Went 4 to *Vsenoshnaya*. Went to a panikhida in Petrograd with Mama, O and T. Nastenka's mother died. Sat with Mama after we got home.

+7

11 September Sunday

Went to *Obednya* 4. After that was with Shvybz at the new infirmary. Breakfast, tea and dinner 4 with Mama. Were 4 at the G[rand] P[alace]. We drove in the motorcar along the boulevard. T read to me. Got my lessons ready. Went 4 to the sisters' infirmary and played ruble.

Pierre Gilliard to Maria—

Mogilev, Sunday 11 September, 1916. Madam and dear pupil! I thank you for the letter with all my heart. I am glad that my retelling of the "Mysterious Hand" interested you. In your letter, the sentences are formed rather well, but you still have a lot of orthographic mistakes. Look carefully at the enclosed sheet of paper with corrections. I advise you to even copy the corrected words.

For the next lesson, prepare one of the exercises which I pointed out to you, or you can write to me again, answering the following questions. Did you have a lesson with Madam Conrad? What did you do at the lesson? Which faery tale or story did you read? Are you currently reading anything in French? Do you go to your infirmary often? How many wounded officers and soldiers do you have

there? Do you go to Her Majesty's infirmary in the evenings? And so forth. Your letter was very entertaining. Grand Duke Dimitri read it and laughed a lot, especially in the beginning and at the end. Prince Igor[37] also read it, as it was brought to me in "The Torch." Did you know, I think that your two cousins, write rather badly in French, they did not notice your mistakes. They even thought that you write very well. When I told them that there are many mistakes, Grand Duke Dimitri looked at your letter again and exclaimed: "Ah yes! Hier is spelled hière, is it not"!!! I laughed heartily, and the grand duke too, he was so happy after all that he found at least one mistake!!! Now you will be able to tease him. Prince Igor forgot his French even more, if that is possible. I advised both of them to hurry up and take French lessons. Mister Gibbs was very touched by your sweet attentiveness and stated that he falls to your feet. Alexei Nikolaevich says that he embraces you . . . slightly. And I beg you to consider me your loyal and loving servant.
Pierre Gilliard

Maria's diary—

+5
12 September Monday
Had arithmetic, Russian and history lessons. Went for a ride with A and Trina. Breakfast 4 with Mama. Went for a drive with O, and Mama with Anya. Got my lessons ready. Had a music lesson. Dinner 4 with Mama and Kiki. We went to the sisters' infirmary and played ruble.

Maria to Nicholas II—

12 September. My dear darling Papa! I am sending you the pictures you wanted, and to Svetlichny too. One of the wounded sergeants from the 4th Hundred has recovered already, but the committee is not allowing him to return to the Hundred, but sending him home to the Caucuses. He is rather unhappy and at first did not even want to agree but they later convinced him. We have not yet played tennis. It's either there is no time, or the weather is bad, raining. Right now, I am sitting in the classroom and I am supposed to have a les-

---

37. Igor Konstantinovich, son of Grand Duke Konstantin Konstantinovich (KR).

son with P.V.P., but he is busy writing the lesson schedule for the winter and is snorting through his nose terribly. He is continuing to write, and I am too. We are now making all sorts of warm clothes for the children who live in Mogilev across from our train. Every time we get back from Mogilev it feels more and more lonesome. You cannot even imagine how I envy P.V.P. who is going to [see] you. But I think he would not allow me [to go instead of him] because as soon as he got to Tsarskoe he caught a dreadful cold. No lesson materialized, P.V.P. only said to do without him. Now there will also be a history lesson, and then I am free and will go riding with Shvybz and Trina. I kiss you and Alexei affectionately and warmly. May God keep you! Your Kazanetz. Yesterday my new commander came to see me for the first time, he told [me] a lot of nice things about the regiment, so I was very happy even.

Maria's diary—

+2
13 September Tuesday
Had German and history lessons. Went for a ride with A and Trina. Breakfast 4 with Mama and Anya. Was at the new infirmary with A and played tennis with Viv'evs de Shestobren and Tolstov. Had tea, were at the *Vsenoshnaya* and dined 4 with Mama. Went 4 to the sisters' infirmary and played ruble.

14 September Wednesday
Went 4 to *Obednya*. Then went to the new infirmary with Shvybz, had *moleben* there. Had breakfast 4 with Mama and Anya. In the afternoon went to the G.P. with T and A. Rode 4 with Mama, Anya. Had tea with the same. Rode with A and Shura. Had dinner 4 with Mama. The same went to Anya's and saw Alya and Grigori. Went 4 to the sisters' infirmary. Played ruble.

15 September Thursday
Had German and French lessons with M. Konrad. The Japanese Prince Kan'in[38] had breakfast with us. I sat with Uncle Georgi and Uncle Pavel. Rode 4 with Isa. Had tea 4 with Mama. There was

38. Prince Kan'in Kotohito was the sixth head of a cadet branch of the Japanese imperial family.

music. Read. Had dinner 4 with Mama and Kiki. Went to the sisters' infirmary, played tennis.

+1/2 / -1
16 September Friday
Were 4 at the *panikhida* for Batushka's soldier son, who was killed. Breakfasted 4 with Mama and Anya. Was at the new infirmary with A. Tea 4 with Mama and Nastenka. Had music. Dinner 4 with Mama. Went to the sisters' infirmary with T and A.

Maria to Nicholas II—

16 September. My golden Papa! It is raining hard. In the morning we 4 went to the Vetka with Isa, where Olga's medical train arrived. There were lots of wounded and the guards too. Wonderful people from the Preobrazhensky regiment, so huge. At 12 o'clock 20 minutes we will go to the Feodorovsky Cathedral, where they will have a panikhida for Batushka's son who was killed. I was thinking of going horseback riding this morning, but the weather is rotten, it is raining and damp. All the leaves are rather yellow here and a lot of them fell. Please thank Derevenko very much for the pictures. It was very nice to see Zinovy Ivanovich Ishizaki at breakfast yesterday. He showed Olga a menu from afar, reminiscing about how he wrote to her in Mogilev in Japanese. I sat with Uncle Georgi and Uncle Pavel, so it was nice and not embarrassing. Right now, I must change into black for the panikhida. These days there are always *panikhidas* for someone. Today Nastenka will come to see Mama. We have not seen her since the panikhida. Well, farewell, goodbye. May God keep you +. I hug you tightly and kiss you warmly, and Alexei too. Your Kazanetz. So tiresome that Igor left on a holiday, just when we are not there.

Maria's diary—

17 September Saturday
Had German, French, Madame Conrad and arithmetic lessons. Had breakfast 4 with Mama and Isa. Went to the new infirmary with A. Then 4 went to the Kazansky cemetery and the Brethren [one] for Zolotarev. Had tea and dinner 4 with Mama. Went to

Vsenoshnaya and 4 to the infirmary. Played ruble.—Drank hot chocolate at our infirmary in the afternoon as it was the birthdays of nurses Maltzev and Adamov.

18 September Sunday
Went 4 to *Obednya.* Then went to the new infirmary and G.P. with A. Had breakfast 4 with Mama. Rode 4 in a motor around Bablovo and Pavlovsk. Had tea 4 with Mama and Anya. Olga read to me and Shvybz. Had dinner 4 with Mama and Kiki. Went to the sisters' infirmary. Played ruble. It was snowing.

0
19 September Monday
Had arithmetic, religion and history lessons. Went for a drive with A and Trina. Breakfast 4 with Mama and Trina. Was at the new infirmary during the day with A. After that we 4 went for a drive in a motor. Tea 4 with Mama and Anya. We saw Teglya.[39] Had music. Dinner 4 with Mama. Were 4 at the sisters' infirmary. I sat with Kiknadze and played ruble.

0/-2
20 September Tuesday
Had a German and a history lesson. Went for a drive with A and Trina. Breakfasted, had dinner and had tea 4 with Mama. Was with A at the new infirmary. Went for a drive 4 with Marie P who had breakfast with us. Had music [lesson]. Were 4 at the sisters' infirmary and played ruble.

21 September Wednesday
Had lessons, History, Batushka. Rode with A and Trina. Had breakfast with Mama and A. In the afternoon went to the infirmary with A and played "Bicks" with Tolstov. Had tea 4 with Mama and Anya. There was [a] music [lesson]. Had dinner 4 with Mama, and the same went to Anya's, where Grigori,[40] his wife and a monk were. From there, 4 went to the sisters' infirmary. Played ruble.

39. Shura's sister.
40. Rasputin.

+2
22 September Thursday
Had French, German and history lessons. Breakfasted 4 with Mama
and Anya. Was with O and A at the G[rand] P[alace]. Went for a
drive 4 in a motor and were at E. V. Silaev's where were Lev Z, Lena,
Verochka and Alia. We sat, ate nuts and drank wine. Tea 4 with
Mama and Nastenka. Had music [lesson]. Dinner 4 with Mama.
Went with T and A to the sisters' infirmary and played checkers
and *puzach* with Volodya K. We played ruble.

+2
23 September Friday
Went up to the "Korbo." Had a lesson with Batushka. Breakfast
and dinner 4 with Mama. Was at the new infirmary with A. Played
billiards with Tolya and Ikotsky Tea 4 with Mama and U[ncle]
Niki.[41] Had music [lesson]. Were 4 at the sisters' infirmary and
played ruble.

+3
24 September Saturday
Had a German lesson with M. Konrad and arithmetic. Breakfast
and dinner 4 with Mama. Was with A at the new infirmary. Went
for a drive 4 in the motor. Tea 4 with Mama, U[ncle] Pavel and
Marie. Were 4 at *Vsenoshnaya* with Marie. After that went 4 to the
sisters' infirmary and played ruble, sat with Volodya K.

25 September Sunday
Went to *Obednya*. Then to the new infirmary with Shvybz. Vikt.
Er. returned from Essentuki.[42] Had breakfast and dinner 4 with
Mama. Walked 4 then rode with Trina. Had tea 4 with Mama and
Anya. Read. Rode bicycles around the rooms with A. Went 4 to the
sisters' infirmary. Played ruble.

-3
26 September Monday
Went with Shvybz up the Korbo. Had [a] history [lesson]. Breakfast

41 Grand Duke Nikolai Mikhailovich.
42 Town in Georgia.

and dinner 4 with Mama. Were 4 at the G[rand] P[alace] and afterwards went for a drive in a motor. Was with A at the new infirmary. Papasha, Mamasha and Ergushev arrived. Tea 4 with Mama
and Anya. Had music. We went bike riding. Were 4 at the sisters'
infirmary and sat with Volodya and did puzzles.

+5
27 September Tuesday
Had German and history lessons. Went for a walk with A and Trina.
Breakfast, tea and dinner 4 with Mama. Was at the new infirmary
with A. The 4 of us went for a walk. Had music. Read. Were 4 at
the sisters' infirmary and played ruble.

+3
28 September Wednesday
Had history and religion lessons. Went for a drive with A and Trina.
Breakfasted 4, but Mama was in bed, had tea the same with Anya.
Was at the new infirmary with A. Vikt. Er. was there. Had music.
Dinner 4 and Mama on the sofa. Were 4 at the sisters' infirmary
and played ruble.

+4
29 September Thursday
Had lessons German, M Konrad[43] and history. Breakfast and dinner
4 with Mama on the sofa. Was with O and A at the G[rand]
P[alace]. Went for a drive 4 in a motor. Tea 4 with Mama and Sonia
Dehn. Had music. Went bike riding with Shvybz. Were 4 at the sis-
ters' infirmary where an orchestra [symphony] played. Volhynsk
Regiment.

30 September Friday
Read and wrote. Had breakfast and dinner 4 with Mama on the
couch. Walked 4 and passed by the old infirmary, but did not go
in, as Soloviev has something along the lines of mumps. Had tea
with Mama and Anya. Went to *Vsenoshnaya*. 4 with Mama stopped
by Anya's where Grigori and the Bishops Isidor and Melkhisedek

43. Madame Konrad was the French tutor.

were. Went 4 to the sisters' infirmary, put together a puzzle with Volodya. Played ruble.

-2

1 October Saturday

Were 4 at *Obednya* and after that was with A at the old infirmary where now [are] lower [ranks] and there was a *moleben*. After that to the new infirmary where the officers remain. Breakfast 4 with Mama and M Zizi. Went for a walk 4. The 4 of us were at a concert at the G.P. Tea 4 with Mama and Anya. The 4 of us went to *Vsenoshnaya*. 4 had dinner with Mama and the same were at the sisters' infirmary and played ruble.

+3

2 October Sunday

Were 4 at *Obednya*. After that went with Shvybz to the old and new infirmaries. Breakfast 4 with Mama, Nastenka and Trina. Went to the train and went to Mogilev. Dinner 4 with Isa, Anya, Resin, Kern, Khodarovsky, Botkin, Voeikov and Shvedov. Sat eating nuts and chatting 4 with Shvedov. Went out at Bologoe. Had tea.

+10

3 October Monday

Went for a walk at Yartsevo station. Breakfasted the same as yesterday evening. Went for a walk at Oresh. We arrived at Mogilev. Papa and the whole suite met us. Tea 4 with Papa and Mama. Went with Papa to Alexei whose stomach hurts and was lying down. Played rich rach and *akulina* with him. Went back. Dinner 4 on the train with Papa, Mama, Kiki and Anya. Walked with Papa on the platform.

4 October Tuesday

Went to the First and Second Hundred parade, the infantry row. Ergushev, Lavrov, Gramarik and Ganushkin were transferred to the Convoy. At breakfast sat with Uncle Georgi and Maksimovich. At this time the Cossacks sang and then danced very well. Drove to the woods with Papa and the suite, where we walked. Had tea on the train. Then reviewed Grandmama's medical train. [I] went to Alexei's and played with him. Had dinner 4 with Papa, Mama and Dmitri. Papa read Teffi's[44] stories to us. Had tea.

+3
5 October Wednesday
We were all at *Obednya*. After that were congratulations. At breakfast, I sat with U[ncle] Pavel and U[ncle] Sandro. Went for a walk in the garden. We all had tea at Papa's. Were 5 and Papa at the cinematograph, was among others, "20 Years Among Predatory Beasts," "The Town of Ghent Terribly" [illeg.].

+1
6 October Thursday
We went for a walk with Lavrov. At breakfast I sat with U[ncle] Sergei and Buchanan [English Ambassador]. We drove in motors and on foot to the Dnieper where we put together a fire and went back to the waterfall. Had tea at Papa's. Talked with Blushkin. Dinner 4 with Papa, Mama, Mordvinov and Anya. Hide and seek with the same, Kiki and Blushkin in darkened carriages.

+8
7 October Friday
We went with Blushkin to the woods and made a fire. At breakfast I sat with U[ncle] Sergei and Maksimovich. Went up to the falls on the Dnieper and boiled potatoes, borsch and chestnuts. Had tea at Papa's. Wrote letters. Dinner 4 with Papa and Mama, Anya and Kiki. Mordvinov was here and we played hide and seek with him.

+5
8 October Saturday
Gave all the children some knitted things. Went with Gramatin to a brook in the forest. At breakfast sat with U[ncle] Georgi and Voeikov. All went for a walk in the woods. Had tea at U[ncle] Pavel's at the little house he found. Dinner 4 with Papa, Mama, Igor and Anya. Mordvinov was here. We all played hide and seek and Lavrov too. Toto broke his pince-nez.

---

44. Russian humorist writer; Teffi was the pseudonym of Nadezhda Alexandrovna Lokhvitskaya.

+8
9/22 October Sunday
We were at *Obednya*, ate a sample of the 1st Hundred's food. At breakfast I sat with Ozerov and Maksimovich. We drove on the Bykovsky Highway and stopped not far from the chapel. We went for a walk and saw two trains while the others boiled schi[45] and fried potatoes. Had tea at Papa's. Marsengol [Italian military agent] arrived by train.
I played the guitar and sang. Dinner 4 with Mama, Papa, Isa, Kiki and Anya. We all played hide and seek including Mordvinov and Galushkin.

+7
10 October Monday
Went with Galushkin to our [illeg.] train and arranged all sorts of things out of ropes and cushions. At breakfast, I sat with U[ncle] Georgi and Ivanov. In the day we went to the woods, walked and ate potatoes. Had tea at Uncle Georgi's upstairs at the dacha. Dinner 4 with Papa, Mama, Anya and Mordvinov. Vikt. Er., Aleks-Aleks and Nik.Vas. arrived and we sat with them and went to the train and checked all the things. Later we put out all the lights and called Toto and hid while he looked for us and he fell through the cushions and touched the rope with his nose. Found everyone except Nik. Vas. since it was time for tea. Had tea without [illeg.] very [illeg.] and good.

+6
11 October Tuesday
Lyonya came while we were with Aleks-Aleks, gave sweets, was 18. At breakfast I sat with U[ncle] Georgi and ?. We went to the woods. We went on foot 6 versts for an hour and then 2 versts more. Had tea at Papa's. We had a cinematograph "The Madman in the Mask" "Japanese Spring" "Bear Cub" "Kind Max." We talked amusingly with Vikt. Er. Dinner 4 with Papa, Mama, Anya and Igor. Went for a walk and took Igor home. We went with Vikt. Er., Nik Vas and Serg. Georg. To the train and got ready all the things and made a

45. Type of soup made with sorrel.

scarecrow from my jacket. After that Toto came and looked but couldn't find Tatiana or Nik. Vas. I hurt myself under my hips on the ropes that had been done. After that we had tea.

+4
12 October Wednesday
We sat with Vikt. Er. We chopped wood for a fire. At breakfast, I sat with U[ncle] Georgi and Zhelov. Went to the woods to the old Stavka and went for a walk there. We 4 went back on foot with Toto and Count Grabbe to the train. We all had tea on the train. Said farewell to Papa, Alexei and the others and departed for Ts[arskoe] S[elo]. Dined and had tea 4 with Mama, Anya, Count Grabbe, Vikt. Er., Khodarovsky (P. Iv), Resin, Botkin, Isa and the engineers. Vikt. Er. sat with us in the cabin in the evening, looked at pictures, smoked and chatted.

-1
13 October Thursday
We wrote. Went for a walk at Likhoslavl Station. Breakfasted with the same as yesterday, and dined with them too. Vikt. Er. came to sit with us, smoked and drew. We all had tea. After Tosno Station, Vikt. Er. came to us again and drew me and I him, but of course it didn't go well for me. After dinner we arrived at Tsarskoe Selo. Went with A to the new infirmary and the old. Had tea 4 with Mama. Unpacked.

-2
14 October Friday
We went for a walk with Trina. Breakfast and dinner 4 with Mama on the sofa. Was with A at the new and old infirmaries. We played billiards with Vasiliev and Tolstov. Had tea 4 with Mama and Nastenka. Had music [lesson]. Were 4 at the sisters' infirmary. Sat at Syroboyarsky's. We played ruble.

15 October Saturday
Had lessons, German, French and arithmetic. Had breakfast 4 with Mama and Trina. Went 4 to the G.P., then rode in a motor. Went

to the new and old infirmaries with A. Had tea 4 with Mama and Anya. Went 4 with Mama to *Vsenoshnaya*. Had dinner and went to Anya's, saw Grigori, Mitya, Bishop Isador. Went 4 to the sisters' infirmary. Played ruble. Sat with Syroboyarsky, Rita, Volodya, etc.

-3
16 October Sunday
The 4 of us were at *Obednya* with Mama, after that at the old and new infirmaries. We played billiards with Medvedev. Breakfast, dinner and tea 4 with Mama. 4 went for a drive, and Mama with Anya. We were at Isa's, she is unwell. Tania Ravtopulo[46] came. 4 with Mama went to the sisters' infirmary. Sat with Syroboyarsky and played ruble.

+1
17 October Monday
Had arithmetic and history lessons. Breakfast and dinner 4 with Mama. In the day 4 went to the G[rand] P[alace] and after that went for a drive in the motor. Was at the old and new infirmaries with A. Vikt. Er. came there. Had tea 4 with Mama and Anya. Had music [lesson]. Were 4 at the sisters' infirmary and sat with Syroboyarsky and played ruble.

-2
18 October Tuesday
Had German and history lessons. Breakfast and tea 4 with Mama. Went for a drive with Mama, A and Anya. Was with A at the old and new infirmaries. Had music [lesson]. Sat with Isa who is ill. Dinner 4 with Mama and Kiki. Were 4 at the sisters' infirmary and sat with Syroboyarsky and played ruble.

+2
19 October Wednesday
Had a history lesson. After that was with A at the old infirmary. Breakfast 4 with Mama. Was with A at the new infirmary. 4 went with Mama to the station to meet Papa and Alexei who arrived from

46. Boris's sister.

Mogilev. Went for a walk with Papa, O and A. 4 had tea with Papa and Mama. Had music [lesson]. We went to Isa's. Dinner 4 with Papa, Mama, Anya and Toto. Sat 4 with Toto.

20 October Thursday
Went to Petrograd with Papa, Mama, O and T to the Fortress for the funeral *Obednya* for Grandpapa.[47] Had breakfast 5 with Papa, Mama and Igor. Walked 4 with Papa and Mama [rode] in an equipage. Had tea and went to *Vsenoshnaya*, the same confessed. Had dinner 4 with Papa, Mama and Igor.

21 October Friday
Everyone received communion. Then had tea. Walked with Papa and A. Had breakfast 5 with Mama, Papa and Ioann. Went to the new and old infirmaries with A. Played billiards with A, Medvedev and Lozhnov. Had tea 4 with Mama and Papa. The 2 Makarovs, 2 Derevenko,[48] 1 Derevenko and Tanya Raftopuldo [*sic*] came over for Alexei's cinematograph. Went to *Vsenoshnaya* with Mama. Had dinner 4 with Papa and Mama and Ioann. Went to Anya's with Mama and Papa, and Grigori was there. Sat and had tea.

+3
22 October Saturday
Was with Shvybz at the new and old infirmaries. Played billiards with A, Medvedev and Mordvinov. Breakfast 5 with Papa, Mama and Gavril. Went for a walk 4 with Papa and Mama was in the equipage. Had tea with the same. We went to *Vsenoshnaya* with Papa and Mama. Dinner 4 with Mama, Papa and Gavril. Anya was here. Pasted pictures in the album with Papa.

+3
23 October Sunday
Was with A, A, Papa and Mama at Church. Breakfast 5 with Papa, Mama, Tsvetsynsky and Dmitri. Was with A at the old infirmary. Went for a walk 4 with Papa, and Mama in the equipage. Was with

---

47. Tsar Alexander III, who died in 1894.

48. Kolya Derevenko, Alexei's playmate, and his brother—sons of Dr. Derevenko, the imperial physician.

A at the new infirmary and played billiards with A, Shakh-Nazarov and Dmitriev. Tea and dinner 4 with Mama and Papa. At the cinematograph at Alexei's were the 2 Makarovs, 2 Derevenko, and 1 Derevenko. Anya was here. Papa read a funny story.

+2
24 October Monday
Had lessons—arithmetic, religion, history and Russian. Breakfast 5 with Papa, Mama, Sandro and Petrovsky. Was at the old infirmary with A. Went for a walk 4 with Papa, and Mama in the equipage. Was with A at the new infirmary. Vikt. Er. was there. Played billiards with A, Tolst[oy] and Koltov. Had tea with A. Had English and music lessons. Dinner 4 with Papa and Mama. Anya was here. Papa read theory.

25 October Tuesday
Had English, German, French and History lessons. Breakfast 5 with Papa, Mama and Kiki. Saw Papa and Alexei off [to Mogilev]. Were 4 at Infirmary 11 and Lianozovsko. After that was with A at the new and old infirmaries. Vikt. Er. and Shakh-Nazarov were there. Had tea. Had English and music lessons. Dinner 4 with Mama. We were at Anya's with Grigori, Matryosha and Varya.[49] Were 4 at the sisters' infirmary. Played *bloshki* and ruble.

26 October Wednesday
Had Russian and history lessons. Was with A at the old infirmary. Breakfast 4 with Mama. Were the same at the wedding of Capt of the 57th Trofimov and Nina. Was with A at the new infirmary. Played billiards—me with Shibaev and A with Zhilinsky. Had tea. Had my hair washed. A and I rearranged our room. Dinner 4 with Mama. Were at the sisters' infirmary and played *bloshki*.

+5
27 October Thursday
Had lessons: German, French and history. Breakfasted 4 with Mama and Sonia Dehn. Was with A and O at the G[rand] P[alace] and

49. Matryosha (Matryona) and Varya (Varvara)—two daughters of Rasputin.

then with A at the old and new infirmaries. I played billiards with A, Tolst., and Koltov. Shakh-Nazarov was there. Tea 4 with Mama and Anya. We were at Isa's and then there was music [lesson]. Dinner 4 with Mama. Were 4 at the sister's infirmary. Sat with Syroboyarsky. We played ruble.

+4
28 October Friday
Had English, Russian and religion lessons. Went 4 with Mama, Anya and Isa to Petrograd. Breakfast on the train. Went to the Winter infirmary, 360. After that 4 with Mama went to the Church of the Virgin-Quick-to-Hear. Had tea with the same and Isa, Vish. and others. Had music [lesson]. Dinner 4 with Mama. Were 4 at the sisters' infirmary. Sat with Syroboyarsky. Played *bloshki* with A, Pr. Eristov and Zenchenko.

+2
29 October Saturday
Had lessons—English, German, French and arithmetic. Breakfast, tea and dinner 4 with Mama. Went for a drive in the motor with O and A. Was at the old and new infirmaries with A. I played billiards with Loginov and Shvybz played with Dmitriev. Vikt. Er. was there. 4 were at *Vsenoshnaya*. After dinner we were at the sisters' infirmary and I sat with Syroboyarsky. Played *bloshki* with Petrov, Zenchenko, Prince Eristov and Rita.

+4
30 October Sunday
Were 4 with Mama at *Obednya*. After that was with A at the old and new infirmaries. Played billiards with Zhelinsky and A played rich rach with Koltov. Breakfast, tea and dinner 4 with Mama. Were with the same at the G[rand] P[alace] and there was a concert. Were 4 with Mama at the sisters' infirmary, played ruble and sat with Syroboyarsky.

Maria to Nicholas II—

30 October. My dear Papa darling! Today is already two years that

the dear Grand Palace infirmary exists, and therefore we must go to a concert there. Your friend Lersky will be there, I am happy to see him as he usually tells such nice funny stories. I am now sitting at Mama's. In the morning we went to an early *Obednya* and after that to our infirmary. At first, we went to [see] the lower ranks then the officers. There we played billiards. I played like swine of course, because it is hard without practice. Yesterday Viktor Erastovich came to our infirmary. He wins over everyone in billiards. Time to end as I have to complete [sewing] two shirts for the officers who are leaving our infirmary and are bidding their farewells to Mama at 6 o'clock. I kiss and squeeze you darlings affectionately. May God keep you. + both. Your Kazanetz.

Maria's diary—

0

31 October Monday

Had lessons: arithmetic, religion, history and Russian. Breakfast, tea and dinner 4 with Mama. Was with A at the old and new infirmaries and played billiards with Tolst., and Shvybz with Koltov. The 4 of us went for a ride in a motor. We were at Isa's and played. Were at the sisters' infirmary and sat with Nikiforov and Ulyanov, played ruble.

-3

1 November Tuesday

Had lessons, German, M. Konrad (Fr[ench]) and history. Breakfast and dinner 4 with Mama. Was with A at the old and new infirmaries. Played billiards with Koltov and A with Nekotsky. Vikt. Er. was here. Went for a drive with A and Trina. Tea 4 with Mama and Anya. Had music [lesson]. Were 4 at the sisters' infirmary and sat with Nikiforov and Ulyanov. Played *bloshki* with Zenchenko and Rita with Pr[ince] Eristov.

-7

2 November Wednesday

Had lessons, history and Batushka. Was with A at the old infirmary. Breakfast and dinner 4 with Mama. Was with T and A at the

Gr[and] P[alace] and after that with A at the new infirmary. Played billiards with Longinov and A with Dmitriev. Tea 4 with Mama and Anya. Talked with Alexei on the new telephone at Mogilev. Had music [lesson]. We went to Isa's. Sasha Melikova was there. Were 4 at the sisters' infirmary and sat with Syroboyarsky, Nikiforov and Ulyanov. After that with Mama at Anya's. Grigori and Bishop Isidor were there.

-4

3 November Thursday
Was with A at the old infirmary. Went for a drive with A and Trina. Breakfast and dinner 4 with Mama. There was a *moleben*. Went for a drive 4, and Mama with Anya. Was with A at the new infirmary. Played billiards with Dmitriev and A with Koltov. Tea 4 with Mama and Dmitri. We were at Isa's. We were at the sisters' infirmary. I sat with Nikiforov and Ulyanov.

Pierre Gilliard to Maria—

Mogilev, 3 November 1916. Madam and very dear pupil, I thank you wholeheartedly for your letter that P.V.P. gave me. Now that I am freer, I will be able to write to you often again, and I hope you will have time to answer me in order not to forget your French. I do not thank you for the nasty gift you told Alexis Nikolaevich by phone to give me. I will avenge myself later!!! Your little brother has a pain in his right leg. He does not suffer, but has a fairly strong swelling. It's too bad—everything was going so well and really it's not his fault. Since yesterday everything is white here and when we went for a walk we built a fortress of snow. It is freezing: in the day—5, at night—7, but the air is very good and there is a little sun. I am very happy that the lessons with Mrs. Conrad are working so well; she is an experienced mistress; may I beg you to greet her on my behalf? I have just started my lessons again with Nicholas Pavlovich, because during the trip it was impossible. We worked last night until 11:20. May I pray you, Madam and very dear pupil, to believe me, Your most affectionate and most devoted servant. P. Gilliard

Maria's diary—

-1

4 November Friday

Had a lesson with Batushka. Went for a drive with A and Trina. Breakfast and dinner 4 with Mama. Was with A at the old and new infirmaries. Was at Anna Pavlovna and her husband V's and played billiards with Lozhinov and A with Koltov. Tolst. had an operation. Had tea 4. O had a piano lesson and I accompanied her. Had music. Were 4 at the sisters' infirmary and played *bloshki* and ruble.

-1

5 November Saturday

Had lessons—German, M.K [Madame Konrad,] F[rench] and arithmetic. Breakfast and tea 4 with Mama. Was with A at the new infirmary and played billiards with Dmitriev while A played Loginov. Vikt. Er. was there. Were with Mama at *Vsenoshnaya*. Dinner with the same and Anya. We all went to the sisters' infirmary, sat with Nikiforov and Ulyanov on the heater.

-6

6 November Sunday

Were 4 with Mama at *Obednya*. Breakfast and dinner with the same. Was with A at the old infirmary. Were photographed. Went for a drive with A and Trina. Was with A at the new infirmary, Shakh-Nagarov was there. I played billiards with Dmitriev and A with Loginov. Went for a drive 4 and Mama with Anya. Had tea with the same. We 4 took photos of each other. Went 4 to the sisters' infirmary. Sat with Nikiforov and played ruble.

-4

7 November Monday

Had arithmetic, religion and history lessons. Was with A at the old infirmary. Breakfast, tea and dinner 4 with Mama. Was with O and A at the G[rand] P[alace] and after that with A at the new infirmary. Vikt. Er. was there. Stood in the guest room. There was music and at Isa's. We were at Anya's with Rita, Vikt. Er, Yuzik and Aleks. Aleks. Sat and talked cozily. Had tea. Saw Rita back to the infirmary.

-4

8 November Tuesday

Had German, French and history lessons. Breakfast, dinner and tea 4 with Mama. Was with A at the old infirmary. I played billiards with Koltov and A with Matvievich. Had music and after that with A and T at Isa's. Were 4 with Mama at the sisters' infirmary. Sat with Kasyanov (wounded again) and played ruble.

Pierre Gilliard to Maria—

Mogilev, November 8, 1916. Madam and very dear pupil, I thank you with all my heart for Your latest letter. I will give you some words that you absolutely must learn by heart to avoid some big mistakes. Alexis Nikolaevich is much, much better. He will get up tomorrow and will, I hope, even go out. He has taken lessons today. P. V. P. asks me to let Anastasia Nikolaevna know that General Voiekov reply is as follows. He ordered that the photographs of the Escort be handed to His Majesty. As for the photographs of the general himself, he forgot them in his office at Tsarskoe-Selo and no one can open it. He apologizes to Anastasia Nikolaevna and will send them to her as soon as possible. M. H. [The Mysterious Hand] has arrived in Moscow and there may be cinema on Thursday instead of today, Alexis Nikolaevich is already happy. I hope with all my heart for you that you will soon be able to come to Mogilev, I am looking forward to your arrival! I beg you to believe me, Madam and very dear pupil, Your very affectionate and very devoted servant. P. Gilliard

Maria's diary—

+1

9 November Wednesday

Had lessons—history and religion. Was with A at the old infirmary. Breakfast, tea and dinner 4 with Mama. Was with A at the old infirmary and played billiards with Dmitriev, A played with Ikhotsk. Had music and after that were at Isa's. Were 4 at the sisters' infirmary and played ruble. Were 4 at Anya's with Mama and Grigori.

-1

10 November Thursday
Had lessons, German, French with M.K., and history. Breakfast 4
with Mama and Elena G. Was with A at the old infirmary. Went
for a drive 4 and Mama with Anya. Was with A at the new infirmary
and played billiards with Vikt. Er. and A played with Dmitriev. Tea
and dinner 4 with Mama. Had music. Were 4 with Mama at the
sisters' infirmary and played ruble.

Maria to Nicholas II—

10 November. Papa my dear! Such joy to be going to [see] you. I
was afraid that we would not get to you before winter. Just now I
walked Mama, Olga and Tatiana to the infirmary. I will have a lesson with Batushka, and then I am thinking of taking a walk or else
riding with Shura. In the afternoon we will go to the medical train
named after Mama. They will have *moleben* there and tea with the
Metropolitan. Of course, Loman arranged this. Yesterday we went
to our infirmary with Shvybz. Viktor Erastovich was there too, and
we played billiards with him and one [other] wounded [patient]. It
is terribly nice to see chests in the hallway, gives one the feeling that
we are going soon. This time Nastenka is coming with us. I don't
think Isa is too happy, but I don't care as I like Nastenka more, she
is after all simpler than Isa. Time to end. I will also write to Alexei's
P.V.P., and I kiss you Papa my darling very very affectionately. May
Christ be with you. + Your very own Kazanetz. The pictures which
A. is in—[give] to Alexei, the rest are for you, the ones you wanted.

Maria's diary—

+2

11 November Friday
Had a lesson with Batushka. Went for a walk. Breakfast 4 with
Mama and Isa. We were 4 with Mama at her 's' train number 143.
There was a *moleben* at church. Went for a drive 4 in a motor. Was
with A at the old infirmary. Tea 4 with Mama and Kiki. Packed.
Went to Isa's. Dinner 4 with Mama, Rita and Grigori at Anya's.
Were 4 with Mama at the sisters' infirmary, didn't play *ruble*, be-
cause everyone cheated.

+5

12 November Saturday

Was with A at the new and old infirmaries. Played billiards with Dmitriev and A with Koltov. Parted. Breakfast 4 with Mama, Isa and Trina. Was with A at Znamenie. We went to the train. All had tea. Vikt. Er. sat with us. Dinner 4 with Anya, Nastenka, Kern, Voeikov, Khodorovski and Vikt. Er. The latter stayed on in the evening. We all had tea. Did not fall asleep for a long time because Shvybz was laughing.

+4

13 November Sunday

Sat with Vikt. Er. Breakfast 4 with Anya, Nastenka, Voeikov, Kern, Khadorovski and Vikt. Er. Drew and worked with Vikt. Er. We all had tea. Arrived at Mogilev and met Papa and Alexei and had tea with Papa. Dinner 4 with Papa, Mama, Nastenka and Anya. Sat with Nastenka, the others in the corridor with Vikt Er. Had tea.

+3

14 November Monday

We were at *Obednya*. After that we sampled the 1st Hundred's [food]. Papa went to Stavka while mine wrote. At breakfast, I sat with Maksimovich and Trepov. Went for a walk with Papa in his Governor's garden, worked, played cards. Had tea with the suite. Returned to the train. We wrote. Dinner 4 with Mama, Papa, Nastenka and Anya. Toto was here. We sat with him and Galushkin in the stateroom. We all had tea.

15 November Tuesday

I wrote. Olga played and we sang. At breakfast I sat with Maksimovich and Nilov. Went to see Mordvinov on the Orshinsky Highway by motorcar. Had tea. There was a cinematograph: Military naval picture and the second part of "The Mysterious Hand." "Neutrality" (Sharzh). Dinner 4 with Mama, Papa and Anya. Mordvinov was here. We sat on the wood. All had tea except for Protopopov.

+4 +2
16 November Wednesday
Sat on the wood with Lenka and Stefti. At breakfast, sat with Nilov and Ivanov. Went by motorcar to the Orshinsky Highway. We walked, lit a bonfire and baked potatoes. Had tea at Papa's. Returned to the train. I am sitting at Olga's. Were at a monastery at the miraculous icon of Our Lady of Mogilev. Dinner 4 with Mama, Papa, Anya and Nastenka. Stood with Shurik and walked. Toto was here. Sat with him and Shurik. Had tea.

-2
17 November Thursday
We went for a walk with Shurik and sat with the children. At breakfast I sat with Maksimovich and Voeikov. Went for a walk to the same place. 8 aeroplanes arrived there. After that we walked and drove with Toto. Had tea at Papa's. We wrote. Dinner 4 with Mama, Papa, Anya and Nastenka. Went for a walk in the field with Toto and Vikt. Er. and sat with the same. Olga threw cushions at Toto. Had tea.

+1
18 November Friday
Sat with Vikt. Er. and the children on the wood. At breakfast I sat with Maksimovich and U[ncle] Sergei. We went by motor to the Bykhovsky Highway and went for a walk in the woods. Tea at Papa's. Dinner 4 with Mama, Papa, Nastenka, Anya and Mosolov. Went for a walk with Toto and Galushkin and sat with the same, had tea.

+2
19 November Saturday
We went for a walk with Nik. Vas., Lenka, Olya, Bomos and other children and after that we sat. At breakfast, I sat with Maksimovich and U[ncle] Sandro. We went for a walk on the Orshinsky Highway. Had tea at Papa's. We went to the All-Night Vigil at the monastery. Dinner 4 with Mama, Papa, Nastenka and Toto. We went to visit the children with Toto and Yergushev. My ear was half asleep. Had tea.

+1
20 November Sunday
We were at *Obednya*. Papa went to Stavka and we wrote at his place. At breakfast I sat with U[ncle] Sergei and Gurko (who was at Papa's at Stavka). Went by motorcar to the Bykhovsky Highway and went for a walk. Had tea at U[ncle] Pavel's with all his family. We left the same [people]. We wrote, I played the piano. We dined as usual. We went for a walk with Papa. We visited the children. Lenka's got a baby brother. Sat with Shurik, Halla's wife and Konstantin. Had tea.

-2
21 November Monday
We were at Liturgy. We wrote and Papa was at Stavka. At breakfast, I sat with U[ncle] Sandro and Voeikov. Went for a walk on the Orshinsky Highway. We went there in motorcars. Had tea at Papa's. There was a French doctor, Cresson, released from captivity, who told us many things. I am sitting at Olga's. Dinner 4 with Mama, Papa, Anya and Nastenka. We went for a walk with Papa. Went with Vikt. Er. to Lenka, who was sleeping. Sat with Nastya by the fire and threw coal in it. Zhenya and Halla came.

-2
22 November Tuesday
Went for a walk with Vikt. Er., and played with the children. At breakfast I sat with Maksimovich and U[ncle] Sergei. Went to the highway with Mama and O. Went to 2 cottages. Had tea at Papa's. We were at the cinematograph 2 hours—"The Mysterious Hand" and the comedic "Invisible Thief." Dinner as always. Went with Nik. Vas. to Lenka's [illeg.] to the bonfire, there was also Halla's brother Vanya and foolish Fokla. Had tea.

-4
23 November Wednesday
Went for a walk with Nik. Vas., Lenka, Bomos, Olya and others. At breakfast I sat with U[ncle] Sergei and Sazonov. We went to the Bykhovsky Highway and went for a walk in the woods. The Kiev

train passed through. We broke the ice in the river. Had tea at Papa's. We went to the Monastery with Shurik. Went with ours and others to the train and Khodarovsky. Dinner 4 with Mama, Papa, Anya and Nastenka. Went with Shurik to Lenka's and others. Sat by the fire with Kostya, Halla, Zhenya, Vanya and Fokla. Had tea.

-4
24 November Thursday
We went for a walk with Vikt. Er. and Shurik and the children by the river. We were at Lenka's and said farewell. Papa and A came and we left Mogilev. At breakfast I sat with Dmitriev and Voeikov. Played Nain Jaune with Al, Neylikh and Blüm [military commissar]. We all had tea. I wrote and read. At dinner I sat with Fedorov and Maksimovich. Sat with Mama and Dmitri. Had tea with all.

-3
25 November Friday
We all had tea. Played Nain Jaune with Al, T and Zhilik. At breakfast I sat with Maksimovich and Dmitri. I am sitting in my compartment. Shvybz is busy with Ortipo. We arrived at Tsarskoe. Tea 4 with Papa and Mama. Was with A at the old and new infirmaries. Dinner 4 with Papa, Mama and Kostya. Papa and I pasted in our albums. Anya was here.

-3
26 November Saturday
Papa, Mama and Al, went to the Georgievsky feast day. Was with A at the old infirmary. Went for a drive with A and Trina. Breakfast 4. Went for a drive with Isa. Was with A at the new infirmary. Vikt. Er. was there. Stood with everyone at billiards. Tea 4 with Papa, Mama and Anya. Were 4 with Papa and Mama at *Vsenoshnaya*, dined with the same and went to Anya's where Grigori was and we had tea. Zhenya Makarov spent the day with Al and is sleeping at Zhilik's.

-4
27 November Sunday

Were 5 with Papa and Mama at *Obednya* and had breakfast with the same. Were 4 at the G[rand] P[alace]. Went for a drive with Nastenka. Was with A at the new infirmary. Vikt. Er. and Shakh-Nazarov were there. Tea 4 with Mama and Papa. Was with A at the old infirmary. Did a puzzle with the sisters, Adamov and Peterson. Dinner 4 with Papa, Mama and Baron Vrangel. Pasted albums with Papa. Anya was here.

-5
28 November Monday
Had arithmetic, religion, history and Russian lessons. Had breakfast 5 with Papa, Mama and old A[unt] Olga. Went for a drive with O and Nastenka. Was with A at the new infirmary. Had tea 4 with Papa, Mama and U[ncle] Pavel (who received a cross.) Had English and music lessons. I read. Had dinner 4 with Papa, Mama, Anya, Kiki and Kutaisov. Pasted pictures into Papa's album with him. Anya and Kiki stayed on.

-2
29 November Tuesday
Had lessons—German, French and History. Breakfast 5 with Papa and Mama. Was at the old infirmary with A, I gave the sisters medals for diligence. 4 went for a walk with Papa. Was with A at the new infirmary. Vikt. Er. was there too. Tea 4 with Papa and Mama. Had music and Russian lessons. Was at Isa's and at Nastenka's, her brother Alek was there. Dinner 4 with Papa, Mama and Svechin. Pasted pictures in Papa's album with him. Anya was here.

-1
30 November Wednesday
Had English, history, Russian and religion lessons. Breakfast 5 with Papa and Mama. Was with A at the old infirmary. 4 went for a walk with Papa. Was at the new infirmary with A. Had tea with A upstairs. Had music [lesson]. Prepared my lessons. Dinner 4 with Papa, Mama and A[unt] Ella. Olga read and the others knitted.

Sofia Karangozova[50] to Maria—
[December 1916]
Your Highness, dear Maria Nikolaevna!
I am very grateful to you and touched that you remembered me and offered to take part in such a good deed as the distribution of things to the poor of Tsarskoe Selo.

You also, like our Tsaritsa, with your inexhaustible kindness and your August sisters, who alleviate the sufferings of the afflicted, wish to come to the aid of the destitute.

Believe, Your Highness, that the Lord God will reward you for all this, and all people appreciate the care of the Imperial Family and pray to God for them.

We, the children and I, always gladly help the poor whenever possible, and especially in such a difficult time that we are experiencing, every decent person should deny himself excess and come to the aid of the needy.

By the 1st of December, as you wrote to us, we gladly delivered three things and thirty rubles: 10 rubles each, from each of us: my daughter, my son and me.

My son constantly asks about the health of Her Majesty and all the Most August Family in his letters.

Knowing that all his thoughts are always about the Tsar's Family, I give him the pleasure and inform him all that I know.

I beg you to convey to Her Majesty that my daughter and I send our best greetings and respectfully kiss her hands.

To the Grand Duchesses Olga Nikolaevna, Tatiana Nikolaevna and Anastasia Nikolaevna, send our sincere, heartfelt greetings. Please accept, Your Highness, our best wishes from my daughter and me.
With all my soul,
Your devoted
Sofia Karangozova.

Maria's diary—
-2
1 December Thursday

50. Wife of one of the imperial officers.

Had German and French lessons. The 4 of us, Mama and A[unt] Ella went to a memorial service for Sonia Orbeliani. Breakfast 5 with Papa, Mama and A[unt] Ella. Went for a walk 4 with Papa. Was with A at the new infirmary. Tea and dinner 4 with Papa, Mama and A[unt] Ella. Was at Nastenka's and Trina's. Had music [lesson]. A[unt] Ella left. Pasted pictures with Papa in his album. Olga read Leykin's "Where Oranges are Ripening" and "Visiting the Turks." Anya was here.

2 December Friday
Had lessons, English, Russian and Batushka. Had breakfast 5 with papa, Mama and Count Totleben. Walked 4 with Papa while Mama [went] in an equipage. Went to the new and old infirmaries with A. Played kosti. Had tea with A upstairs. Went 5 to Anya's infirmary. Sasha Makarov's concert, De Lazari and accordion. Had music [lesson]. Prepared homework. Had dinner 4 with Papa and Mama. The same [were] at Anya's with Grigori and had tea. Talked nicely.

-1
3 December Saturday
Had lessons—German, French, English and arithmetic. Breakfast 5 with Papa, Mama and U[ncle] Boris (back from Persia). Was with A at the old infirmary. Went for a walk 4 with Papa and Mama was in the equipage. Was at the new infirmary too. Vikt. Er. was there. Had tea, were at *Vsenoshnaya*, and dined 4 with Papa and Mama. Anya was here. Pasted Papa's albums with him. We read Leykin.

4 December Sunday
Went to *Obednya* 5 with Papa and Mama and the same had breakfast with Toto. Showed Toto our rooms. Walked 5 with Papa. Saw off Papa and Alexei.[51] Went 4 to a concert at the G.P. Had tea 4 with Mama and Anya. Went to the old infirmary with A., played checkers. Stopped by Nastenka's and Isa's. Had dinner 4 with Mam, the same went to the sisters' infirmary. Played checkers with Shareiko.

51. To the city of Mogilev.

-5
5 December Monday
Had lessons, arithmetic, history and religion. Went for a walk with
A and Trina. Breakfast and dinner 4 with Mama. Was at the old in-
firmary with A. Went for a drive 4, while Mama and Anya were in
the sleigh. Was with A at the new infirmary. Tea 4 with Mama and
Anya. Were 4 with Mama at *Vsenoshnaya* and the same went to
Anya's. Grigori, Lili Dehn and Munka[52] were there. Had tea.

6 December Tuesday
Were 4 with Mama at *Obednya*. Breakfast 4 with Mama, Zizi, Isa,
Nastenka, Anya, Count and Countess Benkendorf, Apraksin and
Resin. Went for a drive 4, and Mama and Anya had a sleigh ride.
Was with A at the new infirmary. Tea 4 with Mama and Anya. Was
with A at the old infirmary. Sat at Nastenka's. Dinner 4 with Mama,
the same were at the sisters' infirmary. Played checkers with
Shareiko. Papa appointed Olga Chief of the 2nd Kubansky Plastun
Battalion.

-3
7 December Wednesday
I had lessons—history and religion. Was at the old infirmary with
A. Breakfast and dinner 4 with Mama. Went for a ride 4, and Mama
with Anya. Was at the new infirmary with A. Played dice and ate
nuts. Tea 4 with Mama and Anya. Had music [lesson] and then
were at Isa's. 4 were at the sisters' infirmary. Played *bloshki* with
Ulyanov and A played with Kasyanov. Were with Mama and Syroboyarsky at Anya's.

-4
8 December Thursday
Had lessons—German, French M. K[onrad]. and history. Breakfast
4 with Mama, A[unt] Mavra and Vera. Was with A at the old infirmary. Went for a drive 4, and Mama with Anya. Was at the new
infirmary with A. Had tea 4 with Mama and Anya. Had music [les-
son]. Went to Nastenka's. Nastenka Gudovich was there. Dinner 4

52. Maria "Munya" Golovina, a court lady and one of Rasputin's "disciples."

with Mama and with the same at the sisters' infirmary. played *bloshki* with Rita and Meyer.

9 December Friday
Went to the old infirmary[53] with A. Had breakfast and dinner 4 with Mama. Rode with Isa. Went to the new infirmary with A., played *kosti*[54] and the gramophone. Had tea 4 with Mama and Syroboyarsky, who is going to his reserve platoon. There was music [lesson]. Nastenka and Isa stopped by. Went 4 to the sisters' infirmary, then to Anya's with Mama, Grigori and Lili Dehn [were there].

10 December Saturday
Had lessons, German, French and arithmetic. Had breakfast 4 with Mama and Isa. The same went to the consecration of the barracks infirmary of the 3rd Sharpshooter regiment. Went to the old and new infirmaries with A. Vikt. Er. was at the latter. Had dinner at Anya's with Grigori and at the sisters' infirmary. From the infirmary [went] directly to the train 4 with Mama, where we spent the night, and during the night departed to Novgorod.

Pierre Gilliard to Maria—

Mogilev, December 10, 1916
Madam and very dear pupil, I thank you wholeheartedly for your long letter and ask forgiveness for not having written to you earlier. Anyway, I hope that Tatiana Nikolaevna received my letter this morning with the story of the first episode of the M[ysterious] H[and] which we saw on Tuesday. I cannot send you the printed account of the episodes you ask me for, because General Janin has not yet received them. Next week I'll send you more (this time it was really complicated) because I'm sure you're as impatient as all of us to know what will happen next. I wish you a nice trip to Novgorod! Ah! You thought I did not know where you were going!! It is true that I did not know it yet when I received Your letter. It snowed again today, you should see how we sink! But that does not

53. Maria and Anastasia's infirmary moved to a new location in Tsarskoe Selo.
54. Dice.

stop us from continuing to play brigands fiercely. I sent your regards to P. V. P. and Mr. Gibbes. They thank you and put themselves at your feet. Alexis Nikolaevich is in good health and very merry. He made me write a poster today for Joy -30 kopecks a pound FOR SALE 30 kopecks a pound (for gastronomic use) A dog deaf, blind, without smell, but smelly!!! Good for chitterlings and sausages. Age 4 1/2 years Weight 20 kilos. Contact Corporal Romanoff. He put this poster at the end of a stick that he fixed on the back of Joy. Then He took his dog by the chain and led him to the dining room tonight during hors d'oeuvres. The master and the dog were very successful. Be careful, Marie Nikolaevna, if you continue to tease me, I will avenge myself!!!! I got confused and I had to have Her Majesty repeat Herself I do not know how many times, but there was such an infernal noise in the phone. I beg you to believe me, Madam and very dear pupil,

Your most affectionate and most devoted servant. Pierre Gilliard

Maria's diary—

11 December Sunday
Arrived in Novgorod, there was a Greeting at the station. Went to the Sofiisky Cathedral. There was a Bishop's *Obednya*, then [we] venerated the Relics of various saints. Walked through to the Patriarch's chamber, they have an infirmary downstairs.

12 December Monday
Arrived at Tsarskoe Selo. Went to the old and new infirmaries with A. Had breakfast and tea 4 with Mama. Rode in a troika with Isa. Sat and read. There was music [lesson]. Had dinner 4 with Mama and Grigori at Anya's. Went to the infirmary 4 with the sisters. Played ruble, then checkers with Shareiko.

-4
13 December Tuesday
Had lessons, German, M K[onrad] and history. Breakfast and dinner 4 with Mama. Was at the old infirmary with A. Went for a drive with A and Nastenka. Met Vikt. Er. up there. Was with A at the new infirmary. Played dice. Tea 4 with Mama and Anya. Had music

[lesson]. Were at Isa, Nastenka and Trina's. Went 4 to the sisters' infirmary. Played checkers with Shareiko.

14 December Wednesday
Went for a walk with Trina but came back by motor with Shvybz. Had lessons, history and religion. Was with A at the old infirmary. Breakfast 4 with Isa, dinner 4 with Mama and tea also. Were 4 at the G[rand] P[alace]

-11
15 December Thursday
Went for a walk with Trina on the boulevard and returned from the sisters' infirmary by motor with Shvybz. I had lessons, German, M.K., and history. Breakfast 4 with Mama and Koteiko who came to Baryan from Japan. Was with A at the old infirmary. Went for a troika ride with Isa. Was at the new infirmary and played dice. Tea 4 with Mama and Kiki. Had music. Read. Dinner 4 with Mama. Were 4 at the sisters' infirmary, played with Pr[ince] [illeg.]-Sokolinsky and A with Kasyanov. Sat with Sokolov.

-11
16 December Friday
Had a lesson, religion, and after that was with A at the old infirmary. Breakfast and dinner 4 with Mama. 4 went for a troika ride with Isa. Tea 4 with Mama and Anya. Had music. Prepared my lessons. Were 4 at the sisters' infirmary. Played ruble and after that, checkers with Sokolov.

17 December Saturday
Had lessons, German, M. Kond.[rad], and arithmetic. Had breakfast 4 with Mama. Went to the old infirmary with A. Rode in a troika with O., T., Isa. Had tea 4 with Mama and Anya, the same went to the *Vsenoshnaya* at home and had dinner. After dinner Lili Dehn came over. Bad news. Grigori disappeared since last night. No one knows where he is.

18 December Sunday
Went to *Obednya*. Mama and Anya received communion. Everyone sat with Lili Dehn. Had breakfast 4 with Mama. Sat together again and had tea. Walked with O, A, Lili and Titi. Went to our infirmary with A. Sat. Had dinner 4 with Mama, Anya, Kiki and Lili. Sat all together. Nothing new is known about Grigori, they suspect Dmitri and Felix.

-15
19 December Monday
Had lessons, arithmetic and history. The rest of the time, I sat with Mama. Breakfast 4 with Mama. We sat and had tea 4 with Mama, Anya and Lili Dehn. Grigori was killed. We went to meet Papa and Alexei at 5 but they arrived at 6 and we went to the station again. Dinner 4 with Papa and Mama. Anya came. She is staying at the other end of the house. Later 4 sat with her in her room.

20 December Tuesday
Had lessons, German, M.K., and history. Breakfast 5 with Papa and Mama. Was at the old infirmary with A. Went for a walk 4 with Papa. Was with A at the new infirmary. Tea 4 with Papa and Mama. Had music. Dinner 4 with Papa and Mama. Anya was here.

21 December Wednesday
Went to Grigori's funeral 4 with Papa and Mama and others. He was buried at Anya's construction [site].[55] Had lessons, history and Batushka. Had breakfast 4 with Papa and Mama. Went to the old infirmary with A. Walked with Papa. Went to the new infirmary with A and Vikt. Er. was there. Had tea 4 with Papa and Mama near Alexei, he has worms in his belly. There was a music [lesson]. Went to Anya's, saw Matryona, Varya and Akulina.[56] Had dinner 4 with Papa, Mama and Sandro. Anya was here. Papa read.

22 December Thursday
Went to the old and new infirmaries with A. Had breakfast 5 with

55. Vyrubova was building an infirmary and chapel at the edge of Alexander Park, which was never completed.
56. Akulina Laptinskaya, Rasputin's housekeeper.

Papa, Mama and Toto. Sat at Mama's with Anya, Lili and Zina. Had tea 4 with Papa and Mama. Sat at Mama's. Had dinner 4 with Papa, Mama and Toto. Walked with Toto. Anya was here. Sat and worked.

-5
23 December Friday
Was with A at the old infirmary. Breakfast 5 with Papa and Mama. Went for a drive with O alone. Was with A and T at the G[rand] P[alace] and after that with A at the new infirmary. Tea 4 with Mama and Papa. Sat with Anya. Lili was there too. Dinner 4 with Papa and Mama. Went to Alexei's and Zhenya Makarov's when they were already in bed. Pasted in the album with Anya.

Shura Petrova[57] to Maria—

23 XII 1916
Dear Maria Nikolaevna,
I send you my heartfelt greetings and wishes for the best and merriest feast of the Nativity of Christ and New Year. I haven't seen you for such a long time and miss you. I hope I will be so lucky as to see you in the holidays. I kiss you firmly, if you permit it. Sincerely loving and faithfully yours,
Shura Petrova

Maria's diary—

-12
24 December Saturday
Were 4 with Papa at the Liturgy. Breakfast 5 with Papa, Mama and Kiki. Was with A at the old infirmary. There was a Christmas party in the corridor, for the nannies etc, and afterwards there was a Christmas party at Anya's. After that we were at Nastenka's, then Isa's and Trina's. We had our Christmas party and received lots of presents. Tea 4 with Papa and Mama. Were 5 at *Vsenoshnaya* with Papa and Mama. Dinner 4 with Papa, Mama and Kiki. Anya was here. We all sat together.

-2

57. Perhaps a daughter of their Russian teacher, Pyotr Petrov.

25 December Sunday
Were 5 with Papa and Mama at *Obednya* and breakfasted the same
and at the Svodny Regimental Convoy's Christmas party etc. Food
was brought in and given, and it was good to see all the Cossacks.
Had tea 4 with Papa and Mama. Was with Shvybz at the old and
new infirmaries at Christmas parties. Vikt. Er. and Shakh-Nazerov
were there. Dined 4 with Papa and Mama, the same went to Anya's
where Paraskovia Ivanovna, Mitya, Mara and Varya[58] were.

-6
26 December Monday
Was with A at the old infirmary. Breakfast 5 with Papa, Mama and
Toto. Were 5 with Papa and Mama at a Christmas party. It wasn't
bad. Went for a walk 4 with Papa. Tea 4 with Papa, Mama and
Anya. Was with A at the new infirmary, played dice. Dinner 4 with
Papa, Mama and Toto. Went to say goodbye to Alexei and Zhenya.
Anya sat [with us].

-8
27 December Tuesday
Was with A at the old and new infirmaries. Breakfast 5 with Papa
and Mama. Were with the same at a Christmas party, all were [illeg.]
Yu., V. Er., A. A., S. I. etc. Went for a walk 4 with Papa and T[oto].
Tea 4 with Papa and Mama. Were 5 with Papa in the Red Hall for
a cinematograph at 2: 1708, "The Mysterious Hand," comedies,
and war. Dinner 4 with Papa and Mama. Alexei's arm hurts. Pasted
in albums, O, Shvybz and Anya.

28 December Wednesday
Went to the old infirmary with A. The Metropolitan came over to
praise Christ. Had breakfast 4 with Papa and Mama, Anya and
Groten. Went 4 to the G.P. Walked 4 with Papa. Went to a concert
at the new infirmary with T and A. Plevitskaya was there and
Vaganova danced. Had tea 4 with Papa and Mama, dinner with the
same. Anya was here, pasted in the album with her and Shvybz.—
Alexei was in bed all day, his arm hurts and [he] slept badly.

---

58. Rasputin's wife, son, and two daughters.

-6
29 December Thursday
Was with A at the old and new infirmaries. Breakfast 4 with Papa
and Mama. Were 4 with Nastenka at the Invalids' Home for a
Christmas party. Sat with Alexei. Had tea 4 with Papa, Mama and
Anya. Played with Nyuta's[59] niece Anna Ivanovna. Dinner 4 with
Papa and Mama. Anya was here. Pasted albums with Anya and
Shvybz.

-9
30 December Friday
Was with A at the old infirmary. Breakfast, tea and dinner 4 with
Papa and Mama. Went for a walk with Papa, O and T. Were 4 with
Isa at a Christmas party at the chosen infirmary. After tea 4 went to
Anya's room where Vikt. Er., Shurik and Yuzik were. Sat cozily by
the fireplace and talked, gave out saucers. Anya was here. Pasted
hers and Shvybz's album. Received a letter from my Kolya.[60]

31 December Saturday
Went to the old and new infirmaries with A., played billiards with
Kotov and Tolstov. Had breakfast and dinner with Papa, Mama and
Kiki. Walked with Papa, O and T. Went to the Nanny school
Christmas party with T, A and Nastenka. Had tea 4 with Papa and
Mama. Went to *Vsenoshnaya* with Papa. Read fortunes with Anya,
sharpened wax and peeled the shells. Had tea. Went to *moleben* 3
with Papa and Mama at the house church.

Catherine Schneider to Maria—
Happy New Year dear Maria Nikolaevna.
All the very, very best.
Trina
Tsarskoe
31st Dec 1916

---

59. Nyuta was the nickname of maid Anna Demidova.
60. Presumably Kolya Demenkov.

1917

Alexei to Maria—
Tsarskoe Selo 12
February 1917
My darling sweet Hussar.
Good night! I wish you all the very best.
May the Lord God protect you+!
A firm kiss,
your
Alexei +

Authors' note: On March 2, 1917, Maria's father was on his way home to Petrograd from the military headquarters in Mogilev. Inside his imperial train, the tsar was pressured into abdicating his throne, not only for himself but also for his son Alexei, having been convinced that this would bring internal political peace to the nation already exhausted from war. The abdication became one of the key events that led to the fall of the Russian empire. Grand Duke Michael, in whose favor the abdication was signed, abdicated as well, which signaled the end of the three-hundred-year-old Romanov dynasty.

If there was ever a chance for the imperial family to escape to safety, it was during the next few days, before the tsar arrived back in Tsarskoe Selo and they were all placed under arrest. But as fate would have it, all the imperial children got very ill with measles—all except Maria, who would come down with the illness last. Because of the illness, the children could not be moved, so the family remained at the Alexander Palace, which proved to be one of the "what if" events of history. It took Nicholas almost a week to travel back to the St. Petersburg area, frayed by revolutionary disturbances, and his family.

Maria to Nicholas II—

March 3. 1917 Tsarskoe Selo. Our dear and sweet Papa! I am always with You in my thoughts and prayers. The sisters are still lying in a dark room, while Alexei is already bored with it and therefore lying in the playroom, where they do not shut any windows. Today we molded bullets from tin with Zhilik and he [Alexei] loved it. Mama is full of energy, although [her] heart is not completely in order. I spend almost entire days with Mama lately, because I am the only one now who remains healthy and able to walk. I also sleep with her, to be close by in case something needs to be said or someone wants to see her. Lili sleeps here in the red room near the dining room sofa where Olga used to lie. She is terribly sweet and helps us all a lot. From our windows we can see our Cossacks and soldiers. Yesterday I went around the cellar with Mama, and saw how they all settled in there. There is complete darkness in the cellar as we do not have electricity during the day. The soldiers were very sweet and when we passed by them, they jumped up from the straw where they were resting and greeted Mama. A porter was leading us with a candle and commanded the soldiers "on attention." In the evening I saw Vikt. Erastovich, he said that Vershikov, who was under house arrest like the rest of Convoy in Petrograd, walked here on foot from Petrograd during the night. We all kiss you affectionately and warmly, our dear darling Papa. May God keep you. + Your children. Yesterday afternoon we had *moleben*, they brought Znamenie Mother of God icon from the church to the sisters. We all felt better somehow the entire day after that.—Papa darling, we all heard and believe that the Lord will never abandon the One who did all he could for all of us. We kiss you warmly many times over. God is always with you and our friend in heaven also prays intensely for you, and everyone, everyone—our thoughts of you never leave us even for a minute.

From the 1917 diary of Nicholas Alexandrovich—

9th March. Thursday. Arrived at Tsarskoe Selo quickly and safely—at 11 o'cl. But Lord, what a difference, outside and around the palace, in the park are the guards, and inside, at the entrance are some kind of ensigns!

Went upstairs and there saw darling Alix and the dear children. She looked healthy and vigorous, but they all were in beds in a dark room. But everyone feels well, except Maria who just caught measles recently. Had breakfast and dinner in Alexei's playroom.

Authors' note: By this time Maria also came down with measles.

12th March. Sunday. It started to get warmer. In the morning Benkendorf and Apraksin[1] were here; the latter is leaving Alix and said goodbye to us. At 11 o'cl. went to *obednya*. Alexei got up today. Olga and Tatiana feel a lot better, while Maria and Anastasia are worse, headache and earache and vomiting.

13th March. Monday. It continues getting warmer, the day was semi-grey. Took a walk in the morning for about half an hour. Kept busy with old business. Maria continues to have high temp. 40.6, and Anastasia has earache. The rest felt well.

17th March. Wednesday. The same [kind of] sunny day. Walked from 11 o'cl. until 11 1/2 o'cl. Maria and Anastasia's temp. went up and down alternatively, and also vomiting.

18th March. Saturday. A grey day and a warm spell; in the morning during my walk, there was some wet snow. During the day Maria had [temperature] 40.9 and occasional delirium, in the evening it went down to 39.3 . . .

19th March. Tuesday. Bright day. At 11 o'cl. went to *obednya* with Olga, Tatiana and Alexei. Maria's and Anastasia's temp. went down to normal, and only in the evening Maria's went up a little.

1. Count Pyotr Nikolaevich Apraksin was the secretary of Empress Alexandra.

From the memoirs of Anna Vyrubova—

On 19 March I received a note from the Empress that Maria Niko-laevna is dying and asking for me. . . . For a minute I fought with feeling of pity for the dying Maria Nikolaevna and fear for myself, but the first prevailed and I got up, got dressed and Kotzeba pushed me in a wheelchair through the upper hallway to the children's quarters, whom I had not seen for a whole month. A happy exclamation from Alexei and the older girls made me forget all. We ran to each other, hugged and cried. Then I tiptoed to Maria Nikolaevna. She was lying there, white like linen, her eyes, naturally large, seemed even larger, temperature was 40.9, she breathed oxygen. When she saw me, she made some attempts to pick up her head and started to cry, repeating: "Anya, Anya." I stayed with her until she fell asleep

From the diary of Nicholas II

20th March. Monday. Apparently, Maria's and Anastasia's illness broke, the temp. remained normal; they are weak and slept all day, of course with breaks.

21st March. Monday. Kerensky,[2] the current Minister of Justice, showed up unexpectedly today, walked through all the rooms, wanted to see us, spoke with me for about five minutes, introduced the new commandant of the palace and then left. He ordered the arrest of poor Anya and for her to be taken to the city along with Lili Dehn. This happened between 3 and 4 o'cl. while I was taking a walk. The weather was awful and [it] matched our mood! Maria and Anastasia slept almost the entire day.

22nd March. Wednesday. There was a snowstorm during the night and masses of snow fell. The day remained sunny and quiet. Olga and Tatiana went outside for the first time and sat on the round balcony while I was taking a walk. After breakfast I worked a lot. The youngest ones slept and felt well.

24th March. Friday. A nice quiet day. Took a walk in the morning. During the day Maria and Anastasia were transferred to the play-room.

2. Alexander Kerensky, later head of the provisional government.

Postcard from Maria to Lili Dehn—

Indeed, He Has Risen! Darling Tili, I thank you immensely for your [holiday] greetings, and also send you [good] wishes. I am still in bed as [I have] inflammation in [my] left lung, [it] still has not gone away. Every day they put a compress on my side, and spread iodine so my skin is peeling. [I] tried to walk but [my] legs are like rags and I am swaying awfully, looking so foolish. At one point I had ear ache but [it was] not too bad, now we all talk loudly. I kiss you affectionately three times.
Easter. [2 April] 1917. Maria

Nicholas's diary—

10th April. Monday. The day remained cool. Alexei got a bit of a sore throat and was put to bed. Olga is still in bed, while Maria gets up for a few hours.

Maria to Lili Dehn—

3rd May, 1917. I heartily thank my dear Tili for the sweet little card. I have been wanting to write to you for a long time but somehow was not able. How are you and the little one doing? We all go out in the garden daily. [It is] so pleasant to sit out in the sun. Someone probably already wrote you that we are planting a vegetable garden. It is really fun to dig the soil and cart it around, I already have blisters on my hands. We just had lessons with Olga and Mama. I kiss you and the little one very very affectionately. Your M. Did you have any news from your husband lately?

Maria to Alexandra Feodorovna—

Mama darling!
Evg. Serg. Tanya said that Rita can't write for a few days, but it is not convenient to give it over the phone. Should we send a letter to Olga Porer? because Tanya thinks she is able to write. Have a good morning. Kisses
Maria 12 May 1917 Ts. S.

From the 1917 diary of Nicholas Alexandrovich—
14th June. Wednesday. Dear Maria turned 18 years old today! In the morning took a walk with all the children around the entire park.

Maria to Ekaterina Erastovna Zborovskaya—
8 and 9 June 1917
Dear Katya,
  I thank you warmly for your greetings and dear letter. I am writing to you sitting on the window sill. The sisters have gone for a walk with Papa, the weather is very good, and even hot for Tsarskoe. The lilacs are already wilting unfortunately. I remember the last time, in these days they brought your brother to us at the infirmary, and we met up with each other often. In the afternoon we go for walks and water the garden. We have already eaten our radish and onions, it was most pleasant and they seemed very delicious. My brother runs a lot and douses everyone with water from the pump while we are swinging in the hammock. We usually get drenched but dry out quickly in the sun. Mama sits on the grass and works. I haven't done any handcraft lately as the heat makes me lazy. I am going to bed. Good night.
  Good morning sweet Katya! I have just got up and it is already hot. Trucks noisily fly past the window. Anastasia is sitting here in the room too, writing something and asks me to give you a big kiss. I just imagine how proud your brother is with his role of adjutant. We all send him and the others our big, heartfelt greetings and we often think of him. And what are Yuzik and Serg. Iv. Up to? Will they be with A.A. and the others? While I am writing to you, dear Jimmy is lying by me on the floor. Ortipo is also lying around some-where, dying from the heat. Olga's cat had two appetizing kittens, ginger and gray. I want to cuddle them awfully. They can barely walk yet.
  Is your brother still living with NV? It must be nice for your mother to see all her old acquaintances again. You wouldn't remem-ber any of them. I thank your Mama with all my heart for her greet-ings and remembrance. Send her my big greetings. What a pity Rimma is going to Peterhof right when you are all not there. We

talk about you often and have so many good memories…the sisters send there big greetings and I kiss you. All the best, my sweet.
M
Just had a history lesson with Olga. We work in the corridor because it is hot in the room. Are you still working with the boys?! I forgot to thank you for the pressed rose which smells so wonderfully. Time to finish, we are going to have lunch. Got a letter from A K today which made me very happy. Answered Vera

From the memoir of Pierre Gilliard—
[22nd June 1917] As the Grand-Duchesses were losing all their hair as the result of their illness, their heads have been shaved. When they go out in the park, they wear scarves arranged so as to conceal the fact. Just as I was going to take their photographs, at a sign from Olga Nikolaevna they all suddenly removed their headdress. I protested, but they insisted, much amused at the idea of seeing themselves photographed like this, and looking forward to seeing the indignant surprise of their parents. Their good spirits reappear from time to time in spite of everything. It is their exuberant youth.

From the 1917 diary of Nicholas Alexandrovich—
3rd July. Monday. Muggy, warm day with clouds, but it only rained at dinner time. In the morning, I went for a walk and in the afternoon, piled up the large pine logs in the same place, near the lattice. All four daughters had their hair shaved off, seeing as after the measles their hair was falling out a lot.

Authors' note: In late July, the Romanov family were told that they would shortly be leaving Tsarskoe Selo, to be taken to an unidentified location. The prisoners were hoping to be sent to their beloved Livadia, but all hopes were dashed when they were told to pack warm clothes. On August 1, the former imperial family with a group of their loyal suite members and a team of sharpshooter guards, boarded a train, which headed east, later learning that their final destination was Siberia—a far cry from the warm Crimea. In the Siberian hub Tyumen, Maria and her family were transferred to a steamer called "The Rus" and journeyed to the town of Tobolsk via several rivers. They arrived at their destination on the sixth of August, but had to live on the steamer for another week while the house intended for them was being prepared.

From the 1917 diary of Nicholas Alexandrovich—

9th August. Wednesday. The weather still wonderfully warm. The suite spent the morning in town as usual. Maria had fever, Alexei had some pains in his left arm.

10th August. Thursday. Woke up to rotten weather—rainy and windy. Maria was in bed with fever, and Alexei got an earache in addition to pains in the arm!

Anastasia to V. G. Maltseva,[3] August 10, 1917—
Dearest Vera Georgievna,
We arrived here safely. For now, we are living on the steamer as the house is not ready. As I write, it is wet with rain. M is lying down as she caught a cold, but she is already better now.

From the 1917 diary of Nicholas Alexandrovich—

11th August. Friday. Alexei slept very little, he moved to Alix's room for the night. His ear got better, the arm still hurts a bit. Maria is better.

12th August. Saturday. Again, an excellent day without sun, but very warm. In the morning walked around the deck and read there too until breakfast. Maria and Alexei got up and went outside for fresh air during the day.

Authors' note: On August 13, the family finally left the steamer and were imprisoned at the "Freedom House," the former Governor's mansion, in the center of town.

From the 1917 diary of Nicholas Alexandrovich—

13th August. Sunday. Got up early, and packed our last things immediately. At 10 1/2, I and the children went down to the shore

3. Vera Georgievna Maltseva was a nurse at the Feodorovsky infirmary.

with the commandant and the officers and walked to our new residence. Looked around the entire house, from the top to the attic. Occupied the second floor, the dining room is downstairs. At 12 o'cl. [had a] *moleben* service, and the priest blessed all the rooms with holy water. Had breakfast and dinner with our people. Went to see the house where the suite will be staying. Many rooms are still not ready and look unattractive.

Then went to the so-called garden—terrible kitchen garden, looked over the kitchen and the guard room. Everything looks old and dilapidated. Unpacked my things in the study and bathroom, which is half mine and half Alexei's. Spent the evening together, played bezique with Nastenka.

V.V. Komstadius[4] to Maria—

From my soul, I wish you happiness and much, much joy in your life. I pray to God about it. The children and I thank you very, very much for the cards. We were so happy to get news of you. Please pass on my greetings to your younger sister, to whom I was unable to write as I was sick in bed for two weeks. I am better now, but still weak. Lately there has been heavy rain every day, and practically each and every evening around 5-6 o'clock. In one place there was heavy hail and so round that it completely damaged the bread and the gardens. That was about 18 versts from us. Sincerely loving you, Vera Vlad.[imirovna]

Maria to Vera Vladimirovna Komstadius—

15/VIII/17 [15 August, 1917]. Heartfelt thanks to darling Vera Vladimirovna for the greetings. I hope that you have now recovered completely. It is so tiresome to be ill in the summer, when one wants to be outside in fresh air. I kiss you firmly and wish you all the best. M

Maria to Vera Georgievna Maltseva—

6th September, 1917. Tobolsk. We congratulate you warmly, dear Vera Georgievna with the day of [your] angel[5] and birthday. From

---

4. Vera Vladimirovna Komtadius (nee Malama) was the wife of Major General Nikolai Komstadius, head of the tsar's personal guard unit. She was a relative of Dmitri Malama and also worked at one of the imperial infirmaries.

5. a.k.a. Name Day.

all our hearts we wish you happiness and health. I was happy to hear from you. Thank your sister for the greetings. It is probably nice for you to ride to work together with your sister now. Did you get our letter before our departure? And what are you doing now, and your daughter? Vera E. probably returned from the south already. If you see them, give our regards and thank them for [illeg.]. I kiss you and Lili very firmly. All the best. M.

To: Vera Georgievna Maltseva, Sister of Mercy at [Feodorovsky] Infirmary in Tsarskoe Selo. Tobolsk.
20th September, 1917. I thank you very much, my sweet Vera Georgievna, for the card. I was remembering you on the 28th of August in particular. It was so nice at the infirmary. We remember all of you very very often. Do you ever see the former nurses and Olga Vasilievna? Please pass this letter to Katya. All this time we've had wonderful weather and [it is] even hot in the sun. But today it is snowing and strong wind. Right now, I am sitting in my room. We live in one room all 4, so it is not lonesome. Our windows look over the street and we often look at the passers-by. Well, and what do you do, my dear?

I continue writing on 21st September. The snow is already sitting on the road. And what kind of weather do you have? Is it still warm or cold already? I remember how we used to go to this infirmary last year.—Did you finish embroidering your appetizing blue pillow case with the grapes? Anastasia kisses and thanks you for the card, she will write one of these days. We just took a walk, went to the garden and dug for rutabaga. Here in the garden we only have rutabaga and cabbage. Thank Verochka and Evg. Aleks. very much for the remembering [us], we kiss them affectionately. Do you know anything about the health of Anna Pavlovna? Forgive me for so many questions, but I want to know so much what everyone is doing and how they all are. I wish you all the best, my dear, and embrace you warmly. I hope that you got our letter in time for the holiday. Heartfelt greetings to your sister and all the acquaintances. Do Kolibri and others write to you? How did they settle in at the Infirmary No. 36? Probably it is very cozy, were you there? Well time to end. M.

Tobolsk. 30th September, 1917. Darling Vera Georgievna. Thank you for the postcard from 28 August. I apologize that we did not thank you earlier. How are you? The weather here is sunny, very pleasant. Regards to Verochka and your sister. Are you tired from working? We remember the dear infirmary often, it was so nice. Everyone sends you regards. All the best. I kiss you firmly.

Tobolsk. 4th October, 1917. My darling Vera Georgievna, please give this letter to Katya. How are you? I have not had letters from you in a while. How is Golubev's health now? I feel so sorry for the poor thing. If you see him, give him regards from us and to others we know who remember us. We just returned from outside. We warmed in the sun. Although lessons started, we still sit outside in fresh air a lot. Evg. Aleks. asked to send her our photographs, but I am not sending because almost certainly won't reach [her]. If you write to Kartaeva, then congratulate her for me with 22 Oct. and her girlfriend too. I will be very grateful to you. Since I don't know their address. Time to end. I wish you all the best, darling. I kiss you firmly. M.

Tobolsk. 15th October, 1917. I thank you from my heart, darling Vera Georgievna for the postcards, which arrived, despite the incorrect address, as we live right in the city, in the house of the former governor. I hope that you are now completely recovered. It is so tiresome to be ill and lie in bed. How did you find Roman? He probably grew a lot from last summer. And what is Loshnov doing at D.B.'s? Do you ever see the acquaintances from the infirmary? There is not that much to write about myself, we live as usual. Today at 8 o'cl. in the morning we went to *obednya*. The church is very close to our house, one needs to only walk through the city garden and a street. We just had tea and now sitting all together. My brother is playing with Kolya (son of Vlad. Nik.), whom they allow to come over only on holidays. I send regards to your sister and those acquaintances who have not forgotten us. Did Kartashova write? I wish you health and all the best, my dear. I embrace you warmly for remembering [us]. May God keep you. M.

Ludmila Kozhevnikova[6] to Maria—

Ts. Selo, 17 October 1917

Sweet and dear Maria Nikolaevna,

On Saturday 14th October, we shifted to our new apartment on Peshkovsky Street. I expect you know the street as you often went down it on your walks. We have set ourselves up quite well, even though we haven't yet unpacked all our things. The apartment is twice as big as our former one, so we have different rooms, Marusya and I in one room, Nina next to us but Vera far off from us; we went and visited each other. It was fun to move. An officer we are acquainted with helped us. We live on the second floor. In winter we will go skiing around the field. I haven't had a letter from Katya for ages, but Vera got one not so long ago from Viktor Erastovich. He had been very unwell and got awfully thin. Papa, Mama and my sisters send you, Olga Nikolaevna, Tatiana Nikolaevna and Anastasia Nikolaevna our heartfelt greetings. I kiss you firmly.

Warmly loving you,

Your Ludmila

Our new address:

Tsarskoe Selo, Peshkovsky Street, House 10 Apartment 2

Sweet, dear Maria Nikolaevna. Well, we are already in our new apartment. It is quite nice and cozy, albeit cramped. Of course, it does not compare with our old one from which we were pushed out of. The weather has been good these last days and I have been walking a lot. For 4 days, I managed to go to Sestroretsk where I had a good rest. Sweet and dear Maria Nikolaevna, I am sending you a photo card of myself. I went on the plateau. Nikolai Ivanovich Zolotorev also photographed it last year. I on the left with a dog, Yergushev, Vera, Nina and Katia. We remember all of you so often and terribly want to see you. Darling Maria Nikolaevna, if you have been photographed lately, please send it. I strongly and firmly kiss you, Olga Nikolaevna, Tatiana Nikolaevna and Anastasia Nikolaevna. Papa and Mama send you their heartfelt greetings. Warmly loving you,

Your Ludmila

6. Ludmila Kozhevnikova was a friend of Maria's from Tsarskoe Selo.

Dear Maria Nikolaevna,
Thank you very much for your letter. Well, it is nearly the end of my vacation, yet I was not able to get (all) together at Sestroretsk because I have to go to my aunt's on the 30th for my cousin's birthday. It is good. . . [second page of this letter appears to be missing] . . . they settled down for the night, places for 2, but passengers 3. We are waiting en route for letters, and it will be a pity if they take a long time to come. Sweet Maria Nikolaevna, please pass on the letter from Katya to Anastasia Nikolaevna. Mother and Father send you and your sisters their heartfelt greetings. I kiss you firmly. Your warmly loving, Ludmila

Viktor Erastovich Zborovsky to Maria—

Your Highness, finally I can be certain that this letter will reach its destination, until now it seemed to me that when I wrote, my letters just disappeared into space, which I think was how it happened. We are still sitting in Ekaterinodar—still unable to get ourselves together; Tertzys for now are sitting in Prokhladnaya Village—this is not far from Vladikavkaz. The heat here is unbearable. Katya does not like the heat and therefore is always walking around like a wet hen. Tomorrow she will yell at me terribly that I did not warn her, and that she was not able to write you a letter. But I just now found out about the chance to send a letter and am writing to you at 1 o'clock in the morning, as the officer who is going to Petrograd is leaving tomorrow. Everyone is asking very much for you not to forget us. If the letters reached you more reliably, we would have tried not to allow you to forget us with our letters. I will ask you to send this letter to the Sidorovs. They write often, but were upset that do not get any letters from me. But it is not my fault and feel desperate, as my letters do not get there. Your Highness, please give regards to everyone— or rather not just regards, but thousands of greetings from all of us, who ask again to not forget them. Be healthy and happy.
V. Zborovsky

Authors' note: On October 24–25, the Bolsheviks had overthrown the Provisional Government in a bloodless coup and took power. The Tobolsk prisoners did not learn of this until later and were not immediately affected by these events.

Maria to V.G. Maltseva—
14th November, 1917. Tobolsk. I thank my darling good Vera Georgievna warmly for letters No 3 and 4. It was very pleasant to learn that you are alive and well. How are you feeling after the illness? I hope you did not get too weak. I am very touched by your nice memories and thank you with all my heart for the wishes. I send regards to Olga. Everyone thanks [you] for the greetings as well, [and] send regards to you, Ak. Iv., V. Alek., [and an] affectionate kiss. Klavdia Mikhailovna[7] is giving us lessons in Literature and History, you probably remember her. We have snow on the ground but it is rather warm, it's even melting these days. Our only acquaintance here is the son of a woman on staff, Tolya, who is 6 years old. He reminds us of Vit'ka Vor.[8] We play with him outside and inside, he entertains us a lot. It is so pleasant to play with little ones, as we love children so much. When we went to. . . [letter ends].

Maria to Nikolai Demenkov—
Heartfelt wishes for [your] Day of the Angel and may you have all the best in life. So sad that we have not heard from you in so long. How are you? This is our house.[9] The rooms are appetizing and bright. Our windows face this street (Freedom St.). They had set up bars from the [guard] booth to the little fence where we take walks. We sit on the balcony especially, often. [We] reminisce about the happy times, the games, Ivan. What are you up to? Regards to all who remember us. We are sending warm greetings. May God keep you. M. 22nd November, 1917.

From the 1917 diary of Nicholas Alexandrovich—
6th December. Wednesday. Spent my name day quietly and not like in the previous years. At 12 o'cl. a *moleben* service. The marksmen of the 4th regiment in the garden, former guards, all congratulated me, and I them—with the regiment holiday. Received three name day pies and sent one of them to the guards. In the evening Maria, Alexei and M. Gilliard acted in a very friendly little play "Le Fluide de John;" there was a lot of laughter.

7. Klavdia Bitner, who followed the imperial family to Siberia and was acting as one of the younger children's tutor.

8. "Viktor the Pickpocket" may be one of the fictional characters in a book?

9. A postcard of governor's mansion was enclosed.

Maria to Zinaida Tolstaya[10]—

Tobolsk. 10 December. We live quietly, take walks twice a day as usual. The weather is nice, the other day it was very cold. You must still have warm weather? I am so envious that you can look at the wonderful sea! This morning at 8 we went to *obednya*. We are always so happy when they let us go to church, of course one cannot compare this church with our *Sobor*,[11] but still better than in the rooms. Right now, we are all sitting in our rooms. The sisters are also writing, the dogs are running around and begging to sit on our laps. I remember Tsarskoe Selo so often, and our merry concerts at the infirmary; do you remember how much fun it was when the wounded used to dance; we also remember our walks to Pavlovsk and Your small carriage, the morning rides past Your house. It all seems so long ago. Doesn't it? Well, it's time for me to end. I wish You all the best and kiss You and Dalya affectionately. Heartfelt regards to all your [family]. Maria

The Grand Duchesses to Viktor Zborovsky—

14 December, 1917. Sending you wishes for the holidays and the new year, from all our hearts. May you have lots of happiness and be healthy! Especially during Christmas, we will be with you all our dears, in our thoughts. Did you recover completely now? We are all well. The view on this [postcard] is not familiar to us either. Life is the same here. We study a lot, hence the days pass by rather quickly. When we are free, we sit on the window [sill] and watch the passersby, this is our biggest entertainment [. . .] May the Lord keep you. I wish you all the best. A.[nastasia]
Big regards and wishes for the holidays. Be well. O.[lga]
Heartfelt greetings. We remember you all often. Tatiana.
So sad to spend the holidays so far from you. Sincerest regards. Maria.

10. Zinaida Sergeievna Tolstaya (nee Bekhteyeva) (1877-1961) was the daughter of the famous Russian poet Sergei Bekhteyev (who wrote "The Prayer" dedicated to the imperial family), and a friend to the empress.
11. Feodorovsky Cathedral.

1918

Olga to Lili Dehn—

Tobolsk. 1st January, 1917 [*sic*, should be 1918]. Saturday. My darling Lili! I was so happy to finally hear from you. To tell the truth, I was afraid that you had forgotten us, but glad that I was mistaken. You probably already heard from one of the sisters how we settled here and that it is really awful. A lot of noise, as we constantly sit all together, and then Kolya Derevenko comes to see my brother for the holidays, so you can imagine the raucous and shouting. All the dogs are with us, Jimmy[1] lives in our room, but Ortipo is separate, one is enough, and there are four of us too. Rubella is gone, but we still cannot go outside, neither Maria, nor I. Anastasia is healthy for now. Our Christmas tree is still standing in the corner of the hall and smells wonderful, and does not drop needles at all.

The Grand Duchesses to Tatiana Botkin[2]—

12 January, 1918. Tobolsk. To dear Tanya with best wishes for her Angel Day. Olga, Tatiana, Maria, Anastasia

Maria and Anastasia to Margarita Khitrovo—

Tobolsk. January 14, 1918
Warm thanks, darling Rita for the sweet postcards. We hope that

---

1. Jimmy/Jim was Anastasia's pet Pekinese.
2. Daughter of Dr. Evgeny Botkin, who also followed the family to Siberia.

you had a good holiday. We passed the holidays unnoticed, quietly. We slide on the mountain which was built in the yard all the time now. I have already managed to get myself a lump on my forehead. Kolya, the son of Vl. Nik. comes to my brother and they play together in the yard, and on holidays he stays until the evening; play hide and seek in the dark, etc. We reminisce about the games at the infirmary and at Anya's house, with Lyuba. Did Ksenia get into the institute? Thank you for the news about N.D.

It's time to stop, we will have dinner soon. We kiss you firmly, darling. God bless you.

M.

A.

Thank you very much for the postcard. Kisses. A.

Maria to Ekaterina Erastovna Zborovskaya—

Tobolsk

19th January 1918

From my soul I thank you darling Katya, your mother and Vitya for the congratulations. I didn't write earlier as I was ill with mumps. Now, all of us are better and we already go out into the yard. In the courtyard, we have built a snow mountain, not too big, and we go sliding down it on skis and sleds. We watered it ourselves and so it is not at all even, and we now no longer go down it on sleds, but rather beside the sleds.

Do Vera and her sisters write to you? We sometimes get letters from them. All in all, things are pretty good. It was awfully nice to see your photographs, Vitya looks remarkably smart in his "french" epaulettes. No one wears them here these days, because in town they have started to tear them off, looks terrible, like some kind of convicts. They even take off the cockades.

I am writing to you by the window, warming up in the sun. The weather here is very good, the frost isn't heavy and there is sunshine virtually every day, which warms us much more than in Ts. S. Do you have news from the sisters on whether Rimma had her operation? I hope the holidays went well for you. It was boring for us without you all at Christmas. Warmly greet your mother and everyone. Kiss them firmly. All the best. M

Tobolsk
26th January 1918
I got your letter yesterday, dear Katya, for which I greatly thank you. Such an awfully long time it took for our letters to get through, but good that they arrived, even if they are delayed. Did you get our letter of the 19th of January? We are always so happy when we receive your letters. Do you still work with your mother or did you find a servant? No doubt you had a wonderful time with guests at New Year. The names you ended up with, in my opinion, were not very beautiful. Always, but especially on holidays, we remember you. The last few days we have had a heavy frost and it has been cold in the house, in our bedroom it was -7 and in the drawing room a mere 6 degrees. The firewood was damp and so did not burn at all, only smoked. They have now brought us some new, dry wood. Papa [illegible] for the small stoves. We slide down the mountain, and when there was heavy frost, we had to run into the kitchen, where there are masses of cockroaches, to warm up. I am sending you a picture of we 4's room. I took it in the evening with a flash. Olga's bed is in the corner. I have glued it on so that it doesn't get removed. We are all very grateful for the greetings and send ours. . . . All the best to you, your mother and brothers. I kiss you darling firmly and often think of you. May God protect you. M
Shvybz kisses you.
(In Olga's hand) - Ask Vikt[or] where is Baron [illegible]!
What is the name and patronym of NV's mother?
And where are Mamashka and Papashka?
(in Olga's hand, by the photo of her bed) – It's cozy!

Maria to unknown—

22 February/7 March. Tobolsk. In the evenings we get together to work or play cards—bridge or some other games, though I am particularly interested in [card games]. Papa reads out loud. Pretty often, when all 4 of us get together in a proper mood we sing various nice songs. This always ends up with us loudly imitating *zurna*[3] sounds. Some of us knock against the door or any other object that catches our eye in order to produce more noise [. . .] and create raucous that can be heard almost all over the house.

3. A musical instrument

A.T.[4] to Maria—

M.N. Ekaterinodar [illeg.] 1918. Your Highness! Thank you very much for your congratulations and [illeg.]. My shoulder almost never bothers me. I know very little about my people, they are now in Tiflis, and from there it is so difficult to get news; brother in Persia, sister with her husband in Orenburg, so we are all now almost lost from each other. This postcard shows our main streets; do not think that they are so bad—this is an old picture, now on the site of these small houses there are beautiful buildings and the view is very decent, but nevertheless I am terribly tired of the city and if I had the opportunity, I would have gone somewhere far, far away. Good luck. Mentally always with all of you. God bless you. Sincerely loyal A. T. I am also sending cards at the same time to O.N, T.N. and A. N.

From the diary of Countess Anastasia Hendrikova[5]—

Feb 4. In the evening 'a la porte'/T.N. and Mr Gilliard/and 'Packing Up'/Mar. Nik., Anas. Nik., and Al. N.
(Alexandra Feodorovna's diary: "8:45 Tatiana Mr. Gilliard & Aleksei acted *A La Porte* for the second time—very well & then followed *Packing Up* . Farce in one act by B. Gattan
Dramatis personae:
Mr. Chugwater—Anastasia
Mrs. Chugwater—Marie
Luggage man—Aleksei
Stage manager: S. Gibbs
Awfully amusing & really well & funnily given")

Feb 26: In the evening 'Packing Up' (Mar. Nik and Anas. Nik.)[6]

Feb 18: Services at home yesterday and today. In the evening "The Crystal Gazer"/Mr Gibbes and Mar. Nik./Chekhov's "The Bear."

---

4. Presumably an officer, former infirmary patient

5. Countess Anastasia Vasilievna Hendrikova (1887-1918) was a lady-in-waiting to the empress and a companion to the grand duchess. She went with the family to Tobolsk and was later shot near Perm on 4 September 1918 along with Catherine Schneider "Trina," the empress's lectrice.

6. Source: http://www.librapress.ru/2017/03/Anastasija-Gendrikova-Tobolskij-dnevnik.html.

Authors' note: Life at the governor's mansion continued in cozy domesticity, events in the capitol felt very far away and did not seem relevant. The prisoners continued their daily routine, and if they were treated a bit more harshly now, things were still relatively calm and comfortable. This changed on April 9th.

From the 1918 diary of Nicholas Alexandrovich—

9 April. Monday. Found out about the arrival of the extraordinary authorized [commissar] Yakovlev[7] from Moscow; he settled in Kornilov house.[8] The children imagined that he will come today to do a search, and burned all letters, and Maria and Anastasia even [burned] their diaries.[9] The weather was revolting, cold with wet snow. Alexei felt better and even slept for two-three hours during the day.

10 April. Tuesday. At 10 1/2 o'cl in the morning Kobylinsky showed up with Yakovlev and his suite. I received him in the hall with the daughters. We expected him at 11 o'cl, therefore Alix was not yet ready. He came in, clean shaven face, smiling and embarrassed, asked if I am happy with the guards and the building. Then, almost running he stopped by to see Alexei, without stopping, looked around the rest of the rooms, and, having apologized for bothering us, went downstairs. In the same hurried manner, he also stopped by the others' [rooms] on the rest of the floors. In a half hour he appeared again, in order to present himself to Alix, again hurried to Alexei and went downstairs. This was the extend of inspecting the house for now. We took a walk as usual; the weather was interchangeable, first sunny, then snowing.

11 April. Wednesday. The day was nice and relatively warm. Sat on my favorite greenhouse roof a lot, there the sun warms one nicely. Worked by the hill and on the clearing of the deep ditch along the inner fencing.

---

7. Vasily Vasilievich Yakovlev, Bolshevik commissar put in charge of transferring the tsar from Tobolsk.

8. House adjacent to governor's mansion which once belonged to Merchant Kornilov, members of the suite who followed the imperial family to Tobolsk settled there.

9. Maria destroyed all her diaries except 1912, 1913, and 1916.

12 April. Thursday. After breakfast Yakovlev came over with Kobylinsky and announced that he received an order to take me away, without saying where? Alix decided to go with me and take Maria; it was useless to protest. To leave the other children with Alexei—ill under current circumstances—it was more than difficult! Immediately we started to pack the most necessary things. Then Yakovlev said that he will return for O., T., An. And A., and that most likely we will see them in three weeks or so. We spent a sad evening, of course no one slept that night.

From the diary of Countess Anastasia Hendrikova—

Apr 12: The Sovereign could not postpone the departure, the Empress decided to go with him and Mar. Nik. is also going with them.

From the testimony of E.S. Kobylinsky[10]

At 2 o'clock we entered the hall with Yakovlev. In the center of the hall, next to each other stood the Sovereign and Empress. Having stopped at some distance and bowed to them, Yakovlev said: "I have to tell you (he was speaking to the Sovereign in particular), that I am the extraordinary authorized person from the Moscow Executive Committee, and my authorization consists of the fact that I must take away the entire family from here, but since Alexei Nikolaevich is ill, I received secondary order to leave with you only." The Sovereign replied: "I am not going anywhere." Then Yakovlev continued: "I ask you not to do this. I have to execute this order. If you refuse to go, I will have to use force, or refuse the assignment entrusted to me. Then they may send someone else instead of me, a less humane person. You can be at peace. I am responsible for your life with my own. If you do not wish to go alone, you may bring whoever you want. Be ready. We will be departing tomorrow [morning] at 4 o'clock." With this, Yakovlev once again bowed to the Sovereign and the Empress and left. At the same time, having said nothing to Yakovlev, the Sovereign turned abruptly, and both of them with the Empress they left the hall. Yakovlev headed downstairs. I followed him. But when I was leaving with Yakovlev, the Sovereign made a gesture for me to stay. I went downstairs with

10. Evgeny Sergeyevich Kobylinsky was in charge of the guard in Tsarskoe Selo and Tobolsk.

Yakovlev, but when he left, I came back upstairs. I entered the hall where the Sovereign and Empress, Tatischev and Dolgorukov stood near a round table in the corner of the hall. The Sovereign asked me, where are they planning to take me? I reported to the Sovereign that it is unknown even to me, but based on a few clues from Yakovlev, it is possible to figure out that they want to bring the Sovereign to Moscow. This is why I thought so then: when Yakovlev came to me on the morning of 12 April and initially told me that he will be taking the Sovereign, he said to me that he will return again for the family. I asked him: "When do you think you will return?" To this Yakovlev replied: "Well, let's see? We will get there in about 4-5 days; say, a few days over there, and back; will return in 1 1/2—2 weeks." This is why I reported to the Sovereign that Yakovlev apparently wants to take him to Moscow. Then the Sovereign said: "They must want me to sign the Brest treaty. But I would rather let them cut off my hand than do this." Very anxiously, the Empress said: "I am going too. Without me they will force him to do something again, as they forced him once before," and with this she brought up something about Rodzyanko. Undoubtedly, the Empress was hinting at the Sovereign's act of abdication from the throne. After this the conversation was over, and I went to the Kornilov house.

From the memoirs of Pierre Gilliard—

A bit before 3 o'clock, walking down the hallway I ran into two lackeys who were sobbing. They told me that Yakovlev arrived to announce to the Sovereign that he is being taken away. What is going on? I did not dare go upstairs without being asked and returned to my room. A minute later, Tatiana Nikolaevna knocked on my door. She was in tears and said that Her Majesty is asking me to go to him. I follow her. She [the Empress] confirms that Yakovlev was sent from Moscow in order take the Sovereign away, and that the departure will take place this night: "The Commissar promises that nothing bad will happen to the Sovereign, and that if anyone wishes to accompany him, there will be no objections. I cannot allow the Sovereign to go alone. They want to separate him from me, like last time, and push him into [doing] something bad, causing him to feel anxiety for the lives of his dear ones . . . The Tsar is necessary to them; they know very well that he alone represents Russia . . . together we will be able to resist more strongly, and I must be next to him during this trial . . . But the boy is still so ill . . . what if there are complications . . . My God, what awful torture! . . . For the first time in my life I do not know what to do. Every time I had to make a decision, I always felt that the answer would be given to me from above, and now I feel nothing. But God will not allow this departure, it cannot, it must not happen. I am convinced that this night there will be an ice drift. . ."

At this moment Tatiana Nikolaevna intervened into the conversation: "But, Mama, if Papa will be forced to leave after all, one must make some kind of decision! . . ." I supported Tatiana Nikolaevna, saying that Alexei Nikolaevich feels better and that we will take good care of him. The Empress, was obviously tortured by doubts; she paced back and forth in the room and continued speaking, but mostly to herself rather than to us. Finally, she came over to me and said: "Yes, it is better this way; I will be going with the Sovereign; I entrust Alexei to you. . ." The Sovereign returned in a minute; the Empress rushed to him with the words: "It is decided— I am going with you, and Maria will go with us." The Sovereign said: "Fine, if you wish. . . ." I went down to my room, and the entire day passed in preparations. Prince Dolgorukov and Doctor Botkin, as well as Chemodurov, Anna Demidova and Sednev will accompany Their Majesties. It was decided that eight officers and soldiers from our guard will go with us. The family spent the second half of the day by the bed of Alexei Nikolaevich. In the evening, at 10 1/2 o'clock we went upstairs to have tea. The Empress sat on the sofa, with her were two daughters. They cried so much that their faces were swollen. We all hid our torment and tried to appear calm. We all had a feeling that if one of us breaks down, the rest will break too. Sovereign and Empress were serious and focused. It was apparent that they were willing to sacrifice everything, including their lives, if the Lord, in His inscrutable ways, would demand this to save the nation. Never before had they shown us more kindness and caring. . . . At eleven and a half o'clock, the servants gather in the large hall. Their Majesties and Maria Nikolaevna are saying goodbye to them. The Sovereign embraces and kisses all the men, the Empress—all women. Almost everyone is crying. Their Majesties leave; we all go downstairs to my room. At three and a half o'clock in the morning equipages are driven in the yard. These are most awful *tarantasses*.[11] Only one has a top cover. We find some straw in the back yard and line the *tarantass* floors with it. We put a mattress into the one intended for the Empress. At four o'clock we go upstairs to Their Majesties, who leave the room for a minute to see Alexei Nikolaevich. The Sovereign, Empress and Maria Nikolaevna say goodbye to us. The Empress and Grand Duchesses are crying. The Sovereign seems calm and finds a cheering word for each of us; he embraces and kisses us. While saying goodbye, the Empress asks me not to go back downstairs and stay with Alexei Nikolaevich. I head over to him, he is crying in his bed. A few minutes later we hear clamor of equipages. The Grand Duchesses are returning to their rooms upstairs and pass by their brother's door, sobbing.

From the memoirs of V.V. Yakovlev—

[12 April] All the residents of the house were up and about. In all corners of the house one could hear sobbing. The Romanov daughters and their entire "court" staff came out on the porch to see off their "patrons." Nicholas Romanov bewilderingly paced around in his wobbly gait from one person to another, and with sort of convulsive movements crossed his daughters as goodbye. His haughty wife restrained the sobs of those remaining behind. Her every gesture, every word showed that one should not show any weakness in front of the "red enemy."

From the 1918 diary of Nicholas Alexandrovich—

14 April. Saturday. Got up at 4 o'cl, as we were supposed to depart at 5 o'cl., but there was a delay because Yakovlev overslept and besides, he was waiting for a lost package. Walked across Tobol on boards, but at the other bank we had to cross for about 10 *sazhens*[12] in a steamer. We met Yakovlev's assistant—Guzakov, who was in charge of the entire guard on the route to Tyumen. The day became excellent and very warm, the road got softer; but it still shook

11. Type of a flat sleigh or wagon.
12. A sazhen is a unit of measurement of about seven feet.

strongly, and I was concerned for Alix. In the open spaces it was very dusty, and in the forests very dirty. In the village of Pokrovskoe there was change of horses, we stood for a long time just across from Grigori's house and saw his entire family, who were looking out of the windows.

The last change of horses was in the village of Borki. Here E.S. Botkin got very strong kidney pains, they put him in the house for an hour and a half, and then he resumed forward, unhurriedly. We had tea and snacks with our people and the sharpshooters at the village school building. The last leg was slow and with all the manner of military precautions. Arrived in Tyumen at 9 1/4 in the presence of a beautiful moon, with an entire squadron, which surrounded our wagons at the entrance into the city. It was pleasant to end up in a train, although it was not very clean; we ourselves and our belongings had a desperately dirty appearance. Went to bed at 10 o'-clock without undressing, I—above Alix's bunk, Maria and Nyuta in the next compartment.

From the memoir of Pierre Gilliard—

14/27 April, 1918.[13] The coachman who drove the Empress to the first post station, brought a note from Maria Nikolaevna: the roads are ruined, conditions of the journey are terrible. Will the Empress be in any condition to tolerate the trip? What burning anxiety one feels for them!

From the 1918 diary [in English] of Alexandra Feodorovna—

14 (27) April. Saturday. Got up at 4, had tea, packed up, crossed the river at 5 on foot on planks & then on a ferry. Waited ages before driving off, 7:15. (Com. fidgety, runing [running] about, telegraphing).—Lovely weather, road atrocious. Changes horses, again 6 times, & our horsemen oftener, as both days the same men. About 12, got to Pokrovskoe, changed horses, stood long before our Friend's house, saw his family & friends looking out of the window. At village Borki took tea & our provisions in a nice peasant's house.

13. The double dates indicate "old" and "new: style. Gregorian calendar (new style) replaced the Julian calendar (old style) in Catholic countries beginning in 1582. This change was also implemented in Protestant and Orthodox countries after a significant delay. In Russia the change took place after the revolution in 1918.

Leaving the village, suddenly saw Sedov in the street!—Changed our carriage once. Again, all sorts of incidents, but less than yesterday. Stopped in a village school, drank tea with our soldiers. Yevgeny Sergeevich [Evgeny Sergeyevich] lay down as awful kidney pains. When darkness set in one tied up the bells of our troikas, lovely sunset, & moon. Tore along at a wild rate. Approaching Tyumen a squadron on horseback formed a chain around us & accompanied a[s] far as the station crossed the river on a movable bridge, from 3 versts[14] through the dark town. At midnight got into the train. Write 2 [letters] to the children.

From the memoir of V. V. Yakovlev—

On the morning of the [17th] 30th[15] [April] we arrived in Ekaterinburg without any incident. Despite our early arrival, the Ekaterinburg station was overflowing with people. As it turned out, the residents of Ekaterinburg found out about our pending arrival—we had no idea about this. Especially large was the crowd concentrated at the freight platform. Our train was standing on the fifth track from the platform. When they saw us, they started demanding for me to bring Nicholas out and show him to them. There was a roar in the air, and here and there threatening cries could be heard: "Strangle them all!" "Finally they are in our hands!" The guards who stood on the platform weakly restrained the pushing crowd, which started chaotically moving towards our train car. I lined up my guard team around the entire train . . . prepared machine guns. To my great horror I saw that somehow the station commissar ended up at the head of the crowd. He yelled out to me, still from afar: "Comrade Yakovlev, bring the Romanovs out of the train. Let me spit in his face, at least!" The situation was becoming extremely dangerous. The crowd was pushing against us and kept getting closer to the train. Its mood was becoming more threatening. To wait for someone from the Soviet was useless—no one among the local leaders came to our aid, although they were already warned not only of our arrival, but also of what was going on at the train station! It was necessary to take some decisive measures. I sent comrade Kasyan to the station head, with a demand to immediately put a freight train

14. A Russian measure of length, about 0.66 mile (1.1 km).
15. Yakovlev was using new style dates.

between the platform and our train, and then send our train towards Ekaterinburg II [station] as soon as possible. The shouts were getting more insistent. Persuasions did not work. The crowd kept demanding to see the Romanovs more and more insistently. In order to at least temporarily restrain them until Kasyan returns, I shouted loudly to my lined-up guards: "Prepare the machine guns." The pushing crowd fled, but threatening shouts towards me could be heard. The same fat commissar with a big stomach yelled in a frenzied voice: "We are not afraid of your machine guns. We have prepared cannons against you. See them sitting on the platform." I looked in the direction he was pointing. Indeed, three-inch muzzles were moving there, and someone was swarming nearby. While we were exchanging these niceties, trying to somehow stall for time, Kasyan returned, he was able to obtain from the station head an execution order for our demand, despite the chaos happening at the station. Right after Kasyan's arrival we saw that a freight train was moving towards us. In a few minutes we were behind a wall of train cars, isolated from the crowd. Shouts and curses could be heard towards the machinist, and while the rushing people were trying to get to our side through the buffers of the freight train, we, having an attached locomotive, took off and disappeared among endless tracks of the Ekaterinburg train station, and in 15 minutes were already in complete safety of II Ekaterinburg.

From the 1918 diary of Alexandra Feodorovna—

17/30 April. Tuesday. Yekaterinburg. Stood ages & moved up & down with the train whilst our two com. Yakovlev & Guzakov spoke with the Sovdep[16] of here. At 3 were told to get out of the train Yakovlev had to give us over to the Ural Region Soviet.
Their chief took us three in open motor, a truck with soldiers armed to their teeth followed us. Drove through bystreets till reached a small house, around whi.[ch] high wooden pailings [pilings] have been placed. Our soldiers not allowed to accompany us. Here a new guard & officer & other civilians, looked through all our baggage. Valia not yet let in. got our lunch at 4:30. (rations) fr. an hotel, *borcht*[17] & a dish, we 3, Nyuta in the dining room, then sitting

16. Soviet department.
17. Soup traditionally made with beets.

room in wh. sleep Yevgeny Sergeevich & our two men. (Canaliza-
tion does not work.)—Had tea at 9:30. Then one brought beds for
the others & found us a basin. Went to bed at 11. Weather was glorious, so warm & sunny. Nicholas read the Bible to us.

From the 1918 diary of Nicholas Alexandrovich—

17 April. Tuesday. Another marvellous warm day. At 8.40 we arrived
in Ekaterinburg. For about three hours [we] stood at one station.
There was major altercation between the local and our commissars.
In the end the former won, and the train moved to another—freight
station. After an hour and a half of standing still, we came out of
the train. Yakovlev transferred us to the local regional commissar,
with whom the three of us got into a motor and drove down de-
serted streets to the house that was readied for us—Ipatiev's. Little
by little our belongings also arrived, but Valya was not allowed in.
The house is nice, clean. They assigned us four large rooms: corner
bedroom, lavatory, close by a dining room with windows looking
over the garden and view of the lower part of vegetable garden, and
finally an open hall with an arch instead of doors. We could not
unpack our things for a long time, as the commissar, the commandant and the officer of the guard still had not been able to inspect
our luggage chests. The inspection later was similar to customs, very
strict, down to the last bottle from Alix's travel first aid kit. This
made me explode, and I sharply expressed my opinion to the commissar. By 9 o'cl. we finally settled in. Had dinner at 4 1/2 from a
hotel, and after clean up, had tea for dessert.

We settled this way: Alix, Maria and I in the bedroom all three,
the lavatory is shared, in the dining room—N. Demidova, in the
hall—Botkin, Chemodurov and Sednev. Near the entrance is the
room of the officer of the guard. The guards were staying in two
rooms near the dining room. In order to get to the bathroom and
W.C., one had to pass by a guard by the door of the guardroom.
Around the house a tall picket fence was erected two *sazhens* away
from the windows; there, a chain of guards was standing, in the garden as well.

From the 1918 diary of Alexandra Feodorovna—
Yekaterinburg. 18 April/1 May. Ipatiev house. Wednesday. Sunny morning again. 25° in the sun. Remained in bed because of enlarged heart, tired & head ache. 1:15. The others got soup & eggs brought. I had some good bread. Marie read to me *Spir. Readings*. 3:30. Tea, bread & Maltz extract.[18] Marie read to me, Nicholas sat at his writing table also in our bedroom. Reading & writing. 8:45. tea. Wrote to the children. Our Commandant is Avdeev[19] (acc.[ompanied] us fr. Tobolsk it seems) his aid[e] Ukraintsev (former soldier was a beater when Misha went shooting near Borzhom.)[20] (as a little boy Olga played with him at Gagri 15 years ago),—he works in a fabric [factory], receives 300 a month, has a large family. ♥ 3[21]

Maria to Anastasia—
Ekaterinburg, 18 April/1May. Christ Is Risen! I send you my greetings for the feast of light, my sweet Anastasia. We arrived here by car after the train. We had breakfast at 4.30 in the dining room. Only unpacked our things in the evening, because the luggage was searched, even the "medicines" and the "candy."[22] After two days in the cart, with bumps, our belongings were in a terrible state. Extraordinary thing—the frames and perfume bottles were not broken, only the top of the Malzeket[23] spilled out, which stained the books, but Nyuta and Sednev put everything back in order. Even inside the bags, there was dust and dirt and all the wrapping paper was untidy and torn. We had tea together at 9.30 in the evening. After that we rested a little; we set cots up ourselves and went to bed at 11 o'clock. Papa read to us, the Gospel of the week. Mama teased Mashka, imitating, with success, Pankra[tov]'s[24] enthusiasm, but despite all of that, everything again is "a little depressing."

We have not unpacked everything, because we were told that we would be moved to another place. I am not going to write to anyone

18. She probably meant "malt extract," which is something like the marmite spread.
19. Alexander Avdeev (Avdeyev) was the first commandant at the Ipatiev house.
20. Town in Georgia.
21. Alexandra had a pain scale for her heart, 1-5.
22. Code word for jewelry.
23. Probably perfume.
24. Commandant in charge of the Ekaterinburg prisoners.

else, so please give my Easter wishes to all and tell them that I send them regards with all my heart. Tell Madelen and the others how we live.

My best wishes to my dear Shvybz. May God protect you. Your M. [To the left of Maria's signature, Alexandra wrote]: Your old Mama. Ekaterinburg, 19th April/2nd May, 1918. [To] An.[astasia] N.[iko-laevna] Christ Is Risen, my little and dear soul. I kiss you three times. I hope you receive all my little eggs and icons. We think about you all the time and dream about the happy day when we will see each other again. Have you received all our letters? It is already one week and we have not seen each other and we have written every day. It is silly, what is there to write about, but we cannot write everything. There were some amusing incidents. Every night I wish you good night's sleep. And you? In the entire house there is no water and we wait a long time for the *samovar*[25] to be brought, which is slow to heat. Mama has her meals on the cot and I have mine with Papa, Nyuta, Evg. Serg., Sednev[26] and Chemod[urov] in the dining room and Nyuta sleeps there. She sends regards to all of you. Do little Tresses[27] and the "good Russians" still take walks together?

Christ Is Risen! 19 April/2 May, 1918. Ekaterinburg. I kiss you fervently thrice, darling, and remember you. Today [Mama's] health is better I think, the others took a walk for an hour in the tiny garden, were very happy. [They] brought water in a barrel, so Papa can take a bath before dinner. I swung on the American swing with Nyuta, walked back and forth with Papa.—Mama is lying down on a cot today, a bit better, but head and heart ache. They asked us to make a list of everyone who will arrive with you—I hope we did not forget anyone—I don't know whom Isa will bring. We must explain the reason [to have] each person with us. How very complicated everything is, 8 months of living a peaceful life and now everything is starting again. I feel such pity for you, that you have to pack and resolve [everything]. I hope that Stepan is helping. [I wish] only to have some news from you. May the Lord keep you + Maria

25. Heated metal container traditionally used to heat and boil water in Russia.

26. Ivan Dmitrievich Sednev was the imperial cook who followed the family. He was killed by the Bolsheviks in 1918, shortly before them.

27. Possibly referring to a peasant messenger boy.

Anastasia to Maria—

24 April/7 May. Tobolsk. Indeed, He Is Risen! My dear sweet Mashka. We were so terribly happy to get the news [from you] and shared our impressions. I apologize for writing crookedly on the paper, but this is just my foolishness. What we rec.[eived] from An. Pav. was very sweet; [sends] regards, etc., to you. How are you all? Sashka and so on? You see, of course that there is always a massive number of rumors; well and you sometimes understand how hard it is and one doesn't know whom to believe and sometimes it's all so disgusting! As they only tell us half of it, but not the rest, and that's why we think he is lying. Ks. Mikh. [*sic*] Bitner comes and spends time with the Little One. Alexei is so sweet; he eats and tries so [hard] (remember how it was at the little bench when you were here?) We take turns having breakfast with Alex.[ei] and making him eat, although there are days when he eats without needing to be told. Dear ones, in our thoughts we are with you all the time. It is terribly sad and empty; I really don't know what possesses me.

The baptismal cross is with us, of course, and we got your news. So. The Lord will help and does help. We set up the iconostasis awfully nicely for Easter, all in spruce, which is the way they do it here, and the flowers. We took pictures. I hope they come out. I continue to draw, not too badly they say; it's very pleasant. We swung on the swing; boy did I laugh when I fell off so splendidly! Yes, quite! I told the sisters so many times last night, that they are sick of hearing about it, but I could tell again and again, although there is no one left to tell. In general, there is a whole trainload of things to tell you all. My Jim caught a cold, and coughs, so he sits at home and sends regards. There was such incredible weather! One could shout from the pleasantness of it. Strangely enough, I tanned more deeply than anyone else, a regular Arab woman! But these days I am boring and not pretty. It's cold, and this morning we froze, although we were inside, of course, and didn't go out. I very much apologize: I forgot to extend good wishes to all you dear ones for the holiday; I kiss you all not thrice but lots of times. My dear, all of us thank you for the letters. There were demonstrations here too, but they were not much of anything. We sit here together as always, but you are missed. Tell precious Papa that we are very grateful for the figs; we are savoring them. I apologize of course that this is such a jumbled letter; you understand that my thoughts are racing and I can't write anything and so I put down whatever comes to mind. Soon we will go for a walk; summer hasn't come yet and nothing is blooming, but things are starting to come up. You know, I want to see you so much, it's sad. I go for walks and then I'm back. It's boring whether you go out or not. I swung [on a swing]. The sun came out but it's cold and my hand can barely write. Your regards were transmitted to us word for word, and we send you big thanks and the same. In the evenings we sit around; yesterday we read fortunes using the book. You know which one. Sometimes we work. We do everything they ask. A kiss to you, and to your dear ones, and much else I won't elaborate on, for you will understand. Thought about it already some time ago. Russa,[28] although sweet, is strange and makes one angry, for she doesn't understand and simply can't bear it. Once I was almost rude, a real cretin. Well, it looks like I have written enough foolishness. Right now, I will write some more, and then I will read it later, during free time, that is. For now, good-bye. I wish you the best, happiness, and all good things. We constantly pray for you and think, Help us Lord. Christ be with you, precious ones. I embrace all of you tightly and kiss you. A.

Olga to Maria—

[Telegram 24 April/7 May, 1918]. To the Chairman of Ekaterinburg Regional Executive Committee for Maria Nikolaevna Romanova. 19 o'cl. 31 min. from Tobolsk. All grateful Easter cards little one slowly recovering feels well kiss affectionately Olga

Maria to Tobolsk—

Ekaterinburg, 26th April/9th May, 1918. Thank you, our little souls, for the telegram which we received yesterday before dinner; we are very happy, because this is the first news we received from you since we [have been] here.[29] We are happy to learn that you received our letters. Do you remember, Shvybz, our special corner near *Feodorovsky Sobor*, of T.G. [?] and of his students "Bokche"

---

28. Perhaps a nickname for one of the servants.

29. They received previous letters written from Tobolsk late or not at all.

and of others; the story of the parrot that Al.[exei] told us and [which] always pleased Nyuta? We began to look like Vl.Al., do you understand? Do not forget that one of you asks for the address of P.Iv. and Styopa. Our life continues without changes. Yesterday we walked for such a long time in the little garden, because the weather was better and the sun warmed us—this reminded us of last summer at Tsarskoe Selo. We thought a lot about you, when we were listening to a polka, at the station waiting room. Afterwards, someone sang a duet. Does Maksimochin still sing so loudly that the entire Tobolsk can hear? It is a shame that we do not know the words to "I do not mind." You could probably ask for the words and of other songs. Time goes so fast, that I have not had the time to read, not even once, the words of the songs that we have written down. Write to M. Zizi and Maria Nik. and tell them that we kiss [them] and think about them. I hope that Ch. wrote to all the sisters. Have you had news from Zinochka? While I write, Papa organizes his cigarettes that were packed loosely together during the voyage but were not totally damaged. Papa kisses you all. A big "good morning" to A.A.[30] You will see him tomorrow for sure. We have retained good memories of him. What do Baby and the others do? [. . .] We think about everybody with affection. We talk a lot about you and think about you all the time, dear ones. We wait for a letter from you. I kiss you affectionately, my precious ones. May the Lord protect you+++ Your Masha. It seems to me that you are being formal in using "Vous" in your letter. What became of Jimmy, Joy and Ortipo?[31]

Maria to Tobolsk—

Ekaterinburg, 27th April/10th May, 1918. Yesterday, we did not have time to send the letter because the guards were changed three times. I hope that today the letter is sent. All new guards come inside and check everything. Each time, Mama is obliged to get up from bed and meet the guards in her dressing gown. Yesterday an extraordinary event happened: Nyuta and I washed Mama's hair. Everything went well and her hair was not tangled, but I don't know

30. Alexei Volkov.
31. Three dogs they brought with them.

what is going to happen today and everything is, for sure, going to come undone. The water here is very good, almost as good as in Tsarskoe Selo. In the bath tub the water looks light blue. Yesterday we went for a walk, like every day, till tea time. The sun was very warm, just like in Tobolsk, and in the evening, it penetrated the window of the second floor. We hope Kolya comes to play with you. I am finishing the letter because there is nothing else to say. I hold you in my arms, my little souls. Warm wishes to everybody. May Christ be with you + Masha

Ekaterinburg. 27 April/10 May
We miss the quiet and tranquil life in Tobolsk. Here there are unpleasant surprises almost daily. Just now the members of regional committee were here and asked each of us how much money has with him, we had to sign off. As you know that Papa and Mama did not have even one kopek with them, they signed, none, and I [had] 16 r. 75 k. which Anastasia gave me for the journey. From the rest they took all the money for safekeeping, leaving each just a little, giving them receipts. They warn us that there is no guarantee from new searches. Who would have thought that after 14 months of captivity they would treat us this way? We hope that it is better for you, the way it was when we were there.

28 April/11 May. Good morning my dears. We just got up and heated the stove as it got cold in the rooms. The wood is crackling cozily. Reminds one of a frosty day in T.[obolsk].—Today we gave our dirty laundry to washer woman, Mama's shawl was washed and very well at that, and dust rags. For a few days now, our guards are the Letts. It is probably not very cozy by you, everything is packed. Did you pack my things, if you haven't packed the birthday book then try to write to N.T. If it doesn't work out then its fine. Now you will probably arrive soon. We know nothing of you, really waiting for a letter. I continue to draw everything from the book Tem[?]. Maybe it would be possible to buy white paint? We have very little of it left. In the autumn Zhilik obtained really good one from somewhere, flat and round. Who knows maybe this letter will reach he house on the eve of your departure. May the Lord bless your journey

and keep you from all evil. Would terribly like to know who will be escorting you. Our thoughts and prayers surround you, just to be together again. I kiss you all affectionately, darlings, my dears, and bless you +

Heartfelt regards to all and those who remain too. I hope that Al. feels stronger again and that the journey won't tire him out too much. Mama

We will take a walk this morning as it is warm. They are still not allowing Valya in. Tell Vl Vas. and others regards. I really regret that I did not have the chance to say goodbye. It will probably be terribly sad for you to leave T. [obolsk] the cozy house etc. I reminisce about all the cozy rooms and the garden. Do you swing on the swing or did the board break? Papa and I kiss you warmly darlings. May god keep you. I send regards to everyone in the house. Does Tolya come over to play? All the best and have a good journey if you are leaving already. Your M.

28 April/11 May, 1918. Good morning my dears. We just got up and kindled the fireplace, as it got very cold in the rooms. The wood is crackling cozily, reminds [me] of a freezing day in Tobolsk. Today we gave our dirty laundry to a washing woman. Nyuta also became a washer woman, washed Mama's kerchief, very well, and the dust rags. For a few days now, our guards are Latvians. It's probably not cozy for you, everything is packed. Did you pack my things, if you have not packed the book for births, then please ask N.T. to write. If it does not pan out, that is fine. Now you will probably be arriving soon. We don't know anything about you, really waiting for a letter. I continue drawing everything from Bem's book. Would you buy me some white paint? We have very little of it left. In the autumn, Zhilik got from somewhere a very nice one, flat and round. Who knows, maybe this letter will get to you just before your departure. May the Lord bless your journey and may He save you from all evil. Would like to know terribly who will be escorting you. Affectionate thoughts and prayers surround you—only to be together again sooner. I kiss you affectionately, my dear sweet ones and bless [you] +

Testimony of Ipatiev house[32] guard Strekotin—
The prisoners constantly tried to start conversations with the red guards. Once, during a walk, the Tsar quietly approached me and said: "Tell me, is this a large city—Ekaterinburg?"—"About as big as Moscow"—I responded, and having tossed the rifle up on the belt, I walked away.

Maria to Zinaida Tolstaya—
Ekaterinburg, 4/17 May, 1918. Christ Is Risen. My dear Z., Good wishes to you for this bright holiday. I apologize for [writing] so late, but we departed right before the holidays. It was very unexpected for us. Alexei happened to be sick, so the sisters had to stay with him. They are supposed to arrive here soon. Tell Rita that not that long ago we saw the little Sedusha. Today is three weeks since we left Tobolsk. It is so sad to be without the others, especially now during the holidays. We have settled in nicely here. The house is small but clean, shame that it's right in the city so the garden is rather small. When the others arrive, not sure how we will settle, there are not that many rooms. I live with Papa and Mama in one, where we spend almost the entire day. Just now we went out into the garden, the weather is grey and it is raining. On the way, the weather was wonderful. We used horses for 260 versts until Tyumen. The roads were awful, we were jolted terribly. The paper with which our things were wrapped rubbed out in places. Tobacco fell out of the cigarettes. But strangely no glass broke. We took the medicines with us and arrived safely. Rode for two days, stayed the nights in villages. Took horses across the Irtysh, and walked across the Tura on foot and a few *sazhens* to the banks—in a ferry. Mama withstood the journey surprisingly well, but now of course feels tired and has a headache almost daily. Doctor Botkin came with us, the poor man had kidney colic on the way, he was suffering a lot. We stopped in a village and they put him to bed there, he rested for two hours and continued with us. Luckily the pains did not happen again. And how are you all? The sisters wrote that we got news from you. If you want to write to me, my address is: Ekaterinburg, the

32. The house where the prisoners were held belonged to engineer Ipatiev; it also became known as "The House of Special Purpose."

Regional Executive Committee. To the Chairman, to be given to me. Have you had any news from Tili? Regards to all yours and Nik. Dm. I kiss you, Rita, and the children affectionately. I wish you all the best. May the Lord keep you. It was terribly sad that we were not able to go to the cathedral even once and venerate the relics of St. Ioann of Tobolsk.

Maria to Elisabeth Feodorovna—

5 May. Ekaterinburg. He Is Risen Indeed! We kiss you dearest, three times. Thank you very much for the eggs, chocolate, coffee. Mama drank her first cup of coffee with great pleasure, it was very good. It's very good for her headaches, and as it happens, we had not taken any with us. We learned from the newspapers that you have been sent away from your convent and were very sad for you. It is strange that we should all end up in the same province under arrest.[33] We hope that you will be able to spend the summer somewhere out of town, in Verkhoturie or in some monastery. We have so missed having a church. My address: Ekaterinburg, The Regional Executive Committee, To the Chairman for transmission to me. May God keep you + Your loving goddaughter

Maria to Tobolsk—

10 May. This morning we are going for a walk, as it is warm. Valya Dolgorukov is still not allowed to see us. Greetings to others. I am so sorry I was not able to say goodbye to them. You must be very sad to leave Tobolsk, such a pleasant house, etc.; I remember the cozy rooms and the garden. Do you play on the swing, or did the plank already break? Papa and I kiss you lovingly, my dears. May God keep you. I send greetings to everyone in the house. Best wishes and a safe journey if you are already leaving. Your Maria

Testimony of Ipatiev house guard Yakimov—

So, we were guarding Tsar Nicholas Alexandrovich with his family. All lived at the Ipatiev house, that is: The Tsar, his wife Alexandra Feodorovna, son Alexei and daughters—Olga, Tatiana, Maria and

---

33. Grand Duchess Elisabeth was sent to Perm, later to be transferred to Alapaevsk (briefly stopping in Ekaterinburg), and was ultimately murdered there along with other extended family members, the day after Maria and her family were executed, on July 18, 1918.

Anastasia. The non-family members who lived with them were: Doctor Botkin; "lady-in-waiting" as we called her, Demidova; the cook Kharitonov, and lackey Trupp. Botkin was older, grey, tall. He wore a blue set: jacket, vest and pants, starched undershirt and tie; short boots on his feet. Demidova was a tall, plump blonde, about 30-35 years old. She dressed well, not like a servant. She definitely wore a corset: by her figure one could tell that she was tightened. . . . The cook was about 50 years old, short, stocky, strawberry blond [hair], dark moustache, not very long, he shaved his beard on his cheeks and chin, leaving it under and around the moustache; on one cheek he had a mole with long hair growing out of it. He wore a black jacket with a solid standing collar, black pants, short boots. The lackey was about 60 years old, tall, thin. He shaved the hair on his head and face. Wore some sort of a jacket, dark-grey pants and boots. Also, with the imperial family lived a boy, around 14 years old. I do not know his name. He was tall, thin, with a white face, long straight nose, wide mouth, thin lips, eyes not particularly large but deep set. He wore a dark-grey jacket with a standing collar, pants and short boots made from the same material, but I had also seen him in long boots.

Testimony of Ipatiev house guard Strekotin—

The ex-emperor always wore the same military khaki uniform . . . he was taller than average, thick, fair-haired, with grey eyes, lively and impetuous, he twirled his ginger moustache often. The Tsare-vich—Alexei, wore the same [uniform] as the Tsar in the same colonel rank, [he was] brunet, with black unhappy eyes, thin, ill-looking. His severe untreatable illness completely paralyzed both of his legs, apparently even before the revolution, which was why he was always carried outside by the Tsar himself. He carefully picked him up, pulled him close to his wide chest, and the other would grab his father's thick short neck with his arms, while his thin, whip-like weak legs hung limply. Two of the daughters were blonde with grey eyes, of medium height and looked very much alike. They were always together, and both seemed merry and talkative. The other two young ladies did not look like each other. One

of them—Tatiana,[34] a plump, healthy looking brunette. The other,
i.e., the eldest Olga,[35] was taller than average, thin, pale faced, ill
looking, she did not take a lot of walks in the garden, did not so-
cialize with any of her sisters, mostly stayed near her brother. The
daughters always dressed well, changed dresses often, and acces-
sorized with gold and diamonds.

Testimony of Ipatiev house guard Yakimov—

About the Tsar, Avdeyev talked with malice. He cursed him in any
way he could, called him "bloody" and "bloodthirsty." The main
thing he cursed him for was the war: that the Tsar wanted this war
and for three years he spilled the blood of the workers, and that
masses of these workers were shot in this war and also for the strikes.
From his words we were to understand that he received the appointment as Commandant of the House of Special Purpose as a reward
from the revolution, because he prevented Yakovlev from taking
away the Tsar. And it was obvious that Avdeyev was very satisfied
with this appointment. He was so happy when he talked at a rally,
and promised the workers: "I will take you all to the house and show
you the Tsar." Avdeyev was a drunkard. He loved drinking and
drank all the time, . . . here [Popov house][36] and at the Ipatiev house.
His associates drank with him. One time, Avdeyev got so drunk
that he fell over in one of the lower rooms of the house. Right at
this time, Beloborodov arrived and asked for him. Someone among
Avdeyev's associates lied that he stepped out. But the way he ended
up on the lower floor was after visiting the imperial family in this
drunk state, he went to see them that drunk. While drunk, they
[Avdeyev and associates] made a lot of noise in the commandant's
room, yelled, slept in a pile, wherever they fell, and made the place
a dirty mess. Sang songs which could not have been pleasant to the
Tsar. They sang "You fell victim in a fatal battle," "Let us reject the
old world," "Walk together, comrades." At times when Avdeyev was
absent, a member of the imperial family petitioned Moshkin with
some request, and he always said that they need to wait until

34. Strekotin probably means Maria.
35. Strekotin probably means Tatiana.
36. House near Ipatiev's where the guards stayed.

Avdeyev returns. When Avdeyev came back and Moshkin passed on the request, Avdeyev had the response: "To the devil with them!" Returning from the imperial family's rooms, Avdeyev would often tell us that he refused one of their requests. This refusal apparently gave him pleasure. He talked about it happily. For example, they asked him to permit them to open windows, and he was telling us how he refused it. I don't know how he referred to the Tsar directly, but behind his back he called him "Nikolashka."

Testimony of Ipatiev house guard Yakimov—

Nothing was left of my ideas about the Tsar which I had before I became a guard. I started to think differently of them after I saw them with my own eyes. I started to feel pity for them as human beings. In my head an idea was born: let them escape; what can I do to allow them to escape. I never told anyone, but I had an idea to talk to the doctor, Derevenko, who used to visit them. But then I was wary of him, thought I don't know what kind of person he is. His face had no expression when he was leaving them, and he never said a word about them. So, I was too wary. Before I got hired as a guard, having not seen or known them, I was also somewhat guilty towards them. Avdeyev and the comrades would be singing revolutionary songs at times, and I would sing along with them a bit. But once I saw what's what, I quit all that, and almost all of us, if not all, used to criticize Avdeyev for that.

Testimony of Ipatiev house guard Strekotin—

The prisoners were taken outside for a walk twice a day, at 10 in the morning and at 4 in the afternoon. 30 minutes each time. At this time, in the garden and in the yard, the guard was increased from among the volunteers in the team, there were always plenty of volunteers. The prisoners did not all always go outside for a walk. In particular, most rarely went out the four people who were imprisoned along with the imperial family. Another who rarely went out, and never for long, was the Tsaritsa. She was serious, haughty and silent. The Tsar was almost always wearing the same military uniform with a cockade in his military hat. The same with the Heir. The Heir was always carried by the Emperor himself during walks, he sat him into a wheelchair and wheeled him around the garden, stopping on paths to give him pebbles, he [the Heir] then tossed them into bushes, or he [the Emperor] picked flowers for him, or branches from bushes.

Testimony of Ipatiev house guard Yakimov—

The imperial family's meals were brought from Soviet Cafeteria, the one on the corner of Voznesensky and Main Prospect. . . . But later, still under Avdeyev, they were allowed to cook their own meals at home. Provisions for this were delivered from the Regional soviet by some special delivery man. The nuns from the monastery brought them milk, eggs and bread. There were prayer services in the house, but the entire time I stayed at the house, there were only three services. Twice they were given by the priest Storozhev and once by the priest Melendin. But there were services before us. I know this because I was the one who went to get the priests when there was to be a prayer service. During Avdeyev, there were two services at the house while I was there.

Testimony of Father Ioann Storozhev[37]—

On Sunday, 20 May/2 June, 1918, I performed the usual liturgy service at the Ekaterininsky Cathedral, and just having returned home at 10 o'clock in the morning, settled in to have tea, when someone knocked at the front door of my apartment. I personally opened the door and saw in front of me a soldier of nondescript appearance, with a red face and small shifty eyes.[38] He was wearing an old jacket of khaki color, on his head—a worn military cap. There were no epaulets, nor cockade, of course. No weapons could be seen on him.

To my question of what he needs, the soldier responded: "You are requested to perform a service for Romanov." Not understanding whom he is referring to, I asked "Which Romanov?," "You know, the former tsar," he explained. From subsequent discussion it turned out that Nicholas Alexandrovich Romanov is asking to perform the next *obednitsa*—"[39] He wrote over here asking for some

37. Priest from the nearby Voznesensky church. The slashes (/) in the text are in the original.
38. This was Yakimov.
39. A shortened version of the liturgy, which can be said either by priest or laity. There is no communion at an obednitsa service.

kind of *obednitsa* service" the visitor announced. Structured *obednitsa* is usually performed for the military when for one reason or another it is not possible to perform a liturgy. Normally this prayer service is combined with a subsequent liturgy, but is significantly shorter, as after *obednitsa* no Eucharist is offered. Having agreed to perform the service, I noted that it would be necessary to bring a deacon with us. The soldier insistently objected for a long time against inviting a deacon, stating that "the commandant" ordered to bring only one priest, but I insisted, and together with this soldier we went to the Cathedral, where I got everything needed for the service, invited deacon Buimirov, with whom, accompanied by the same soldier, we went to the Ipatiev house. Since the time the Romanov family was placed here, the house was surrounded by a double plank fence. The cabby stopped near the first outer wooden fence. In front walked the soldiers who accompanied us, behind them the deacon and I.

The external guard let us pass; having been delayed for a short time near the gate locked from within, on the side of the house that earlier belonged to Solomirsky, we entered behind the second fence right at the gate of the Ipatiev house.

Here stood numerous young men armed with rifles, dressed in general civilian clothes, on their belts hung hand grenades. These armed men apparently were the guards. They took us through the gates into the courtyard and from there through a side door into the ground floor of the Ipatiev house.

Having ascended the staircase, we entered the upstairs towards the main door, and then through the hallway—into the study which "the commandant" occupied. Everywhere, on the stairs as well as on the platform, and in the front room were guards—the same type of young men armed with the same rifles and hand grenades in civilian clothes.

Inside the commandant's actual room, we found two middle-aged men, who were wearing tunics. One of them was lying in bed and seemingly sleeping, the other was silently smoking cheap cigarettes. In the center of the room there was a table, on it a *samovar*, bread, butter. On the piano, which was also in this room, there were rifles, hand grenades and some other things. It was dirty, messy, disordered.

At the moment of our arrival the commandant was not in this room. Soon some young man arrived, wearing a tunic, khaki pants with a wide leather belt with a holster in which was a large revolver; this man's appearance was that of a typical "workman." I did not notice anything unusual, nothing outstanding, attention grabbing or sharp either in this man's appearance, or his behavior. I soon guessed, rather than understood, that this gentleman is "the commandant of the house of special purpose," as the Ipatiev house was referred to by the Bolsheviks during the time the Romanovs were imprisoned there. The commandant stared at me silently, without greeting, I saw him for the first time and did not even know his surname, and now memorized it. To my question about which service we need to perform, he replied "they are asking for *obednitsa.*" Neither I, nor the deacon engaged in any conversation with the commandant but I only asked if I would be allowed to offer *prosfora* to the Romanovs after the service, which I showed him. The commandant quickly looked over the *prosfora* and after a long thought returned it to the deacon, saying: "it can be given to them, but I must warn you there will be no other conversations." I could not help but respond that I do not plan to have any conversation at all. My response apparently bothered the commandant a bit and he said a few times "That's right, no other ones besides those about religious subjects." We got dressed with the deacon in the commandant's room, meanwhile the bucket with burning coals was brought into the commandant's room by one of Romanovs' servants/not Chemodurov,—this one I never saw at the Ipatiev house, but met him later, after the Bolsheviks left Ekaterinburg/. This servant was tall, I remember, in a grey suit with metal buttons. . . . Having dressed in holy vestments, taking with us all that was necessary for the service, we walked out of the commandant's room into the hallway. The commandant himself opened the door which led into the hall, letting me go in first, with me walked Father Deacon, and the commandant entered last. The hall into which we entered through an arch was connected with a smaller room—a sitting room, where close to the front corner I noticed a table set up for the service. But I was distracted from looking at the hall and the sitting room because as soon as we stepped into the hall we saw that three figures walked from the window: they were Nicholas Alexandrovich, Ta-tiana Nikolaevna and another older daughter, but which one exactly I did not have a chance to see.

In the next room, separated from the hall by an arch, was Alexan-dra Feodorovna, two younger daughters and Alexei Nikolaevich. The latter was lying down on a [folding] cot and I was amazed by his appearance: he was pale to a point of transparency, thin, and he surprised me by his great height. In general, his appearance was ex-tremely sickly and only his eyes were lively and bright and looked at me with obvious curiosity—a new person. He was dressed in a white undershirt and covered with a blanket down from his waist. His bed stood by the right wall from the entrance, just past the arch. Near the bed stood an armchair, in which Alexandra Feodorovna sat, wearing a loose dress, of dark lilac color.

There were no jewels on her at all, and I did not notice any on the daughters either. Alexandra Feodorovna's great height was no-ticeable, as was her manner of holding herself, the manner that can-not be called anything but "majestic." She sat in an armchair but got up energetically and steadily when we entered and exited, as well as when during the service I preached "peace to all," read the Testament or when we sang the more important prayers.

Next to Alexandra Feodorovna's chair, farther along the right wall stood both their younger daughters, and then Nicholas Alexan-drovich himself; the elder daughters stood in the arch, and a bit away from them, behind the arch in the hall stood: a tall older gen-tleman and some lady/they later explained to me that this was Doc-tor Botkin and Alexandra Feodorovna's maid. Farther down stood two manservants: the one who brought us the bucket, and the other, whose appearance I did not notice and do not remember. The "commandant" stood in the corner of the hall by the farthest win-dow the entire time, hence at a rather decent distance from the parishioners. No one else at all was either in the hall, or in the room past the arch. Nicholas Alexandrovich was dressed in a khaki tunic, the same color slacks and tall boots. On his chest was an officer's St George Cross. There were no epaulets. All four daughters wore dark skirts and simple white blouses. Their hair was cut rather short in the back; they looked cheerful, and I must say, almost merry.

Nicholas Alexandrovich impressed me by his firm gait, his calmness and especially his manner of looking directly and openly into one's eyes. I noticed no sign of emotional oppression in him. It seemed to me that I saw some barely noticeable grey hairs in his beard, the beard was longer and wider when I was there this first time than on the fourteenth of July; when it looked to me like Nicholas Alexandrovich cut the beard all around. As for Alexandra Feodorovna, her appearance was somehow tired, even sickly. I forgot to mention one thing that constantly caught my attention—the special respect to my holy rank with which every member of the Romanov family bowed in response to my silent greeting to them at the exit of the hall after the service ended. The service—*obednitsa*, we performed in front of the table set up in the center of the room behind the arch. The table was covered with a silk cloth with ancient Russian style design. On the table, in proper order and the usual church symmetry stood numerous icons. There were small, medium and very small folding icons with vestments—all these of unique beauty in their ancient style and workmanship. There were simple icons without vestments, among them I noticed "Our Lady of the Sign [*Znamenie*]"/Novgorod, "It Is Truly Meet" icon, I cannot remember the rest.

I also noticed the icon of The Mother of God, which at the 20th May service took center place. This icon was apparently very ancient. I am afraid to insist, but I think this image was referred to as "Feodorovskaya." This icon was in golden vestments without jewels. This icon is not among those you showed me,—neither are folding ones, nor "*Znamenie*" nor "It Is Truly Meet," they are not here. The icon you are showing me without vestments, only with a metal frame, with a torn off crown—it is not called "Feodorovskaya" but "Kazanskaya"—this I insist on categorically. This icon was not at the first or at the second service, neither on the table nor on a wall. Having stood up at our spots in front of the table with the icons we started the service, and the deacon spoke the *ectenia*[40] petitions while I sang. Two female voices sang along with me/I think it was Tatiana Nikolaevna and one other among them/, occasionally Nicholas Alexandrovich sang along in a low bass/he sang "Our Fa-

40. Litany.

ther" this way for instance and etc./The service passed cheerfully and well, they prayed very zealously. At the end of the service I did the usual "release" with a holy cross and for a minute stopped in bewilderment: should I approach the parishioners with the crucifix so they could kiss it, or was this not allowed, and with this wrong step I could perhaps create difficulties for the Romanov family in being able to satisfy their spiritual needs by having future services. I snuck a look at the commandant, to see what he was doing and how he would feel about my intention to approach with the crucifix. It seemed to me that Nicholas Alexandrovich also threw a quick look towards the commandant.

The latter stood in his spot, in the farthest corner and calmly stared at us. Then I took a step forward and simultaneously Nicholas Alexandrovich approached the cross first with firm and even steps, without moving his steady gaze away from me, and kissed the crucifix, behind him approached Alexandra Feodorovna and all four daughters, while I myself approached Alexei Nikolaevich lying in his bed. He was looking at me with such lively eyes that I thought "doubtless he will now say something," but Alexei Nikolaevich silently kissed the crucifix. Father deacon gave him and Alexandra Feodorovna each a *prosfora*. Then Dr Botkin and the aforementioned servants—the maid and two manservants, approached the crucifix.

We undressed in the commandant's room, folded our things and went home, having been escorted through the gates and past the guards to the fence by some soldier.

Testimony of Ipatiev house guard Yakimov—

One thing I witnessed first-hand of the life of the imperial family: they used to sing sometimes. I had the chance to hear their spiritual singing. They sang the Cherubic hymn. They also sang some secular song. I did not hear the words, but the melody was sad. . . . I heard only female voices, never any male ones. . . . During the [prayer] service, from a distance I heard female and male voices: they must have sung themselves.

Testimony of Ipatiev house guard Strekotin—

The Tsar had a habit of coming over to the window and staring at the garden intensely, he ignored the guards' warnings. The red guard Safonov, V.Ya. decided to teach the Tsar a lesson. Once he warned him but the latter continued to stand at the window, so Safonov took aim at him, and when the Tsar turned around, apparently intending to walk away, he shot towards the ceiling right by the window. . . After this the Tsar never again approached the window.

In the garden, hammocks were hanged for them, but they were used almost exclusively by the daughters. The prisoners often attempted to start conversations with the guards, especially the daughters and the Tsar. They said for example: We are bored, it was merrier in Tobolsk. What is your name? Can you guess what this little dog's name is? (they always brought dogs outside with them, which lived with them, I think two or three dogs). Or: What is this? What is this for? They even showed photographs. For example: in one photograph, together with all the imperial daughters was Rasputin. Of course, any conversation with the prisoners was forbidden, but there was still some talk. Especially difficult was the indoor upstairs post where the prisoners lived. There, almost every minute, the prisoners walked by the guard post, and the daughters especially would smile at the guard every time and start a conversation, they would stop at the post and it was all very repulsive and annoying. I stood at that post only once, and declined after that.

Testimony of Ipatiev house guard Yakimov—

When the [guards] moved into the Ipatiev house, they started to steal the Tsar's belongings. They would often go to the cupboards and take things from there into big bags, which they drove away in automobiles or horses. They brought these things to their houses.

Testimony of Ipatiev house guard Strekotin—

The most eager to talk were the daughters (except Olga). . . When they approached the red guard Sadchikov, N.S. with this type of talk, he rudely responded: "There is no need to distract me, you can just stomp along." They looked at each other fearfully, and continued walking along the path silently. Sometimes they lay down in the hammocks, and one would ask: "Swing me," and if someone dared come over, she would unavoidably say: "I am bored."

Testimony of Ipatiev house guard Yakimov—

I had the chance to see all the members of the family and everyone who lived with them. I saw them in the house, when they walked by to go to the lavatory or outside walking in the garden. They walked to lavatory past the commandant's room via the entrance hall and guard post No 1. They could have walked through the room where the kitchen was located, but for some reason they never went that way. If the Heir was already outside, they took the stairway which leads downstairs from the lavatory, then through the porch to the yard and from the yard into the garden. But when the Heir was going outside, then they all walked through the main entrance to the street, then through the main gate to the yard and into the garden. I never spoke to either the Tsar or any members of his family. I only saw them. These meetings were silent. Only once I heard and saw the Tsar talking with Shishkin. They were walking in the garden. The Tsar was walking around the garden. Moshkin sat in the garden on a small sofa. The Tsar approached him and started talking about the weather. The Tsar was no longer young. His beard had some grey in it. I saw him in a tunic, belted with an officer's belt with a buckle. The buckle was yellow, and the belt was yellow. Not light yellow, but dark yellow. The tunic was khaki. The same khaki color were his pants, and old worn looking boots. His eyes were nice, kind, as was his entire face. In general, he gave the impression of being a nice person, simple, sincere and talkative. He looked like he wanted to talk to us. The Tsaritsa did not seem anything like him. Her gaze was stern, her figure and manners were those of a proud and haughty woman. At one time a group of us talked about what we thought of all of them, that Nicholas Alexandrovich was a simple man, while she was not simple: and that she looked like a Tsaritsa. She appeared older than him. On her temples grey hairs were noticeable, her face was not that of a young woman, but of an old one. He looked younger compared to her. It seemed that Tatiana was similar to the Tsaritsa. She also looked stern and proud like her mother. The rest of the Daughters: Olga, Maria and Anastasia did not have any haughtiness. One could tell by looking at them that they were simple and kind. The Heir was always ill, I cannot say anything about him. The Tsar would carry him out to the wheelchair, and in it he was covered by a blanket.

Once Yurovsky took over the house, immediately he set up a machine gun post in the attic. Put a new guard post in the backyard. Ended the drunken antics. I never saw him drunk or drinking. But he did change something else, which worsened conditions for the imperial family. He decreased deliveries from the nunnery, or completely stopped them, I can't remember.

Authors' Note: On June 14, Maria turned 19 years old. Many years later, a story was published in one of the Western Romanov biographies about a guard named Skorokhodov, who smuggled in a cake for Maria's last birthday in June of 1918, and was consequently dismissed from his post, after being caught alone in a "compromising position" with Maria.[41] This narrative must be addressed, because there is absolutely no first-hand evidence that anything like this ever happened. The story of the cake seems to have originated with one of the executioners, Pyotr Ermakov, whose accounts have subsequently been proven to be extremely unreliable. Ivan Skorokhodov was indeed a guard at the Ipatiev House, but he left due to illness and hospitalization rather than dismissal.[42] In early July, the new commandant Yakov Yurovsky installed a different guard team at the Ipatiev house, which led to hyper-monitoring of fraternization between the guards and prisoners in their final days. Breaking any rules, no matter how minor, resulted in the violator being immediately thrown into a local jail. This is another reason that makes the "cake" incident extremely unlikely.

The "cake" myth also served as a basis for stories about Maria being "shunned" or "frozen out" by her family members for her alleged inappropriate behavior, but once again, there is no evidence for this whatsoever. Parts of a note written by Yakov Yurovsky about a conversation with visiting clergy, which was cited as a source for this, have been misconstrued and used to imply that something un-

41. "Fate of the Romanovs," King, G. and Wilson, P., 244-245. John Wiley & Sons, 2003.
42. "Ispoved' Tsareubiyts," Veche, M., 2008, 470

toward happened between Maria and a guard. It was quoted that the priest who conducted the last service for the family stated that "one must give a pass [for inappropriate behavior] to an imperial soul." However, the original Yurovsky note mentions nothing of the sort—the pertinent part reads: "I invited the Priest and the Deacon. When they had got dressed in their vestments in my commandant's office, I told them that they could perform the Service according to custom, but warned them there must be no conversation. The Deacon declared, 'This is what happened before and not with such important people. If one messes it up, it can cause a scandal, but in this situation, we can sort it out in a good spirit.'"[43] It is unclear what the myth of Maria's inappropriate behavior and consequent shunning was based on, other than perhaps faulty translation in the original publication that referenced the alleged incident.[44]

The same book also used the recollections of V. N. Netrebin, another guard at the Ipatiev house, as a source of this pervasive myth.[45]

E.S. Botkin to his brother Alexander[46]—

Ekaterinburg, 26 June (9 July), 1918. My dear, good friend Sasha, I am making the last attempt to write a real letter,—at least from here,—although this caveat is completely redundant; I do not think that it is in the cards for me to ever write from anywhere else again,—my voluntary imprisonment here is limited to my existence on this earth. In actuality, I have died—dead to my children, my friends, my work. . . . I have died, but have not been buried yet, or rather was buried alive,—whichever you prefer: the consequences are almost identical, i.e. both one and the other have their negative and positive sides. If I were literally dead, that is to say, anatomically dead, then according to my faith I would know what my children

43. Yurovsky, unpublished memoirs, 1922, APRF, f. 3, op. 58, d. 280.

44. This incident will be addressed in more detail in an upcoming book focused on debunking numerous Romanov myths.

45. Recollections of V.N. Netrebin, who was part of the inner guard at the Ipatiev house, about the execution of the imperial family, written down for Uralstpart (Autograph), F. 41 Op. 1 D. 149 L.167-174 Воспоминания В.Н. Нетребина, состоявшего во внутренней охране дома Ипатьева, о расстреле царской семьи, написанные для Уралистпарта (Автограф), ЦДООСО Ф. 41 Оп. 1 Д. 149 Л. 167-174 (с об.).

46. Dr Botkin started this letter on the date indicated but continued writing it on subsequent days. It is thought that he was writing the letter at midnight of 16-17 July, when he heard the knock on his door, which was why the letter ended abruptly. It was never mailed and was found at the Ipatiev house after the murders.

are doing, would be closer to them and undoubtedly more useful than now. I rest with the dead only civilly, my children may still have hope that we will see each other sometime in this life, while I, other than thinking that I can still be useful to them somehow, do not personally indulge myself with this hope, do not humor myself with illusions, but look directly into the face of unadorned reality. Although for now, I am as healthy and fat as always, to a point where I feel disgusted every time I look in the mirror. I only console myself with the thought that if it would be easier for me to be anatomically dead, then this means that my children are better off, because when I am separated from them, it always seems to me that the worse off I am, the better off they are. And why do I feel that I would be better off dead,—I will explain this to you with small episodes, which illustrate my emotional being. The other day, i.e. three days ago, when I was peacefully reading Saltykov-Schedrin, which I often read with pleasure, I suddenly saw the face of my son Yura in diminutive size, as if from far away, but [it was] dead, in a horizontal position, with closed eyes. . . . The last letter from him was on 22 March o[ld] s[tyle], and since that time postal connection from the Caucasus, which even earlier faced great difficulties, probably stopped completely, as neither here nor in Tobolsk had we received anything else from Yura. Do not think that I am hallucinating, I have had these types of visions before, but you can easily imagine, how it was for me to experience this particular thing in the current situation, which in general is quite comfortable, but to have no chance not only to go to Yura, but not even to be able to find out anything about him. Then, only yesterday, during the same reading, I suddenly heard some word, which to me sounded like "Papulya,"[47] which was uttered in Tanyusha's[48] voice, and I almost broke down in sobs. Again, this was not a hallucination, because this word was uttered, the voice was similar, and not even for a second did I think that this was my daughter speaking, who was supposed to be in Tobolsk: her last postcard was from 23 May—5 June, and of course these tears would have been purely egotistical, for myself, that I cannot hear and, most likely will never again hear that dear little voice and feel that affection that is so important to

47. Diminutive affectionate term for "Papa."
48. Botkin's daughter, Tatiana.

me, with which my little children spoiled me so. Again, the horror and sorrow which gripped me during the vision I described were purely egotistical too, since if my son had truly died, then he is happy, but if he is alive, then it is unknown what kind of trials he is going through or is fated to live through. So you see, my dear, that my spirit is cheerful, despite the torment I live through, which I bear, just described to you, and cheerful to a point where I am prepared to do this for many more years. . . . I am encouraged by the conviction that "one who bears all until the end is saved," and the awareness that I remain loyal to the principles of the 1889 graduates. Before we graduated, while still students, but already close friends who preached and developed the same principals with which we started life, for the most part we did not view them from a religious point of view, I do not even know if too many of us were religious. But each codex of principals is a religion already, and for some it is most likely a conscious thing, while for others subconscious,—as it basically was for me, as this was the time of, not exactly uniform atheism, but of complete indifferentism, in the full sense of the word,—it came so close to Christianity that our full attitude toward it, or at least of many of us, was a completely natural transition. In general, if "faith is dead without work," then "work" cannot exist without faith, and if faith joins any of our work, then this is just due to special favor from God. I turned out to be such a lucky one, through the path of heavy trials—the loss of my firstborn, the year-and-a-half-old little son Seryozha. Since that time, my codex has been widened and solidified significantly, and I took care that each task was not only about the "Academic," but about the "Divine." This justifies my last decision as well, when without any hesitation I left my children completely orphaned, in order to do my physician's duty to the end, like Abraham did not hesitate to sacrifice his only son to God on His demand. I strongly believe that the same way God saved Isaac, He will save my children too and be a father to them. But since I do not know how He will save them, and can only find out about it in the next world, my egotistic torment which I described to you, due to my human weakness, does not lose its torturous severity. But Job did bear more, and my late Misha always reminded me about him, when he was afraid that I, bereft of my dear little children, would not be able to bear it. No, apparently, I can bear it all, whatever God wills to burden me with. In your letter, for which I ardently thank you once more (the first time I tried to convey this in a few lines on a detachable coupon, hopefully you got it in time for the holiday, and also my physiognomy—for the other?), you were interested in my activities in Tobolsk, with a trust precious to me. And so? Putting hand on heart, I can confess to you that there, I tried in every way to take care of "the Divine, as the Lord wills" and, consequently, "not to shame the graduates of year 1889." And God blessed my efforts, and I will have until the end of my days this bright memory of my swan song. I worked with my last strength, which suddenly grew over there thanks to the great happiness in the life [we had] together with Tanyusha and Glebushka,[49] thanks to the nice and cheerful climate and relative mildness of winter and thanks to the touching attitude towards me from the townspeople and villagers. As a matter of fact, in its center, albeit a large one, Tobolsk presents as a city that is very picturesquely located, rich with ancient churches, religious and academic institutions, [but] at the periphery it gradually and unnoticeably transitions into a real village. This circumstance, along with noble simplicity and the feeling of self-respect of Siberians, in my opinion gives the relationships among the residents and not visitors, the specific character of directness, naiveté and benevolence, which we always valued and which creates the atmosphere necessary to our souls. In addition, various news spreads around the city very fast, the first lucky incidents for which God helped me be of use brought out such trust towards me, that the number of those wanting to get my advice grew with each day, up to my sudden and unexpected departure. Turning to me were mostly those with chronic illnesses, those who were already treated again and again, [and] sometimes, of course, those who were completely hopeless. This gave me the opportunity to make appointments for them, and my time was filled for a week or two ahead in each hour, as I was not able to visit more than six—seven, in extreme cases eight patients per day: since all these cases needed thorough review and much and much pondering. Who was I called to besides those ill within my specialty?!

49. Botkin's son Gleb.

To the insane, to those asking to be treated for drunkenness; [they] brought me to a prison to see a kleptomaniac, and with sincere joy I remember that the poor wretch of a lad, who was bailed out by his parents on my advice (they are peasants), behaved decently the rest of my stay. . . . I never denied anyone, as long as the supplicants accepted that certain illnesses were completely beyond the limits of my knowledge. I only refused to go to those recently fallen ill if, of course, they needed emergency help, since, on the one hand I did not want to get in the way of regular physicians of Tobolsk, which is very lucky to have them in the capacity and most importantly, quality of relations. They are all very knowledgeable and experienced people, excellent comrades and so responsive that the Tobolsk public is used to sending a horse or cabby to the doctor and receive him immediately. More valuable is their patience towards me, who did not have the ability to fulfill these types of requests, but on the contrary, was forced to make them wait a long time. It's true that soon it became commonly known that I never refuse anyone and keep my word sacredly, a patient could wait for me with peace of mind. But if their illness did not allow them to wait, then the patients went to local physicians, which always made me happy, or to Doctor Derevenko, who also possessed their vast trust, or they headed to the hospital, and this way it would happen that when I arrived at a time of prescheduled appointment, I did not find the patient there, but that was always convenient, since most of the time my schedule was so extensive that I wasn't able to accomplish everything, at times debts formed, which I paid off when I did not find someone there. To see [patients] at the house where I was staying was inconvenient, and anyway there was no room, nevertheless from 3 until 4 1/2—5, I was always home for our soldiers, whom I saw in my room, the walk-through room, but since only our own [people] passed though there, it did not discomfort them. During the same hours, my town patients came to see me too, either for a refill of a prescription or to make an appointment. I was forced to make exceptions for peasants who came to see me from villages tens or even hundreds of versts away (in Siberia they don't pay attention to distance), and who were in a hurry to get back. I had to see them in a small room before the bathroom, which was a bit out of the way, where a large chest served as an examining table. Their trust was especially touching to me, and their confidence, which never betrayed them, that I will treat them with the same attention and affection as any other patient, not only as an equal but as a patient who has every right to my care and services, gave me joy. Those who were able to spend the night, I would visit at the inn early the next morning. They always tried to pay, but since I followed our old codex, of course I never accepted anything from them, so, while I was busy in an *izba*[50] with a patient, they hurried to pay my cabby. This surprising courtesy, to which we are not used to at all in large cities, was occasionally highly pertinent, as at times I was not in a position to visit patients due to lack of funds and fast-growing cab costs. Therefore, for our mutual benefit, I widely took advantage of another local tradition and asked those who had a horse, to send it for me. This way, the streets of Tobolsk saw me riding in wide bishop's sleighs, as well as behind beautiful merchant trotters, but most often drowning in hay in most ordinary burlap. My friends were equally varied, which perhaps was not to everyone's liking, but it was no concern of mine. To Tobolsk's credit I must add that there was no direct evidence of this at all, and only one indirect, which in addition was not unquestionable. One evening the husband of one of my female patients came to see me with a request to visit her right away, because she had strong pains (in the stomach). Luckily, I was able to fulfill his wish, albeit at a cost to another patient, for whom I did not schedule a visit, but rode with him to his house in a cab in which he came to get me. On the way he starts to grumble at the cabby, that he is not going the right way, to which the latter reasonably respon. . . [letter ends abruptly]

Testimony of Ipatiev house guard Yakimov—

Something confusing happened with the priest. The prayer service under Yurovsky happened just once. This was on Saturday, 13 July[51] [30 June], Yurovsky called me to him and instructed me to find a priest. First, he asked me which priests are serving. I named f. Meledin and f. Storozhev. Then he asked me to get one of them. Back then Meledin lived the closest, so on that same Saturday

50. Peasant house generally made of logs.
51. From here on, the dates used are in the new style.

evening I asked him. In the morning. . . Yurovsky [found out] and
sent me to tell Meledin not to come, [to tell him] that *obednitsa* was
canceled. And if he asks who canceled it, "tell him that it was them,
not I. Instead of Meledin, go ask Storozhev," [he said]. . . . So, I
went to Storozhev and asked him. What this meant, I do not know.

Testimony of Father Ioann Storozhev—

On 30 June/13 July I found out that the next day, 1/14 July, on
Sunday, f. Meledin had to perform a liturgy at the Ipatiev house,
that he already had a warning about this from the commandant,
and the commandant at the time was infamously cruel, a certain
Yurovsky—former military medic.

I assumed that I would replace f. Meledin at the cathedral and
perform a liturgy for him on 1-14 July. Around 8 o'clock in the
morning on 14 July, a soldier came to see me, and requested for me
to serve *obednitsa* at the Ipatiev house. At 10 o'clock, I was already
at the Ipatiev house with deacon Buimirov. Inside, behind the fence,
at the bottom of stairs and inside the house, there were lots of armed
young men, standing on guard. When we entered the commandant's room, we saw disorder, dust and mess. Yurovsky was sitting
at the table, drinking tea and eating bread with butter. Another man
was sleeping on the bed, fully dressed. Having entered the room, I
said to Yurovsky: "The clergy was invited here, so here we are. What
do we need to do?" Yurovsky directly stared at me without a greeting, and said "Wait here, then you will serve *obednitsa*." I asked
"*Obednya* or *obednitsa*?" "He wrote *obednitsa*," said Yurovsky. When
we dressed and a bucket with coals was brought in, Yurovsky invited
us into the hall for service. I was the first to enter the hall, then the
deacon and Yurovsky. Simultaneously, Nicholas Alexandrovich with
two daughters came in through a door that led into inner rooms.
Yurovsky asked Nicholas Alexandrovich: "Are all of you gathered?,"
Nicholas Alexandrovich answered firmly "Yes—all." Ahead, behind
the arch, already standing were Alexandra Feodorovna with two
daughters and Alexei Nikolaevich, who was sitting in a wheelchair,
wearing a sailor jacket. He looked pale. Alexandra Feodorovna,
wearing a dress, looked livelier than in the past. Olga Nikolaevna,
Tatiana Nikolaevna, Maria Nikolaevna and Anastasia Nikolaevna

were wearing black skirts and white blouses. Their hair reached their shoulders in the back.

To me, Nicholas Alexandrovich, as well as his daughters, looked exhausted this time. During the service the family members arranged themselves [this way]: Alexandra Feodorovna's chair stood next to the wheelchair of Alexei Nikolaevich, which was farther away from the arch, hers was a bit behind his. Behind Alexei Nikolaevich stood Tatiana Nikolaevna. Olga Nikolaevna, Maria Nikolaevna, Anastasia Nikolaevna stood near Nicholas Alexandrovich, who took his usual place on the right side of wall arch. Behind the arch, in the hall stood Doctor Botkin, the maid and three servants. At the far corner window stood Yurovsky. We performed the service at the table set up in the center of the room behind the arch. This table was covered with a silk cloth with ancient Russian style design. On the table, in proper order and the usual church symmetry stood numerous icons. There were small, medium and very small folding icons with vestments—all these of unique beauty in their ancient style and workmanship: "Our Lady of the Sign [*Znamenie*]," "It Is Truly Meet," the Icon of the Holy St Ioann of Tobolsk. . . .

In front was a large plant and to me it looked like among its branches was an icon called "Savior Not Made By Hands," in the usual style, without vestments. The deacon and I started the *obednitsa* service. The ritual of *obednitsa* is usually performed for the military, when for one reason or another it is impossible to do a liturgy. In its substance this prayer service is similar to the ritual of liturgy, but is significantly shorter, as at *obednitsa* the Holy Eucharist is not offered. According to the ritual of *obednitsa*, it is customary to read "at rest with the saints" at a certain point. For some reason instead of reading, the deacon sang this prayer. But as soon as we started singing, I heard that the Romanov family members, who were standing behind us, fell to their knees, and here I suddenly felt a deep spiritual comfort afforded by shared prayer. On an even deeper level one felt this when at the end of the service I read a prayer to the Mother of God, where in highly poetic touching words the supplication of a tormented person is expressed to support him in his sorrows, to give him strength to bear with dignity the cross sent by God.

After the service all kissed the Holy Cross. When I was leaving and walked very close by the former Grand Duchesses, I heard barely audible words "Thank you." Silently the deacon and I reached the art school building, and here he said to me, "You know Father Protoirei,[52]—something happened with them in there." In these words, there was confirmation of my own impression, I stopped and asked him why he thinks so. "Not sure. It is as if they are different somehow. And no one sang." And I must say that for the first time no one in the Romanov family sang with us at the prayer service on 14 July. What an amazingly subtle perception of the situation. Only now do we know what happened to the family from the testimonies of the eyewitnesses. But those who performed the service understood with a joint perception of the praying people. As far as deviation from the canon law in following the ritual of *obednitsa*: singing "at rest with the saints" represented a funeral service for those praying while they were still alive! How this happened, for what reason—is only known to the Supreme Being, but it happened just prior to the murder of the prisoners of the House of Special Purpose. They had their funeral service. That evening was blessed: it passed in warm sincere conversations.

Testimony of Ipatiev house guard Yakimov—

On 15 July, Monday, in our barracks at the Popov house the boy who lived with the imperial family appeared, he used to take the Heir around in his wheelchair. It caught my attention then, the other guards also noticed it. Nevertheless, no one knew what it meant, why the boy was brought here. But it was undoubtedly done on Yurovsky's orders.

From the report of Yakov Yurovsky—

[On] 16 [July] . . . A telegram was received from Perm about extermination of the Romanovs, and at 6 o'cl in the evening Filipp Goloschekin signed for it to be enforced. At midnight, a truck for moving the corpses was supposed to arrive. At 6 o'clock, the little cook Sednev was taken away, which really worried the Romanovs and their children. Dr Botkin came over to ask, what brought this

52. Archpriest.

on? He was told that the boy's uncle, who was arrested, had escaped, now he has returned and wants to see his nephew. The next day the boy was sent to his hometown/I think in the Tulsk province/.

Testimony of Ipatiev house guard Yakimov—
The last time I saw the Tsar and his daughters was 16 July. They were taking a walk in the garden at four o'clock in the afternoon. I cannot remember if I saw the Heir at this time. I did not see the Tsaritsa, she did not go out then.

From the testimony of Yakov Yurovsky—
[16 July] . . . Meanwhile, all the preparations were made: 12 men were selected/including the Latvians with revolvers, who were sup-posed to execute the sentence/. 2 of the Latvians refused to shoot the girls. When the truck arrived, everyone was sleeping. We awoke Botkin, and he [awoke] all the rest. The explanation was given as follows: "in light of the disturbances in the city, it was necessary to move the Romanov family from the upper floor to the lower one.

Testimony of Ipatiev house guard Yakimov—
[17 July] . . . Just after midnight, old style time, or after 2 new style time, which the Bolsheviks changed to two hours forward,—some people came down into the lower rooms and started walking to-wards the room marked "I" on the map of the lower floor [the cel-lar]. In front walked Yurovsky and Nikulin. Behind them walked the Sovereign, the Empress and the daughters: Olga, Tatiana, Maria and Anastasia, and also Botkin, Demidova, Trupp and the cook Kharitonov. The Sovereign himself was carrying the Heir. Behind them walked Medvedev and the "Latvians," i.e. the ten men who lived in the lower rooms who were recruited by Yurovsky through the Extraordinary [committee]. Among them were two Russians with rifles.

From the report of Yakov Yurovsky—
[17 July] They dressed for about a half hour. Downstairs a room with wooden paneling was chosen to avoid ricochet/all furniture

242 MARIA ROMANOV, THIRD DAUGHTER OF THE LAST TSAR

was taken out from it. The team was ready in the room next door. The Romanovs did not suspect anything. The commandant went to get them personally, alone, and brought them down the stairs to the lower room. Nicholas carried Alexei in his arms. The rest carried with them little cushions and various small things. Having entered the empty room, A.F. asked: "so, there is no chair? May we not sit?" The commandant ordered two chairs to be brought in. Nicholas sat Alexei on one, A.F. sat on the other. The rest were ordered by the commandant to line up.

When they lined up, the team was called in. After the team entered, the commandant said to the Romanovs, that in light of their relatives' continuous offense on Soviet Russia, Ural-ispolkom[53] made the decision to execute them by shooting. Nicholas turned his back to the team, facing his family, then, as if he realized what was happening, turned to the commandant, with the question "what? what?." The commandant quickly repeated and ordered the team to get set. Earlier the team was assigned who will shoot whom and were ordered to aim directly in the heart, to avoid too much blood volume and to finish faster. Nicholas did not utter anything else, again turning to the family, the others uttered a few incoherent exclamations, all this lasted a few seconds. Then the shooting started, which lasted two-three minutes. Nicholas was killed by the commissar himself, immediately after A.F. and Romanovs' people died/12 people were shot in total: Nicholas, Alexei, A.F., the four daughters Tatiana, Olga, Maria and Anastasia, Dr Botkin, lackey Trup [sic], cook Tikhomirov,[54] another cook (Kharitonov) and a lady-in-waiting,[55] whose surname the commandant forgot/. Alexei, their [sic] his three sisters and Botkin were still alive, and they had to be finished off.

This surprised the commandant because they aimed directly into their hearts, it was also surprising that the revolver bullets bounced off someone and ricocheted like hail around the room. When they tried to finish the girls off with bayonets, the bayonet could not go through the corsage. . . .[56]

---

53. Urals executive committee (abbreviation).

54. It is unclear whom he meant here, there was only one cook: Kharitonov.

55. The maid Anna Demidova.

56. He meant corset.

Then [we] started carrying out the corpses and loading them into the truck, covering with cloth, in order to prevent blood seepage. That's when theft started; was forced to get 3 reliable comrades to guard the corpses during the transfer/the corpses were carried one by one. . . .

Authors' note: As the bodies were carried out, some accounts suggest that either Maria or Anastasia, or perhaps both, were still alive and began to move and moan and had to be bayonetted to death.

The truck carrying the corpses headed towards Koptyaki forest until it got stuck in the boggy, marshy areas near the mineshaft where Yurovsky originally intended to dispose of the bodies. Sitting around fires near the mineshaft were local peasants who had been haymaking. Yurovsky and his men sent them away before beginning the task of undressing the bodies and removing their valuables. The clothes were burnt and the bodies thrown into the mineshaft. However, the shaft was unable to conceal the remains effectively, the water in the shaft barely covering the bodies, so it was decided to move them.

While looking for a place to better dispose of the bodies, Yurovsky decided to try and burn the bodies, so commanded Voikov to get petrol, kerosene and sulphuric acid with which to disfigure the remains so they would be harder to identify.

When he returned to the mineshaft, work was still ongoing to remove the bodies from it. That night they drove off with the bodies again to find a better place to bury them, but soon became stuck. Planks were laid down to help the truck pass, when Yurovsky, deciding that as it was late at night and no one was around, they should bury the bodies where they were. As a pit was being dug, they tried to burn two of the bodies—Alexei and that of a woman. According to Yurovsky's account it was the maid Demidova, but as it turned out many years later it was, in fact, Maria. A pit was dug near the fire and the remains shoveled in. The other remains were placed into a bigger pit, sulphuric acid poured over the bodies, and then the pit was filled in, finally being covered with the planks they had used to try and move the stuck truck with.[57]

57. Information about the burial is based off Yurovsky's 1934 account of the murders as published in "The Last Act of a Tragedy" by V.V. Aleskeyev, Yekaterinburg, 1996.

Announcement of the shooting of the Tsar, July 1918—

In recent days, the capital of the Red Urals, Ekaterinburg, was seriously threatened by the danger of the approaching Czecho-Slovak bands, while at the same time a new conspiracy by the counter-revolutionaries who had the goal of snatching the Crowned Executioner out of the hands of Soviet power was discovered. In light of this, the Ural Regional Committee decided to shoot Nicholas Romanov, and this was carried out on July 16th. The wife and son of Nicholas Romanov are in a safe place.

The All-Russian Central Executive Committee recognized the decision of the Ural Regional Soviet to be correct.

UNDATED CORRESPONDENCE

Many documents in the State Archives of the Russian Federation fund of Maria Nikolaevna are undated, but we decided to include them here, separately.

Empress Alexandra Feodorovna was often indisposed due to her various ailments. At such times, she and her children sent each other notes. Maria's notes to her mother, which were written in English, have been presented here with Maria's own spelling.

Undated letters from Maria to her mother—

I congratulate dear Mama with Yolka holiday and wish to get well soon. Kiss
Maria

Dear Mama! I congratulate you with your name day. Forgive me that I'm giving you something so disgusting but I don't have anything better.

Darling Mama! I thank you afoull much that you take me so ofoon too diner. It is so sad that He went away for sech a long taem. I wood like to go to znaminia very much as I was not there from the 24th of Decembre. Mary to day is in a very nice humour. Mama darling you don't know wat a nice feeling I had when I came to the [illeg.] I never had such before. I kiss you 1000000 times God is with you angell Mama suit darling beloved Mama. Your own it the Maria P.S. please rite me a we little letter.

My dear darling Mama you don't no how sory I am that you fell bad. It is so oful to se how you safer, you so patient that I can not understand. Anastasia kisses you and is very sad you can't come down, and wishes you, God [illeg.]. Madem direst is am writing in hierest is am afrade to go home in the dark so I sitt on the W.C. packing my [illeg.] in the dark [illeg.] I hope you will soon go to bed and [illeg.]. God [illeg.]. Sleep well. God bless you. Your Marie.

My dear beloved Mama. Has Anya not forgotten to tell Listopad (Autumn) not to come [illeg.], did she find all her servents in her house. God bless you. A big kiss from Kazansha

Mama darling I hope that you did not forget that at Easter in Russia one _____ with the peple, Anastasia kisses you, Papa & Kiki. I kiss you all to. Your loving Kazansha

10th May. My darling Mama! You told me yould like to go to the Holy conbonion [sic] You no is also wonted to go at the beginning of lentn. I hope you will have a nice drive. When we came back from the "Private Dacha" Mengden the frend of Sofia Ivanova, she looks like old "Baba Yaga."[1] I kiss you many times and Papa. Anastasia sends you a "kiss." How I would like to go with you to conbonion the 14. God bless you. Your Marie.

Dear Mama! I have 37 & 4 with a half. I kiss you & Papa very much. Your loving Maria

Dear Mama! How do you fell I hope you slept well thet night and have no pain in your hart or in your hand. Please kiss Anya from me and tell her to keep you quit well when we come. I kiss you ever so tenderly. Your loving Marie

My darling Mama! I hope you will fell better tomorrow. Sleep well and get up quit well. I am so sory not to get your blessing befor going to bed. I am very sory not to sleep with you on bord as I never was with out you on bord. God bless you I [illeg.] and kiss. Marie Darling Mama, I thanks you very much for your letter, I was so

---

1. Old witch from Russian fairy tales.

glad to get it. Pleas kiss Anya very much and tell her to send my love to our Frend. Anastasia thanks you very much for your letter and kisses you many times. 1000 kisses from your loving Marie.

Dear darling Mama! I thank you very much for your note. Kann You go today to curch? Please kiss Anya from me. Maria

I slept very well & my temperature is 36 & 5. I have 3 littel pictures for Anastasia. Please kiss Papa very much. I kiss you very tenderly. Your loving dother [daughter] I thank you dear Mama for the flowers. I kiss you very much. Your loving Maria

I beg your pardon dear darling Mama for all that I meid bad to you, and was very bad and not listen to you. I send kiss.

I send you dear Mama the two fotegrafs you asked. I hope your head wernt ack much in the night, and will pass till tomorrow. Good by God bless you. I and Anastasia kiss you. Your loving Maria.

Dear Mama! You are probably terribly [sick and] tired of Sonia. We need a buckle for Alexei's little horse kushaks[2] for kiata. What did you do with the ring, I hope to go to the cathedral soon. I kiss you and Papa.
Maria.
P.S. I hope to get a response to this letter tomorrow. I hope Sonia will leave soon.

My dear Mama, I am sending you a letter for Papa as I don't want Papa to read my letter in front of Dmitri. Did Papa understand what walk in the woods means? Explain to him what the little note means. Sleep well,
Your Kazanetz.

Dear Mama! How are you feeling today? Please ask Anya to show you the letter I wrote to her. I will tell you how to go to Piter. Kiss, Maria

2. Belt, or rein.

Dear Mama! Tell me if it's true that everyone hates me. I now feel this myself, and I know that I have noticed it a while ago. Mama darling, say that this is the sole truth. I wanted to write this long ago but kept forgetting.
Yours,
Maria

25th March [no year]
My dear Mama! Please kiss Anya. Mama, you told me that chrevo[3] means piglo, but in the new testament: and the infant . . . in her chrevo." Does the infant really get born from the mother? Mama please write to me how it is born. I hope that tomorrow your head wont ache. Where did Anya have dinner? Sleep well and dream about Kiki and everything you wish for. Kiss Papa firmly for me. I kiss you affectionately. May god be with you. Yours Maria

16th October
My dear Mama! How did you sleep? I slept very well, only woke up once. . .

My dear Mama! Do you remember we played one game and there it was written [illeg.]. Mama try and give birth to a baby, I really want it, since usually it's so painful for the mother to give birth and you are now ill, so maybe this means you are having a baby. I will swear on it to everyone on the yacht from you, especially Kiki. Darling Mama, take care of yourself and lie in bed peacefully and go to bed early. I kiss you affectionately. Your Maria
P.S. I will pray for you
My dear darling Mama! How did you sleep and how do you feel? I thank you so much for the little hat.
Your loving daughter who kisses you.
Marie
My dear Mama! How is your head now? Forgive me that I am annoying hour again but I promised Anastasia that if she goes to be soon, I would ask you to allow her to be to bed later tomorrow. Mama darling, don't think that she made that up, it was I who told her, or else she would not want to go to bed. So, mama darling,

3. Womb.

may I, yes? Mama darling, my Mama, you cannot know how I pity you that you are still ill. Today Olga is having her hair washed. Do you like it when they wash your hair. What are you doing, Papa? Mama I'm giving papa cufflinks and cigar box. Mama darling remind me tomorrow that needed to tell you something. Kiss affectionately. Maria

Mama when will N.P. come to Anya? Will he come for the anniversary or not? I would like to see him.

My dear Mama! Forgive me that I am writing you again. Mama I will not see Our friend or . . ? Today I read with Trina and it was written about one man sent to Vt. . . ? Mama what do you think if Trina saw Him would have hit Him or ?. Mama now it is much harder for Him to come see us at home. ? ? I kiss you and Papa affectionately. I kiss you and Papa awfully hard. your daughter who loves you. Maria.

Dear Mama! How are you feeling. I slept well temperature 36 + 1. Ear does not hurt at all. The doctor will come at 10. How did you sleep last night? In the evening at half to 9 Evgeni Sergeevich was here. I kiss you and Papa affectionately.
Maria
P.S. An.[astasia] kisses Papa.

Dear Mama! I congratulate you with the Great Lent. I ask forgiveness Kiss you affectionately, You looked very beautiful in the Russian dress. I hope you will feel well tomorrow. I hug you tightly and Papa and ask him for forgiveness. +
Maria

My dearest Mama, I kiss you affectionately and wish you a good night. It made me so sad to see how much your heat ached at dinner. I prayed for you and hope that you will feel better. I hug you tightly. Your loving Kazanetz.
The Standart
27th June
I kiss Papa firmly.

Dear Mama! I am very grateful for the letter. I hope that you don't have a headache. Alexei said that since you are ill you need a kiss. What are you doing now! I kiss you affectionately.
Maria

My beloved Mama dear! Many thanks for the darling note and telegram. In the morning we studied and I took a walk with Shura. Anastasia still does not have real Becker, but only not much. We now had P.V. lesson. He read Turgenev to us. Excised the eye of the commander of the [illegible] regiment. I kiss you affectionately and love you. Your daughter,
Maria
May God keep you +

Authors' note: All four Grand Duchesses received a large amount of correspondence—not only from family and friends but also from strangers, both in Russia and from abroad. Here is a selection of some of undated letters and other correspondence Maria received and wrote over the years.

Maria to Tatiana—

16th November
Dear Tatiana! How is your health? Do you like Olga's Kastiyan. What are you doing now? I kiss you firmly.
Maria
I congratulate you, dear Tatiana, with Yolka. Forgive me for the nasty looking postcard.
Kiss you
Maria

My darling Tatiana. Sonia Orbeliani is intolerable. She calls on the phone from the morning and pesters—did we get a telegram from Mama? So tiresome. How is Ortipo? In the evening we will ring to see how are you and write to you. Goodbye.
Kisses
Dragoon.

My sweet Tatiana.
We are going to visit you at the infirmary with M. Zizi and I am terribly embarrassed, because in the afternoon there will be a lot of relatives.
On the other side, it is you and your husband Provatorov [referring to a picture on the other side of the card].
I kiss you firmly.
Your Dragoon.

Maria to Grand Duchess Ksenia Alexandrovna—
Dear Aunt Ksenia! How are you doing? It is really nice here. Yesterday Anastasia and I went to a hunt for the first time it was really nice. I sat on [illeg.] with Grinwald, Anastasia with Papa, Olga with D, and Tatiana with Prince Golitzyn. I kiss all those who are with you affectionately. Your loving Maria

Undated letters to Maria from various people:

From Titi Dehn to Maria—
[Child's handwriting, Xmas postcard—Nativity scene]
Dear Maria Nikolaevna. I thank you very much for the charming letter. I firmly kiss your little hands
Titi
Want to see you very much!

Post card with prayer of St John the Warrior[4]—
O mighty intercessor and saint of Christ, John the Warrior! Have mercy upon thy handmaiden who suffers misfortunes, affliction, and all types of adversity. Save her from all evil and protect her from offenders, for thou hast been granted such grace from God.

Catherine Schneider to Maria—
Darling Maria Nikolaevna
My congratulations on the New Year.

---

4. Sent to Maria on a postcard with her picture on it. In the Orthodox tradition, people imprisoned or who are going through sorrows ask the intercessions of this saint. This, while undated, was possibly sent in 1917.

Trina
How is your health? I am as I was, in bed.

Pierre Gilliard to Maria—

Between us, Marie Nikolaevna, if you continue to tease me, I will have revenge!!! I am so tired of having had to repeat this to His Majesty, I don't know how many times, that he has had nothing but a (constant) infernal noise down the telephone.
I beg you to believe me, Madame, my very dear pupil, that I remain your very affectionate and devoted servant,
Pierre Gilliard

Anna Demidova to Maria—

Your Imperial Highness, Grand Duchess Maria Nikolaevna. I congratulate you with the holiday. I expect there will be dances today. I hope you have many dances. Congratulate Shura and Liza with the holiday from me, please. Kissing your hand. Sincerely yours, Nyuta.

To good Duchess Maria Nikolaevna. I congratulate you with the holiday. I wish that you, Maria Nikolaevna receive a lot of presents.
Nyuta

Tatiana Konstantinovna[5] to Maria—

Darling Maria, my husband and I are so moved that you didn't forget, and thank you from the heart for the photographs.
Your Tatiana

Kichkene 1914. Dear Maria! With all my heart I thank you for the nice little card with your congratulations, and for all your good wishes. In my room it smells so nice with different flowers: the Father from Oreanda typed up somewhere the names of the snowdrops and from Koreiz the Yusupovs sent a whole basket of flowers, which I arranged in vases. And now these roses and violets have recovered in the water and are wonderfully fragrant.

---

5. Daughter of Grand Duke Konstantin Konstantinovich.

Mentally hugging you.
Your loving Tatiana.

N. P. Sablin to Maria—

3—IX—15. Dear Maria Nikolaevna!
Thank you very much for your sweet letter. I often think about you
and want to see you all soon. We are all, thank God, healthy and
are having a good time. We get up by 9 o'clock—we drink tea with
the Emperor until 10 1/2 h. and then he receives reports, and we
are there just in case His Majesty needs anything. At 12 1/2 hours
we have breakfast, and at 2 1/2 h. go for a walk. One always has to
go through the city, and everywhere there is a mass of people—they
shout hurray. After the walk, tea, lunch and dice games. Between
tea and dinner, we often go to the city garden,—there is a very beautiful view from it. Yesterday a convoy and a company of the con-
solidated regiment arrived—it seems there are no sailors between
them. What are you doing at Tsarskoe? Does the weather seem
good? It is here too.
I wish you all the best. Tell Her Majesty that I firmly kiss Her hands
and thank her. Do not forget your devoted N. Sablin.

Liza[6] to Maria—

Grand Duchess Maria Nikolaevna. How is your health? I feel much
better, although I get tired of sitting and walking.
On this corridor, I carry the dressings. I firmly kiss your hand and
wish you all the best.
Your loving Liza

Cousin Ksenia[7] to Maria—

50 Grosvenor Square

6. Probably a nurse from the infirmary.

7. Princess Ksenia Georgievna, great-granddaughter of Tsar Nicholas I. This letter from Princess Ksenia would have been written after November 15, 1916, when Countess Nada Torby married HSH
Prince George of Battenberg. The four bridesmaids were Princess Louise of Battenberg, Countess
Anastasia (known as Zia) Torby, and Princesses Nina and Xenia of Russia, the daughters of Grand
Duke George and Princess Marie of Greece and Denmark. In 1917, the Battenbergs relinquished
their German titles. Prince Louis was created Marquess of Milford Haven, Earl of Medina and Vis-
count Alderney, so George and Nada were the Earl and Countess of Medina until 1921, when Louis
died and George succeeded as 2nd Marquess of Milford Haven.

Dear Marie,

How are you? Thank you so much for your letter. Papa wrote to me that he saw you all at Mogilev and that you all went to our dacha. Mama has 3 infirmaries at Harrogate, we sometimes go there to visit the soldiers. We moved here in winter and have a wonderful home. Louise, Zia, Nina and I were what you call bridesmaids at Nadia's wedding. On the third day, she and Georgie went to Scotland. Please pass on this photograph to your Mama and kiss her and the sisters from me. Nina kisses you.

Your Ksenia

Mordvinov and Sablin to Maria—

With all our souls, we thank Your Imperial Highness for your dear attention and good remembering [of us]. His Majesty passed on to us your greetings yesterday. Please accept and pass on our sincere greetings and most warm wishes to Her Majesty and your sisters. Mordvinov. Sablin

Kolya[8] to Maria—

14th June. Dima and I send You our best wishes for Your birthday. Yesterday, we all went for a ride in an equipage, me on horseback; halfway along we got caught in an awful rain and got so wet that we had to stop at the watchman's hut to dry off and wait till the rain stopped. Hope that You are all well.

Your devoted Kolya.

Mama took this picture, sailing on a boat.

Margarita and Dolla[9] to Maria—

Dear Marie,

Thank you and Anastasia for your nice present and pretty card. With lots of kisses from Margarita and Dolla.

Draft of letter ftom Maria to Irène of Prussia—

Dear Auntie Irene

How do you do?

8. An unknown friend of Maria's—unlikely to be Alexei's friend, Kolya Derevenko.

9. Princesses Margarita and Theodora of Greece, daughters of Maria's cousin Alice Battenberg and Prince Christopher of Greece. Sisters of Prince Philip, Duke of Edinburgh.

I saw you in my dream, as if you were standing with us in church. Have you now gone to Toddy's house? Please tell Toddy and Baby that I send them much love. Will Auntie Victoria come this summer to us. I send my love to Helmina.

Aunt Onor[10] to Maria—
Darling Marie—how nice of you to have done all that big cushion for me, thank you so much you have been enormously diligent. Our thoughts are much with you today on Christmas eve and I hope you are all well and will be able to enjoy it. With much love and good wishes for a happy New Year.
Your loving
Auntie Onor

Dearest Marie—thank you so much for your pretty embroidery, how diligent you have been. For Christmas and the New Year, I send you all my best wishes. Yours lovingly
A. Onor
A good Easter kiss dear Marie xoxo Don Lu[11] A big kiss from A.

Princess Margaretha to Maria—
Darling Marie, I hope you all are well. You must have a very nice time in Livadia and I quite understand you are sorry to leave it. Do write a card I would be very glad. 1000 kisses from your loving cousin Margaretha.

Irène of Prussia to Maria—
HERRENHAUS
HEMMELMARK
BEI ECKENFÖRDE
I hope Derevenkos family the cat + kittens arrived safely. Jimmy is very much pleased to be here + runs with us when we ride—we have often to wait + call as he hunts a rabbit or anything that passes our way. Many kisses to you all dear ones. Ever your loving aunt Irène

10. Second wife of Grand Duke Ernst Ludwig of Hesse and By Rhine, Maria's maternal uncle. Born Princess Eleonore of Solms-Hohensolms-Lich (1871-1937), Eleonore died in an aeroplane crash on her way to the wedding of her son Ludwig.
11. Maria's cousins, Georg Donatus and Ludwig, children of Grand Duke Ernst of Hesse and Grand Duchess Eleonore.

Königliches Schloss
Kiel
My dear Marie
I suppose you are very busy preparing for Xmas now—we have just had ours I took some of our presents to Hemmelmark yesterday. We did not go in Uncle's little white motor but in a bigger blue one when more goes into
Many kisses from your loving
Aunt Irène

Alexander Vladimirovich[12] to Maria—

I congratulate you, dear Maria Nikolaevna, with your birthday and with all my beating heart send you wishes for health, good spirits and bright happiness for the future. Al. Vlad.

Princess Louise of Battenberg to Maria—

87 Queen's Gate
London SW
Dear Marie,
I saw in the newspapers that you all went to the bazaar at Offenbach, it must have been great fun. I do wish I had also been there. I suppose you are all very busy with your lessons now and haven't much time to lay patience. I am going to start my French lesson again this winter, but I am sorry to say I never seem to get any better. We have been having very nice weather, but to-day it is rather foggy so I have to write with the light turned on.

Yesterday afternoon Dickie came up from his school to go to the dentist, so Nona and I fetched him at the station and took him there and then brought him here for tea. He had to leave again soon after 5 o'clock. He was allowed to come here because he has been so good at his lessons this term. Papa arrived yesterday for lunch, he was wearing slippers as he is just recovering from an attack of gout, luckily it was a very slight one this time and he got it at sea soon after leaving Gibraltar so he is nearly alright again now.

Mama's fox terrier Spot is here now, he has just come from the country where he has been staying with a sister-in-law of Nona's

12. May have been one of the imperial officers.

while Papa was at Gib[raltar]. He is very surprised at everything in London and is not at all obedient so we have to take him out on a chain otherwise he would sure to be run over. He much prefers men to women, he is quite nice and friendly to us but if he can he goes and sits with the men servants, which is such a pity because he is awfully nice.

We have got the electric underground stations quite near us on both sides which is awfully convenient because one can get so very fast anywhere one wants. It passes underneath our house one can hear it. Sometimes I go for a walk with a niece of Nona's who is my age. She does not always live in London. She is staying with her grandmother, a dear old lady who is always very kind to Dick and me.

The shops are lovely here and one does see such funny people in the streets and such funny clothes the skirts look like pillow cases they are so tight and hats which cover the whole head and hair and muffs bigger nearly than themselves. I always long that a bear or a mad dog would come because they would be so funny trying to run they would be sure to fall on their noses. Now I must stop as I can't think of anything else to write. Lots of love to your Mama, Papa and sisters. Please thank Olga for her letter. Fondest love and kisses from your very loving cousin Louise

Authors' note: The following letter from Louise may have been written in late 1912, or early 1913, as Nona Kerr went to Greece in November 1912 as a volunteer to help Alice with nursing during the First Balkan War. Nona left on March 16, 1913, two days before George I was assassinated at Salonika.

The Mall House,
Spring Gardens
S.W.
Darling Marie,
Thank you ever so much for the nice little mat. It was awfully nice of you to send it to me. I think it very pretty. There must have been a lot of work about and it is so well done. I have sent you a tiny little bottle with lavender water in it, which I thought might amuse you.

I hope you will have a very nice Xmas. I wonder if your holidays have started yet. We are living now in a new house. It is very nice and has got comfortable rooms. Dickie is home now and George was here for Xmas. Nona is still in Greece with Alice, Margarita and Dolla have written us lots of letters whilst Alice was away. They write them quite alone so the spelling is rather odd.

Thank you again so much for your nice present. Lots of love and kisses from Louise

Prince Louis "Dickie" of Battenberg to Maria—

Dearest Marie thank you so much for the nice photo. I have sent Helmine hers. I am so sorry that I haven't got any nice one to send you. I hope you are having a nice time and are enjoying yourselves very much. I saw this airship at Frankfort. Much love from Dick

Grand Duchess Elisabeth Feodorovna to Maria—

+ And joy pours down from heaven:
Christ is risen!
Christ is risen!
Jesus says to her:
Maria! She turns and
Says to Him: Rabbi!
The light of Christ sanctifies all

Lili Dehn to Maria—

I wish you a Happy New Year dear Maria Nikolaevna and from my soul wish you all the very best. Kissing you firmly,
Your Lili

Alexandra Tegleva to Maria—

Beautiful, sweet Maria Nikolaevna!
How are you doing and are you healthy? Do you ride your bike well? Today I saw you in a dream and kissed you tightly. Let me kiss your pretty little hands soon. Your Teglya.

Tolstoy family to Maria—

Dear Maria Nikolaevna, Congratulations on your Name Day, and for our dear Name Day Girl, we all wish you and all you dear ones all the very best, happiness, and joy in the world. We think about you all the time. May the all-merciful Lord protect and bless you. Warmly kissing your hand, eternally loving you, Zina's Mama, sisters and brothers.

Maria's English exercises—

One day we went on the shore. There I, Anastasia and our sailors went to make a fire. We took some stones and put them together. Then we put in the branches and set fire to it. We enjoyed it very much.

My Journey to England

When we came to Cowes, Papa and Mama went on board the English yacht. Then on the next day we all went on shore, there we met Auntie May and cousin Mary. We played and picked shells. In the afternoon, Olga and Tatiana went to town.

Olga and Tatiana bought Anastasia and me two bracelets. I like mine very much. Then we went to Peterhof. After this, we went to the Crimea.

In another letter I shall write how we lived in the Crimea

The Crimea

On the next day after we arrived, we went to the sea. Some days after that we began to bathe, it was very interesting. On Sundays, we went to pay visits. Then we rode on horses on the hills. We enjoyed it very much. One day we went for a drive and at 4 o'clock we went on board the Standart. There we slept one night and, in the day we went to Sebastopol where we stayed one day and one night. There we entered the train, in which we came to Tsarskoe Selo.

SOURCES

Beinecke Library at Yale University
Romanov collection.

Buligin, P. P. *Ubiystvo Romanovykh*. M., 2001.

Eagar, M. *Six Years at the Russian Court.*
www.alexanderpalace.org/eagar.html.

Feodorovna, Alexandra. *Letters of the Tsaritsa to the Tsar 1914-1916.* Introduction by Sir Bernard Pares. 1923.

Hoehnebart, Victor.
Private letter collection.

Hoover Institution at Stanford University
Romanov Papers.

Ispoved tsareubiytz. Podlinnaye istoria velikoi tragedii. Ubiystvo Tsarskoi Sem'yi v materiyalakh predvaritenogo sledstviya i v vospominaniyakh litz, prichastnykh k soversheniyu etogo prestupleniya. M.: Izdatelskiy Dom Veche," 2008.

Khrustalev, V. M. *The Last Diary of Tsaritsa Alexandra.* New Haven, CT: Yale University Press, 1997.

Nepein, I. G. *Pered Rasstrelom: Poslednie Pisma Tsarskoi Sem'yi.* Omskoe Knizhnoe Izdatelstvo, 1992.

Rossiyskiy Arkhiv: Istoria Otechestva v Svidetelstvakh i Dokumentakh XVIII-XX vv. L.A. Lykov

State Archives of the Russian Federation (GARF)
Fund #601 Emperor Nicholas II Alexandrovich.
Fund #640 Empress Alexandra Feodorovna.
Fund #642 Empress Maria Feodorovna.
Fund #651 Grand Duchess Tatiana Nikolaevna.

Fund #673 Grand Duchess Olga Nikolaevna.

Fund #682 Tsesarevich Alexei Nikolaevich.

Fund #683 Grand Duchess Anastasia Nikolaevna.

Fund #685 Grand Duchess Maria Nikolaevna.

Nicholas II, Diaries, 1917-1918.

Yakovlev, V. V. "Transfer of Nicholas Romanov from Tobolsk to Ekaterinburg." F. 601, Op. 2.

Tsarskiy Venetz. Pisma Tsarskoy Semi iz Zatocheniya Veche, 2013.

INDEX